HOWL'S MOVING CASTLE

FROM THE NOVEL BY DIANA WYNNE JONES
SCREENPLAY WRITTEN AND DIRECTED BY
HAYAO MIYAZAKI

3

Main Characters

Iowl's Moving Castle
The Story So Far

Sophie becomes the cleaning lady for Howl's moving castle after he Witch of the Waste turns her into an old lady. Sophie cleans the castle, but she ends up ruining Howl's potions, turning his blond hair black. In utter despair, Howl becomes bedridden. But his troubles run deeper than that. He's been summoned to Kingsbury palace, and he's afraid he will be ordered to fight in the war. Because he swore an oath at the royal sorcery academy, he must cooperate with his former master, the court appointed wizard Suliman. He sends Sophie to pose as his mother at the palace…

Sophie

She looks after the shop she inherited from her father, but the Witch of the Waste turns her into an old lady. She now works at Howl's moving castle as the cleaning lady.

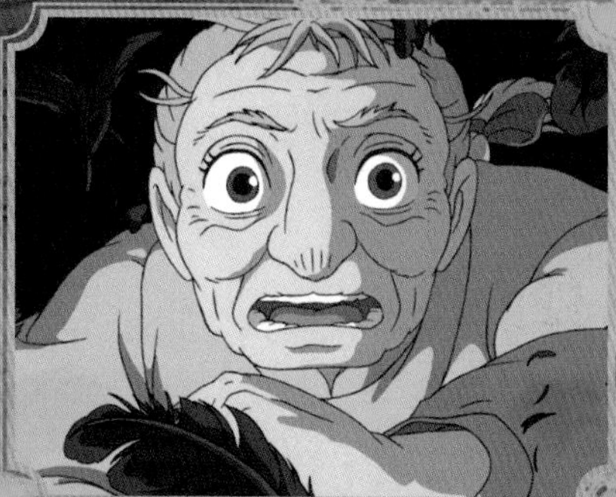

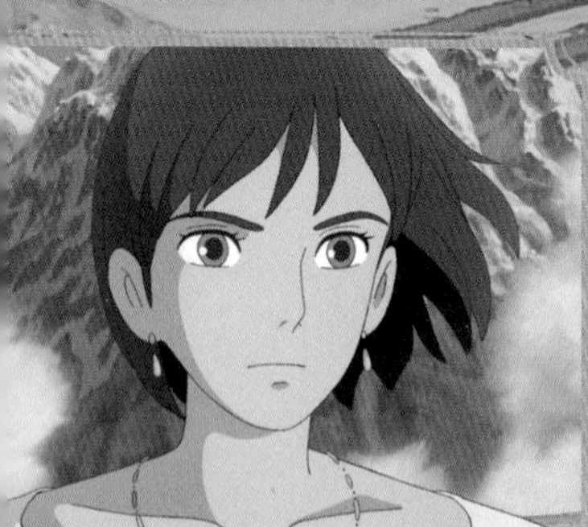

Howl

A wizard and the lord of the moving castle. He is a very powerful wizard, but he uses many aliases in order to live undisturbed. He claims he's a coward, but…

Calcifer

A fire demon. He lives in the fireplace of Howl's castle and powers the castle. He seems bound to Howl by a magical contract.

Markl

Howl's apprentice. studies magic whil running errands. He magically transform himself into an old man when dealing with clients.

The Witch of the Waste

The sorceress who turns Sophie into an old lady. She chases after Howl, but the court appointed wizard Suliman strips the witch of her magical powers.

Turnip-head

A moving scarecrow. Sophie rescues him in the Waste. Sophie came up with this nickname because his head resembles a turnip.

Heen

Suliman's pet dog. He guides Sophie t Suliman in the roya palace.

Suliman

The Kingsbury court appointed wizard. As Howl's former master, she wants Howl to help in the war.

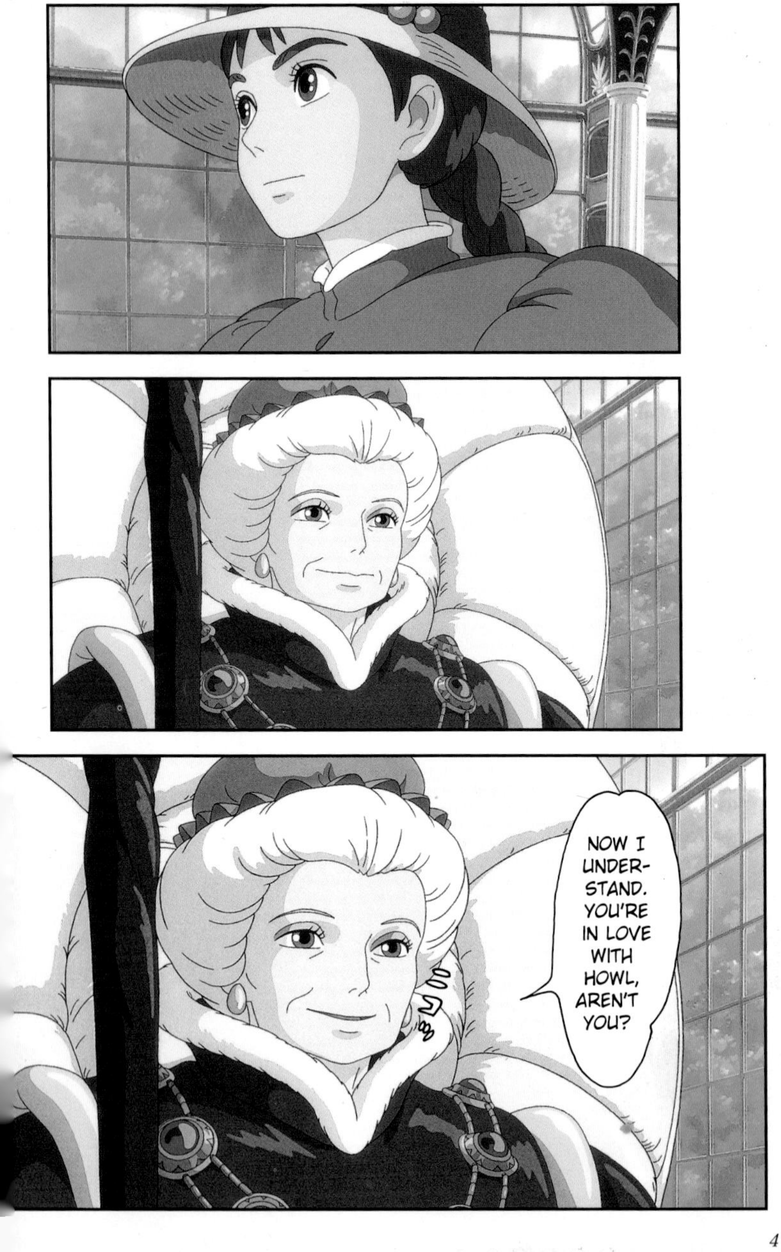
NOW I UNDER-STAND. YOU'RE IN LOVE WITH HOWL, AREN'T YOU?

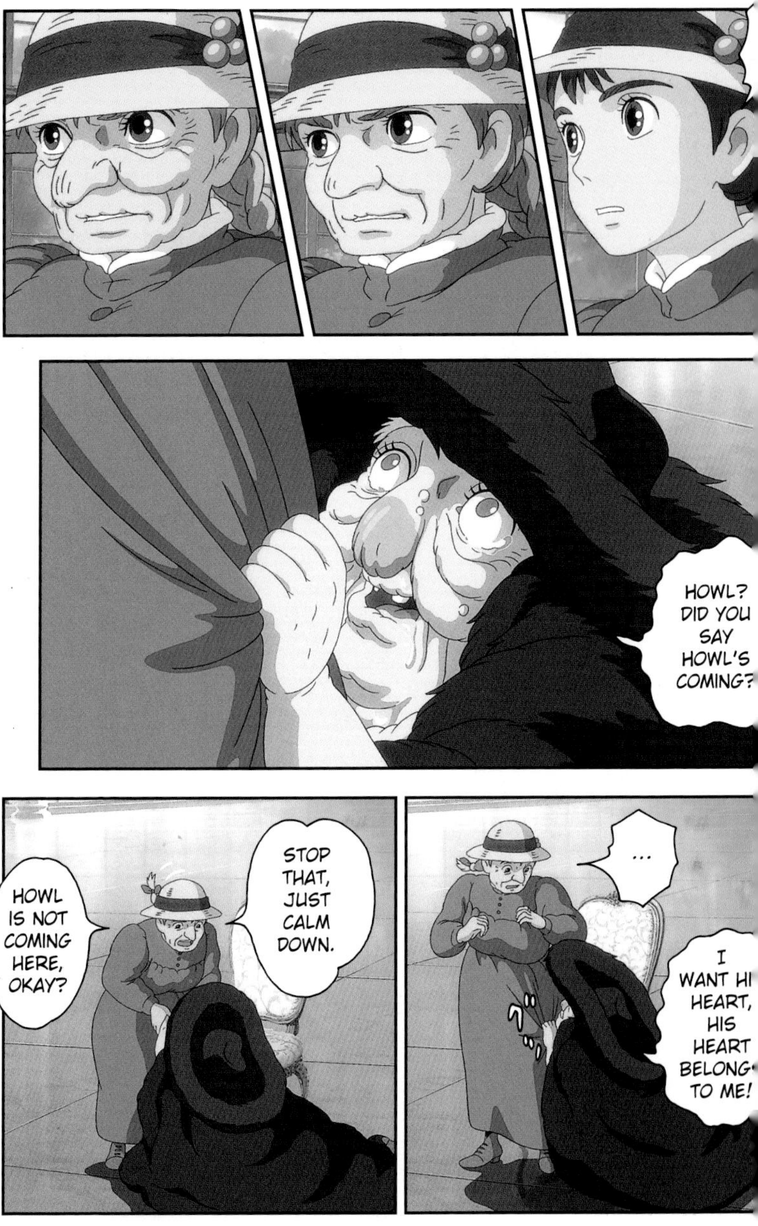
HOWL? DID YOU SAY HOWL'S COMING?
...
I WANT HI HEART, HIS HEART BELONG TO ME!
STOP THAT, JUST CALM DOWN.
HOWL IS NOT COMING HERE, OKAY?

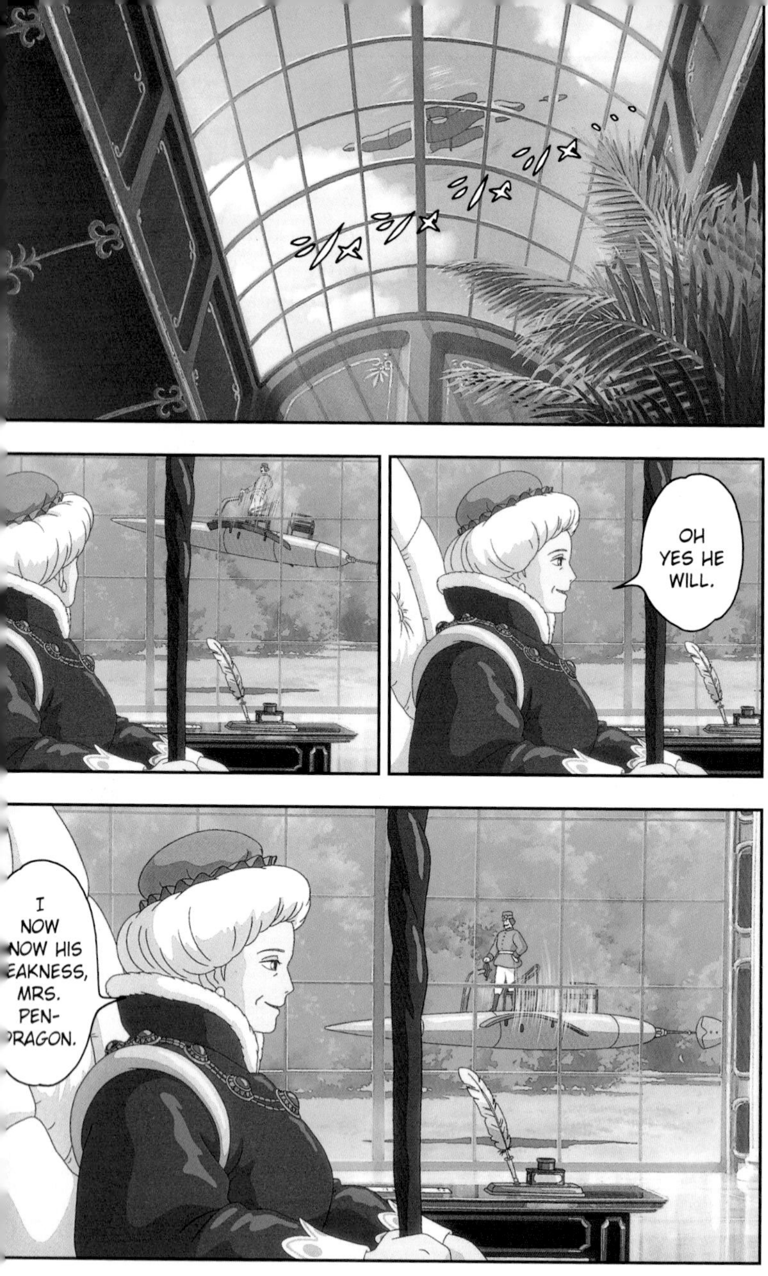
OH YES HE WILL.
I NOW NOW HIS EAKNESS, MRS. PEN- RAGON.

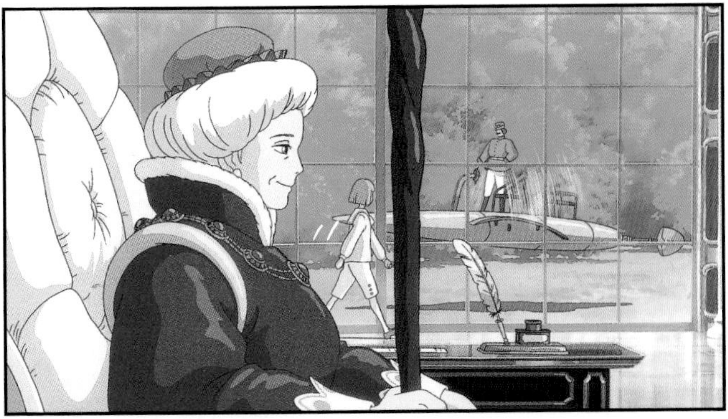

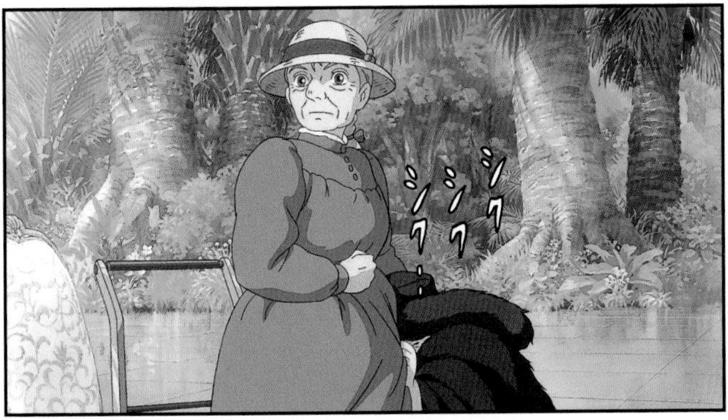
シク
シク
シク

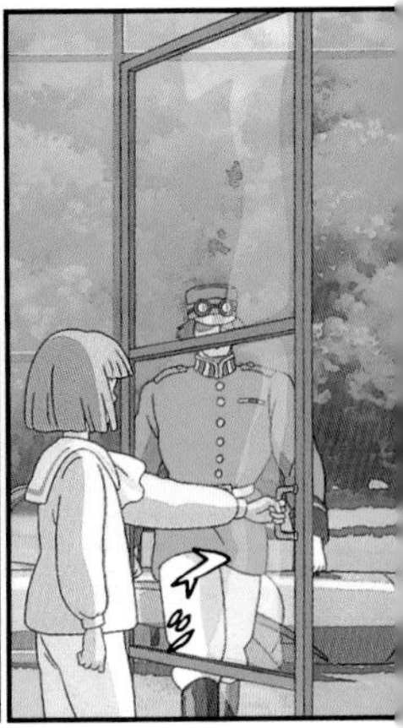
スッ

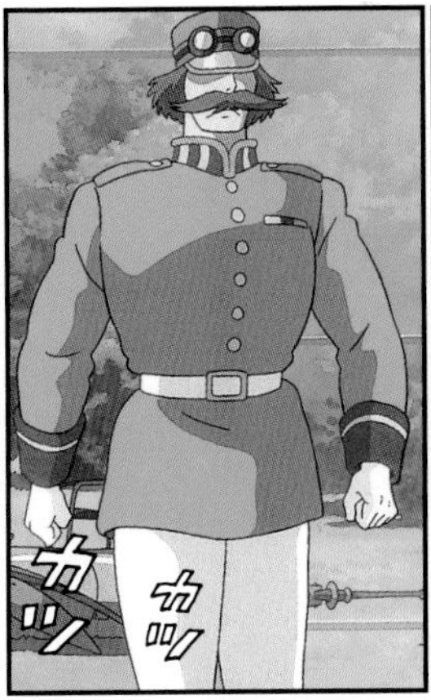
カッ
カッ

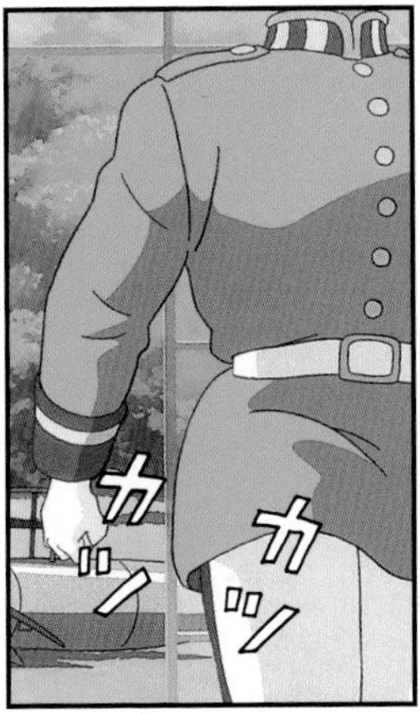
カッ
カッ

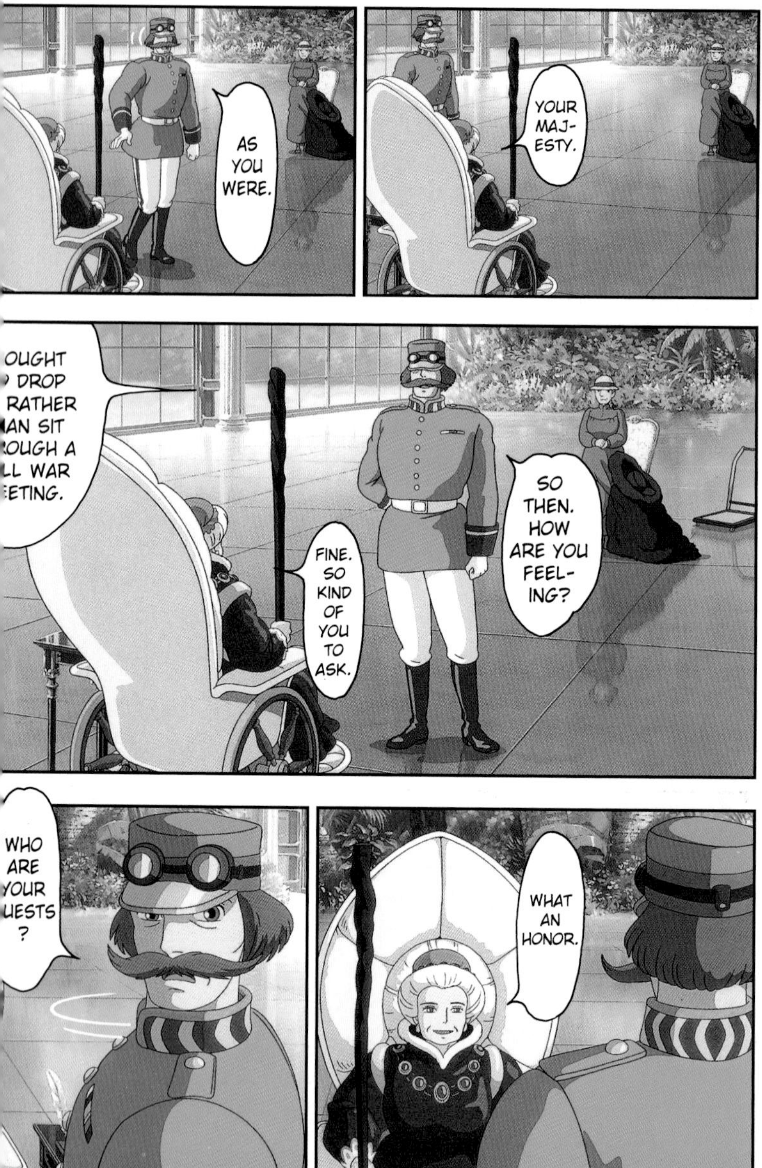
YOUR MAJ- ESTY.
AS YOU WERE.
SO THEN. HOW ARE YOU FEEL- ING?
FINE. SO KIND OF YOU TO ASK.
OUGHT DROP RATHER AN SIT OUGH A LL WAR EETING.
WHAT AN HONOR.
WHO ARE YOUR UESTS ?

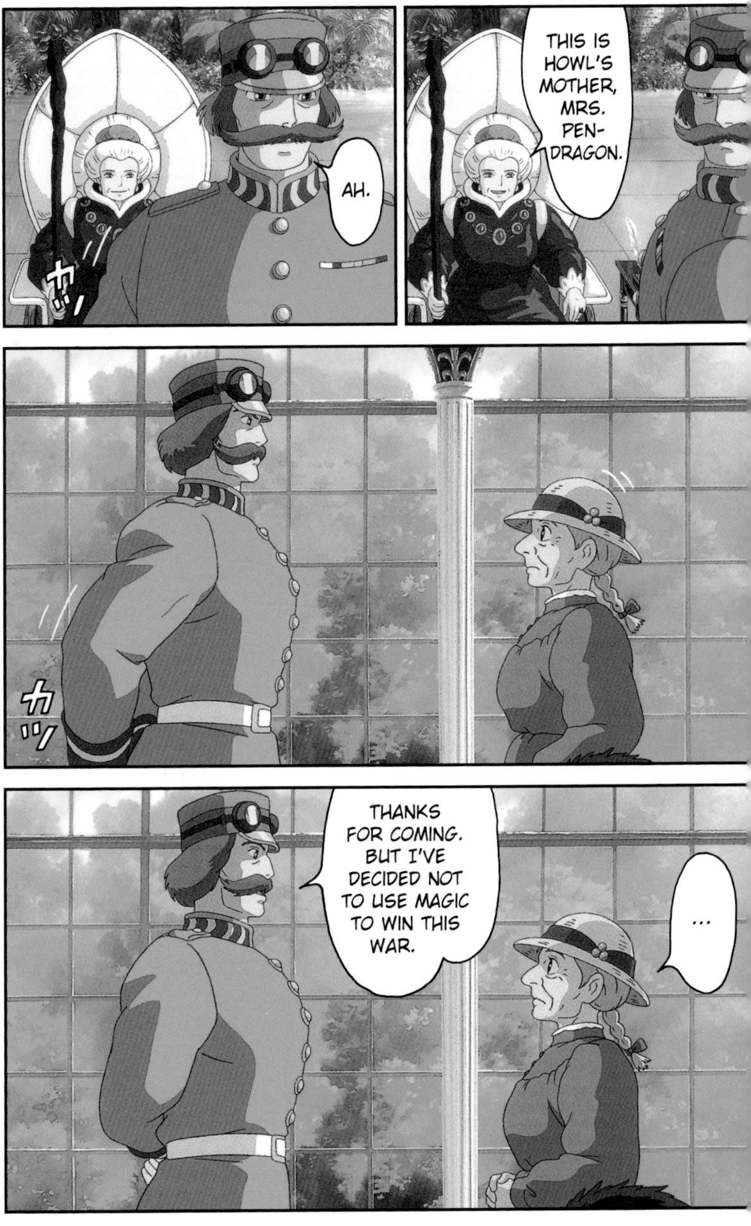
THIS IS HOWL'S MOTHER, MRS. PEN-DRAGON.
AH.
カッ
カッ
THANKS FOR COMING. BUT I'VE DECIDED NOT TO USE MAGIC TO WIN THIS WAR.
...

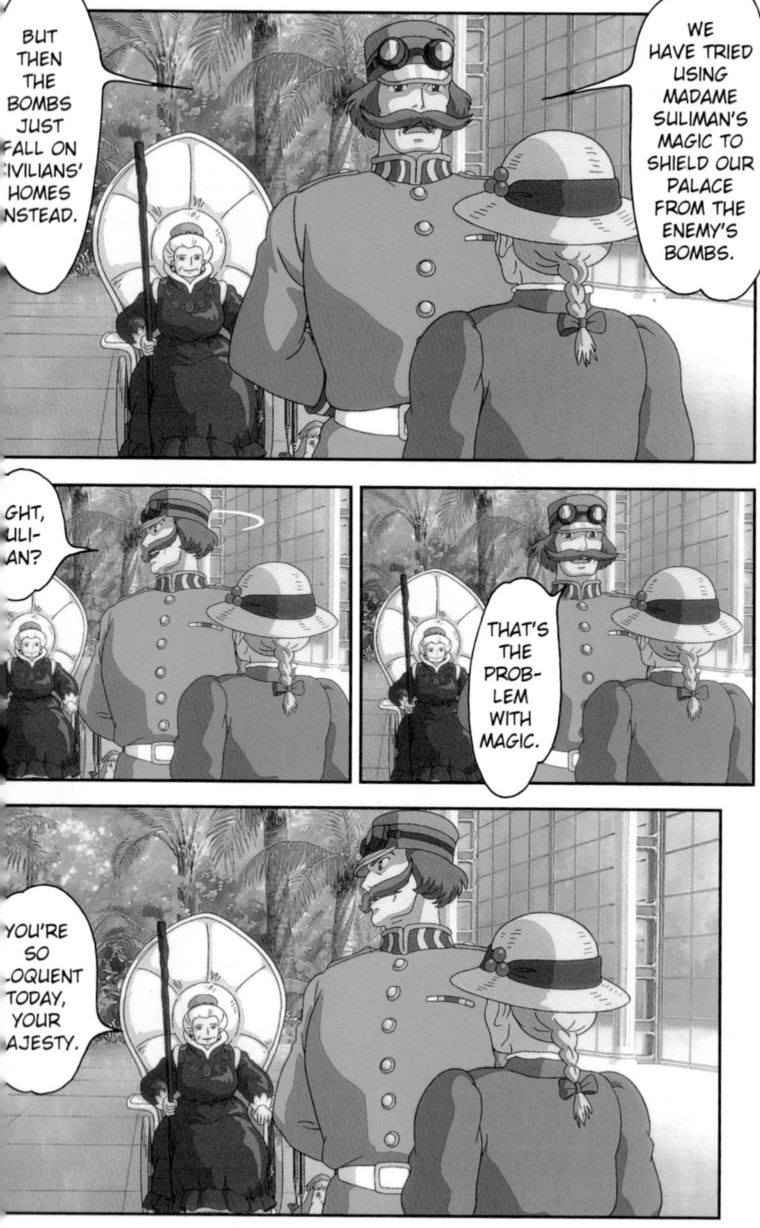
WE HAVE TRIED USING MADAME SULIMAN'S MAGIC TO SHIELD OUR PALACE FROM THE ENEMY'S BOMBS.
BUT THEN THE BOMBS JUST FALL ON IVILIANS' HOMES NSTEAD.
THAT'S THE PROB-LEM WITH MAGIC.
GHT, ULI-AN?
YOU'RE SO LOQUENT TODAY, YOUR AJESTY.

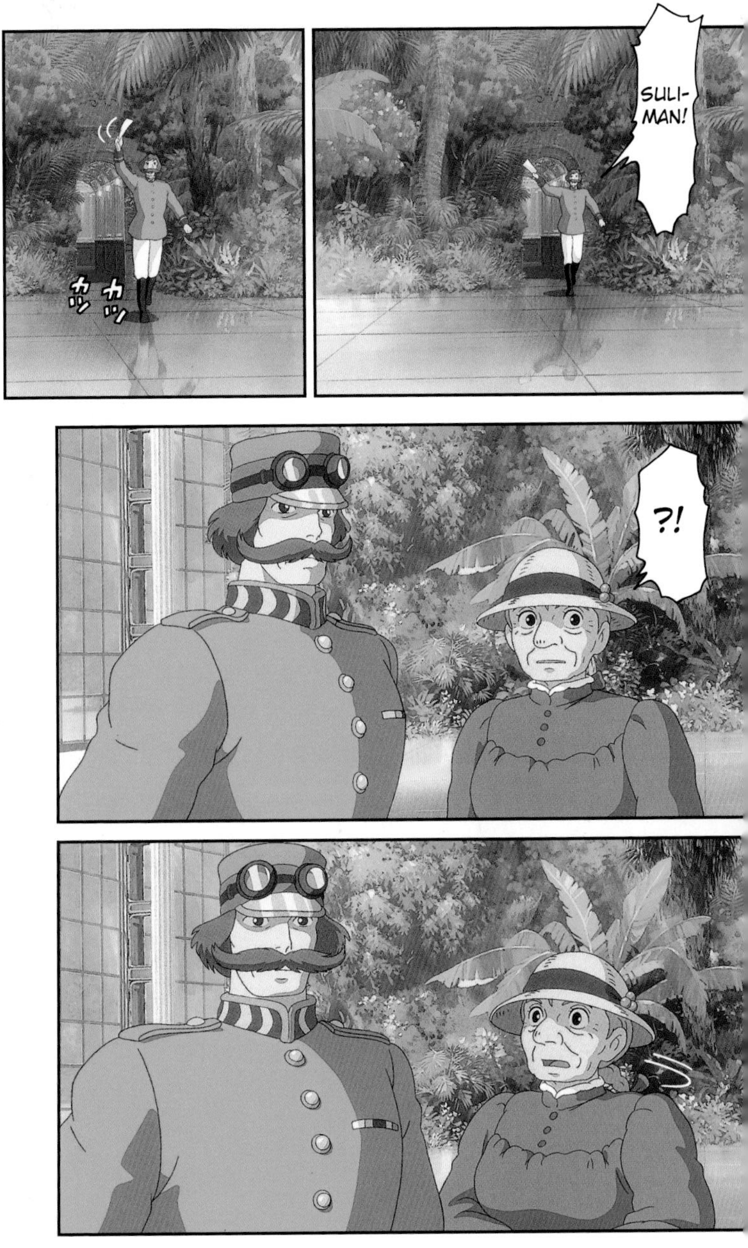
SULI-
MAN!
カッ
カッ
?!

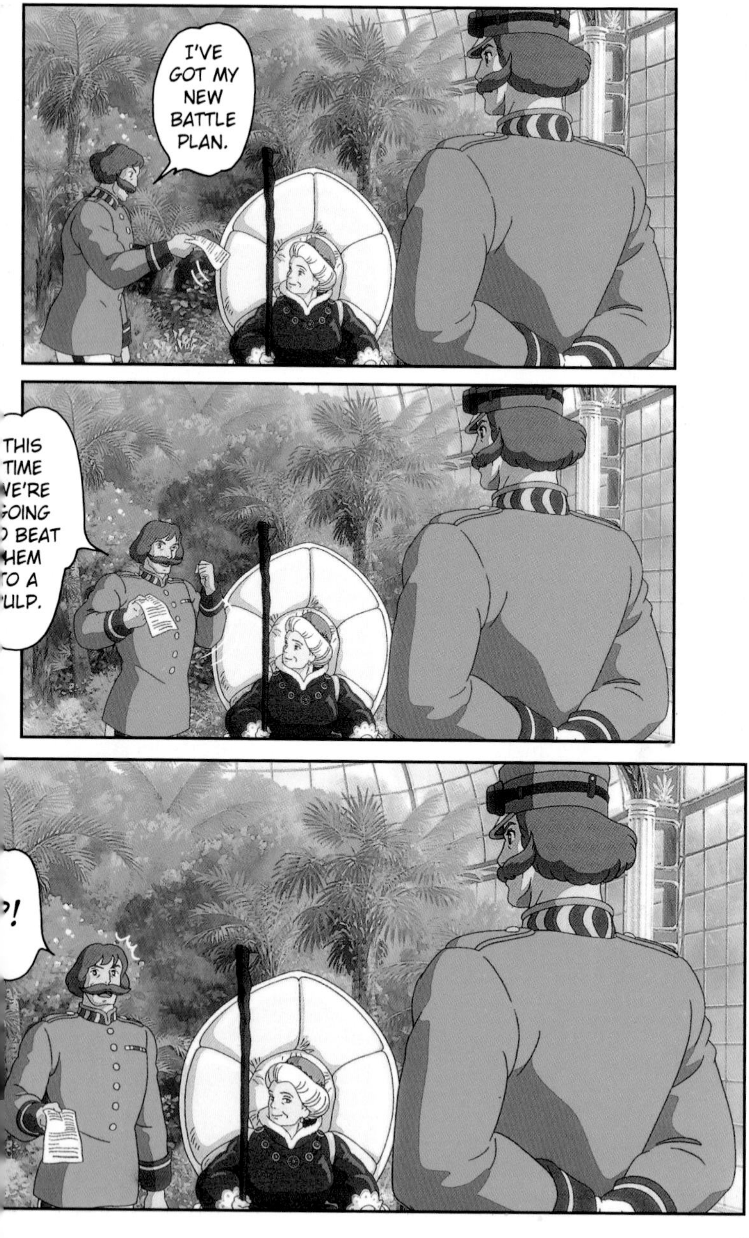
I'VE GOT MY NEW BATTLE PLAN.
THIS TIME VE'RE GOING) BEAT HEM TO A ULP.
?!

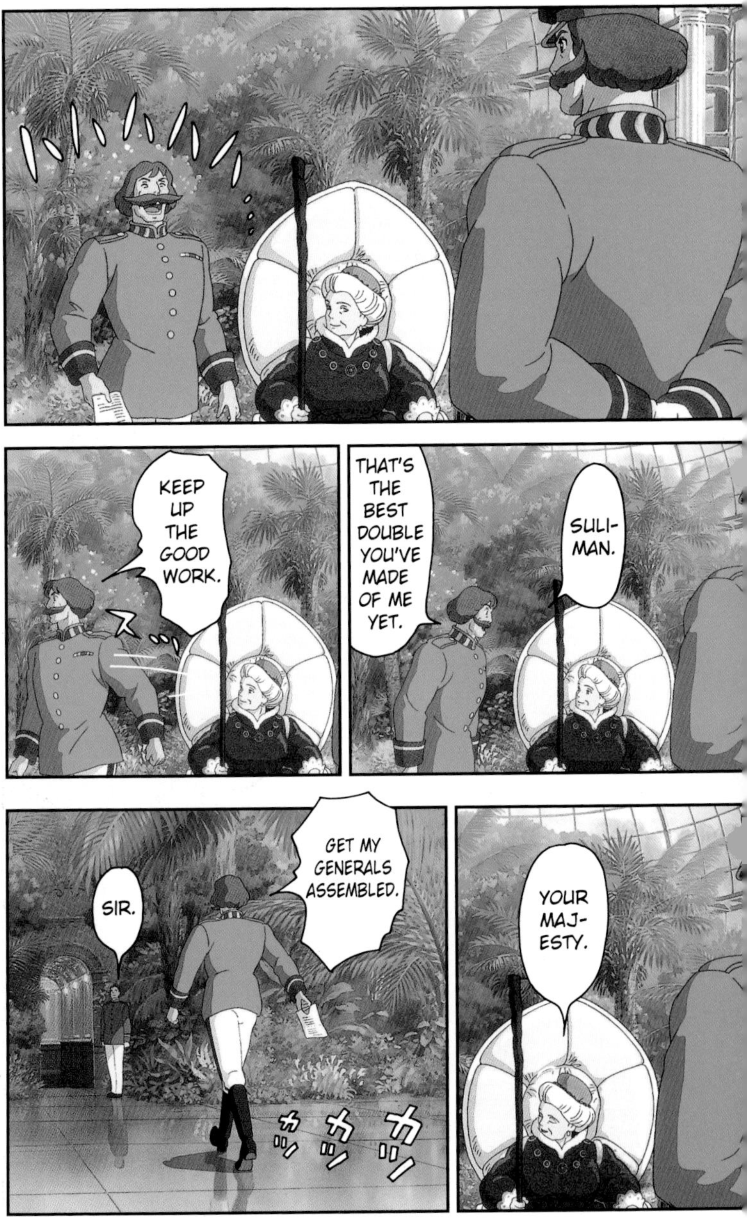
SULI-MAN.
THAT'S THE BEST DOUBLE YOU'VE MADE OF ME YET.
KEEP UP THE GOOD WORK.
ス…
YOUR MAJ-ESTY.
GET MY GENERALS ASSEMBLED.
SIR.
カツン
カツン
カツン

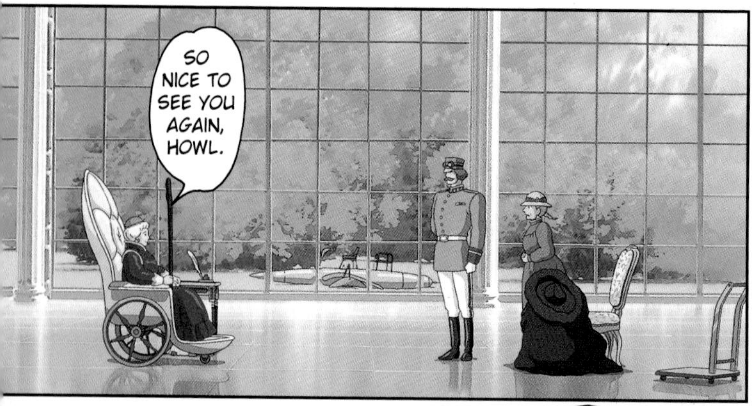
SO NICE TO SEE YOU AGAIN, HOWL.

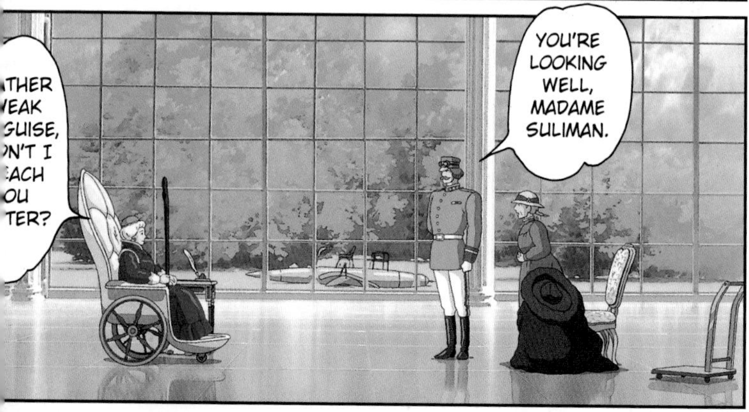
YOU'RE LOOKING WELL, MADAME SULIMAN.
THER EAK GUISE, N'T I ACH OU TER?

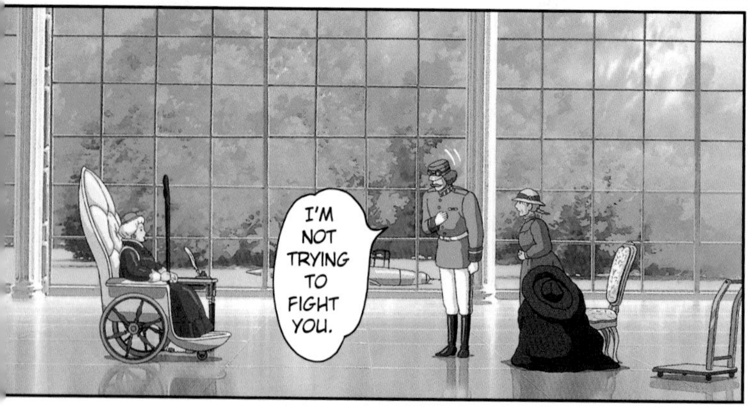
I'M NOT TRYING TO FIGHT YOU.

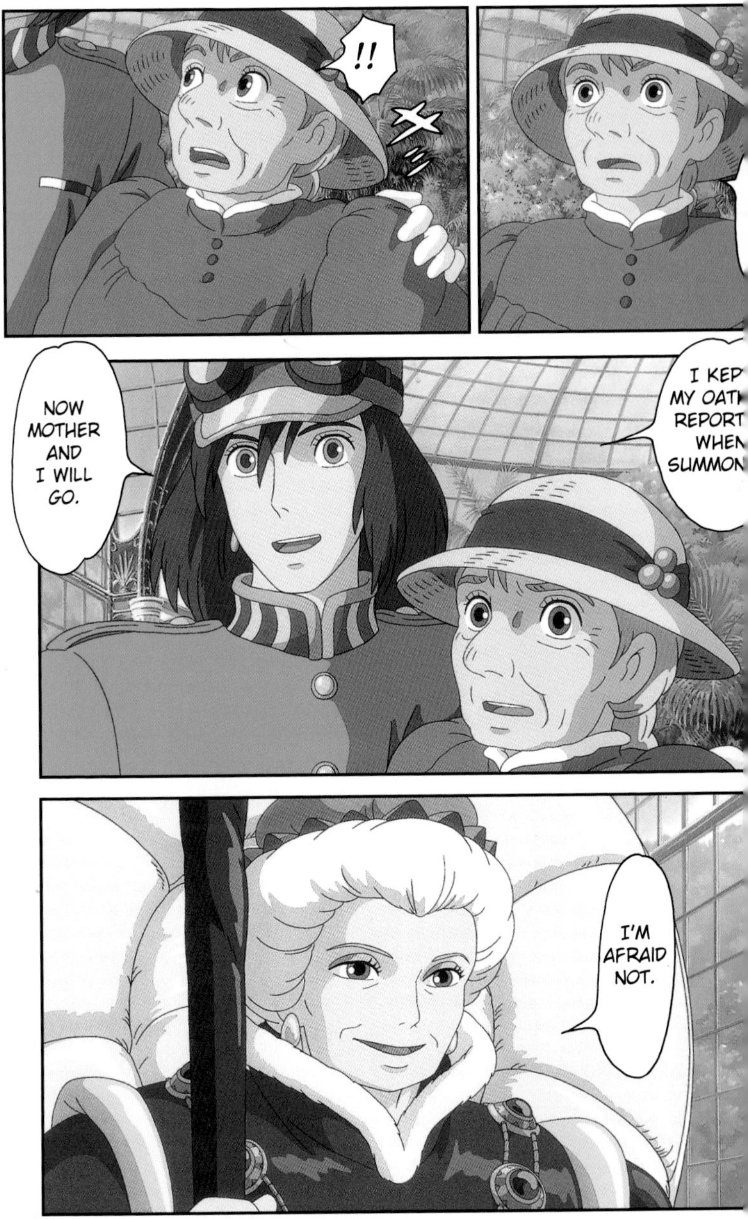
!!
I KEP MY OAT REPORT WHEN SUMMON
NOW MOTHER AND I WILL GO.
I'M AFRAID NOT.

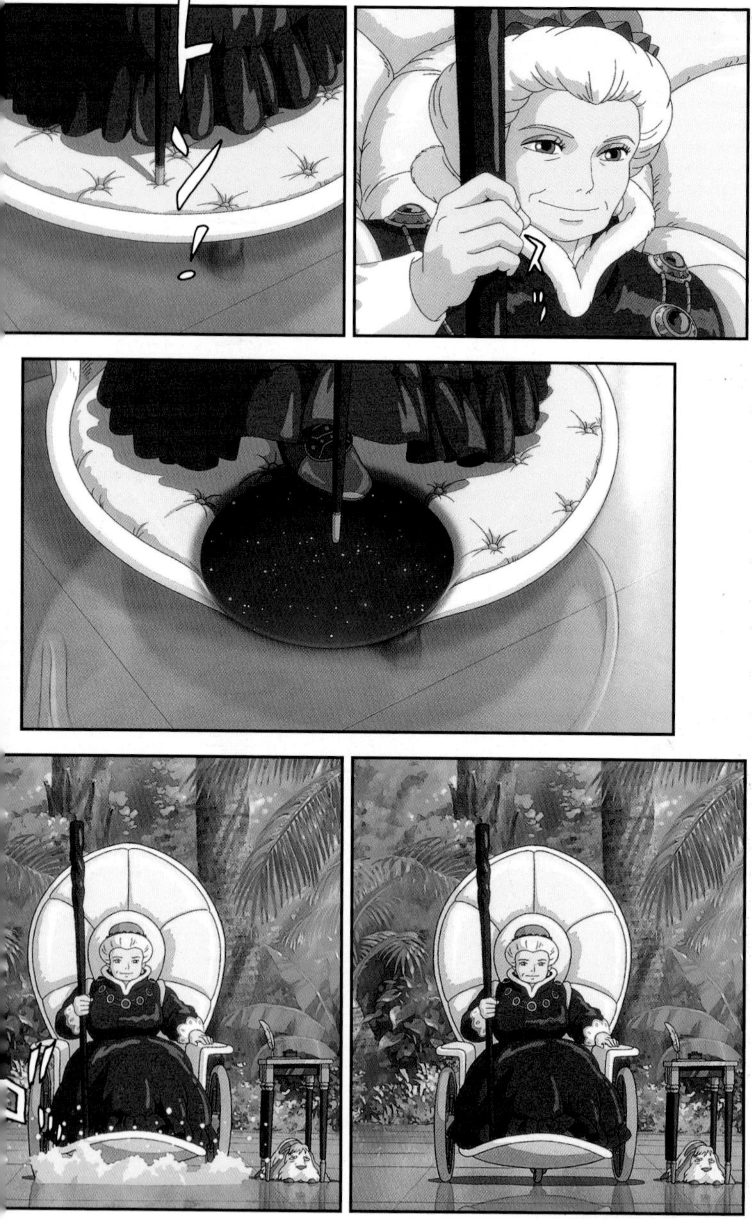
トン!

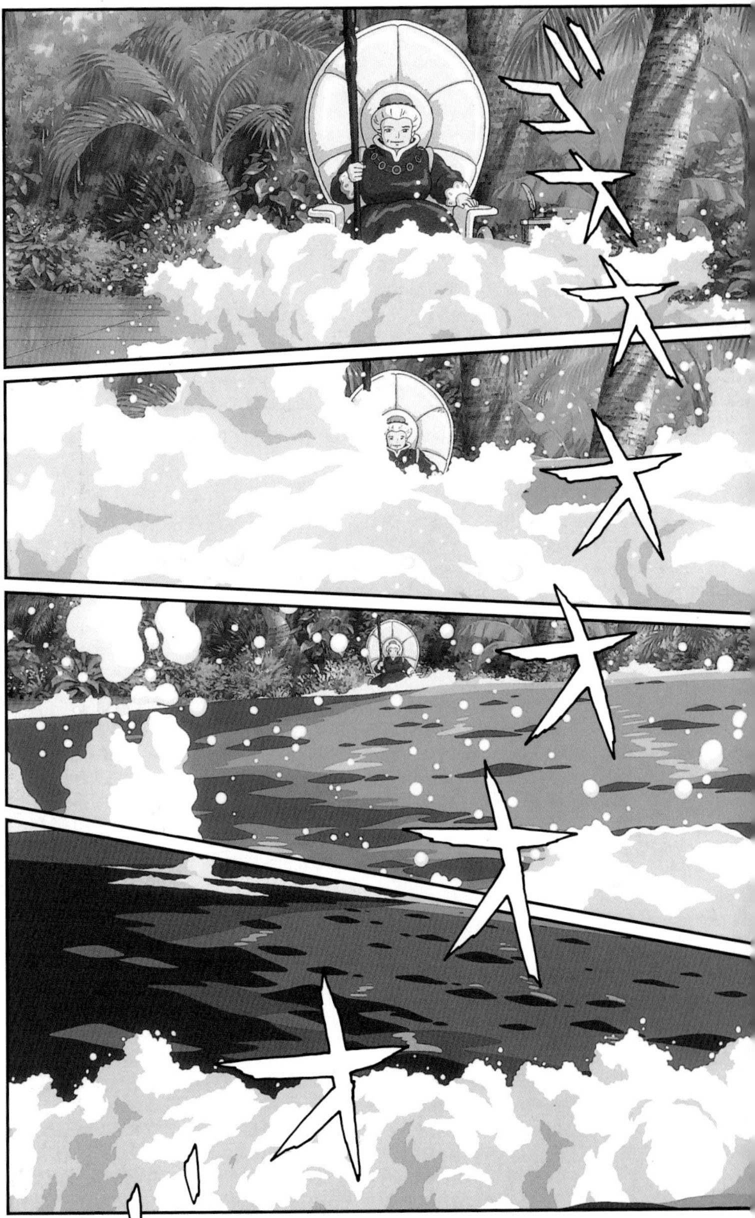
ズスススススス

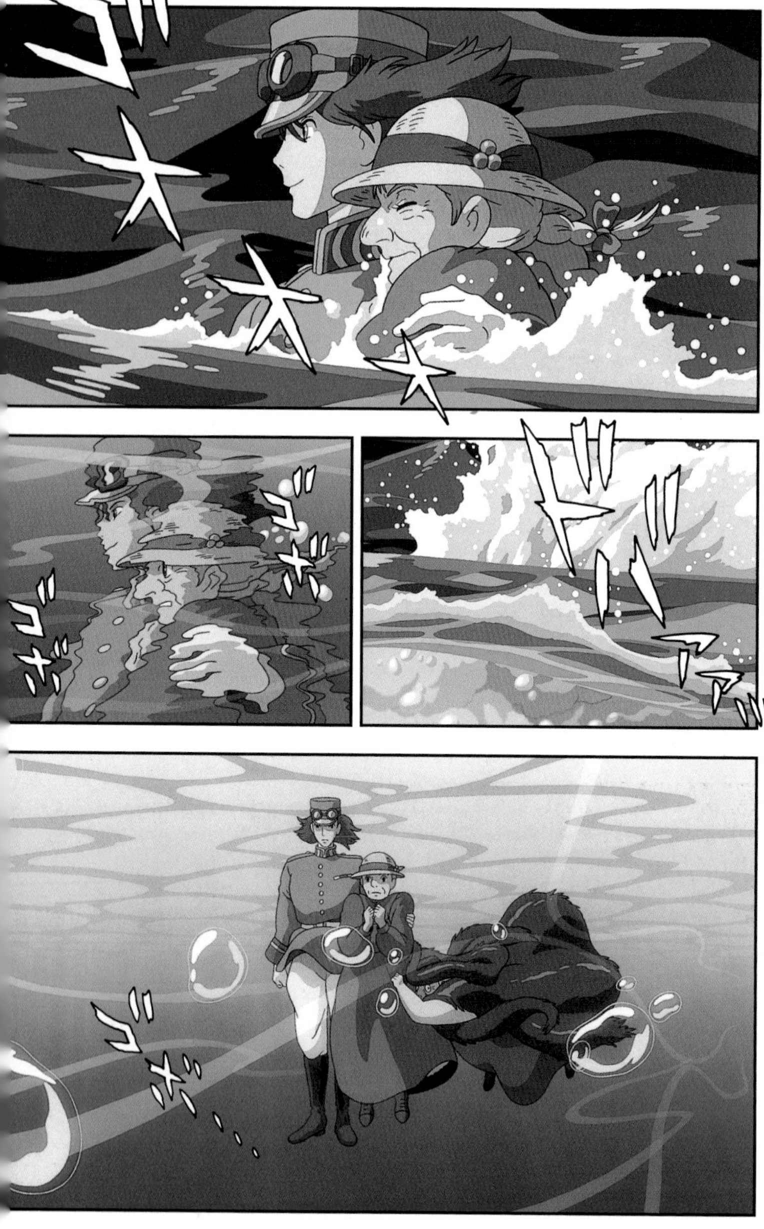
ゴボボボ
ゴボボ
ゴボボ
ゴボボ…

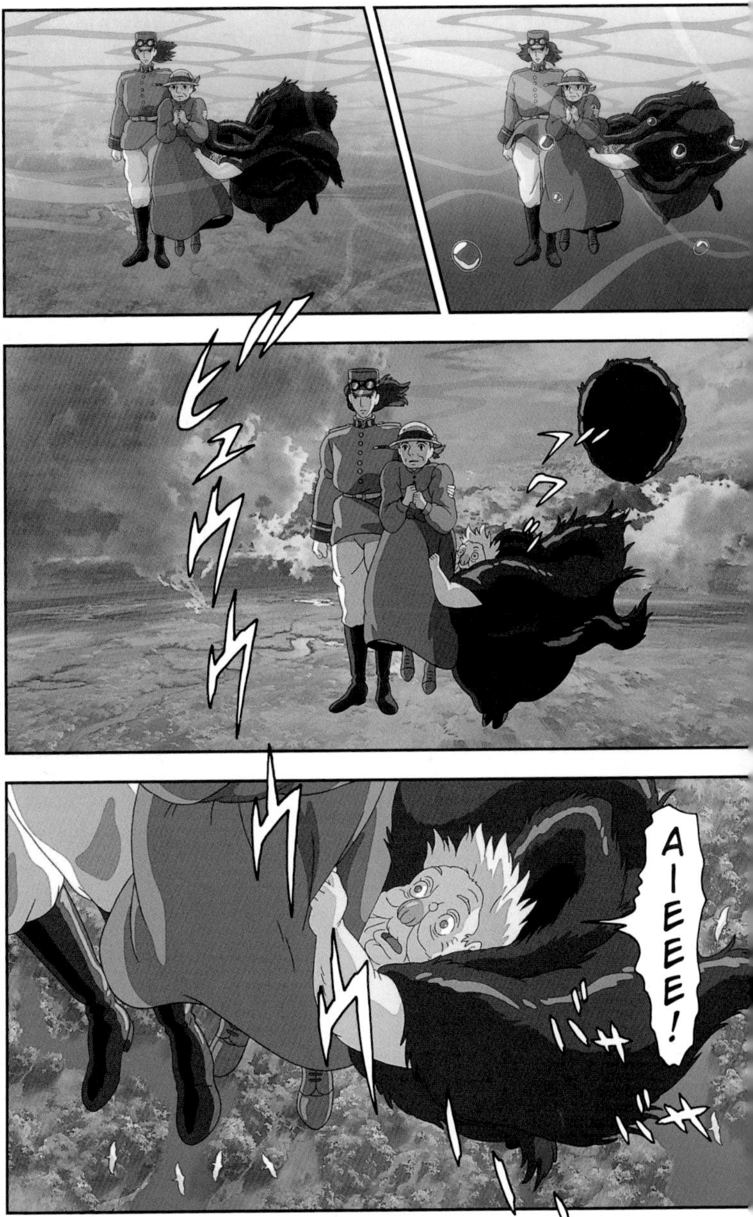
AIEEE!

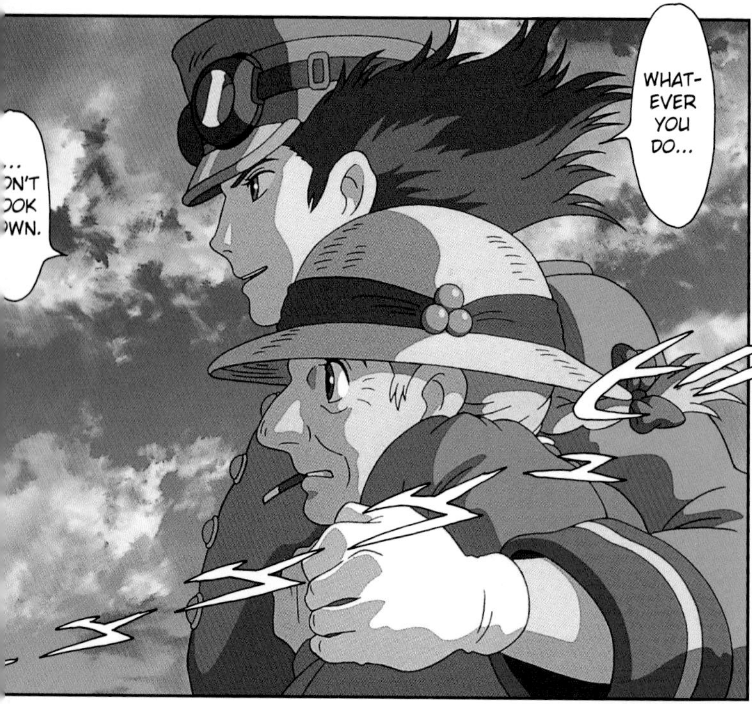
WHAT-EVER YOU DO...
... ON'T OOK WN.

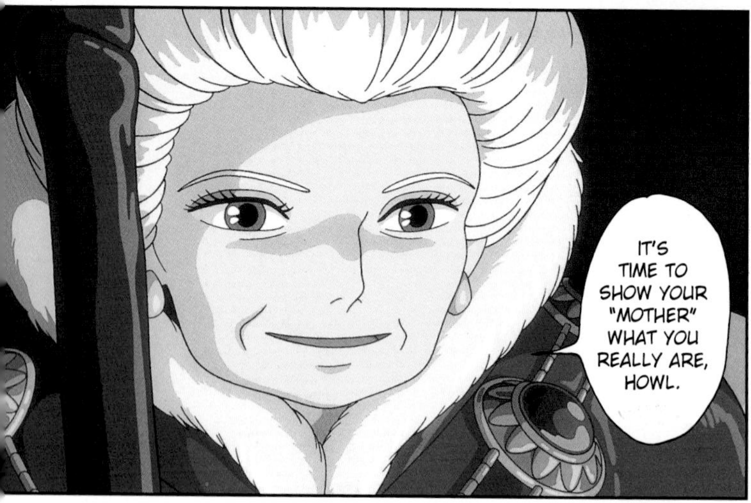
IT'S TIME TO SHOW YOUR "MOTHER" WHAT YOU REALLY ARE, HOWL.

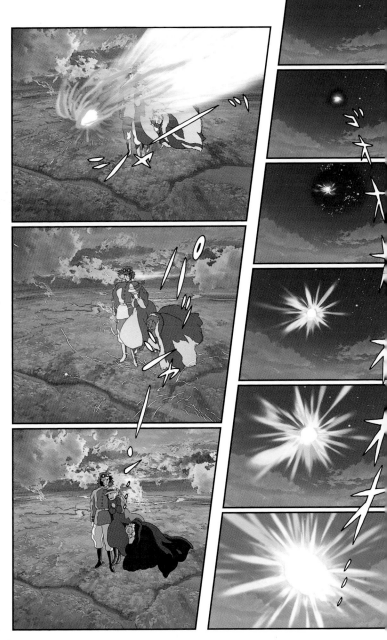

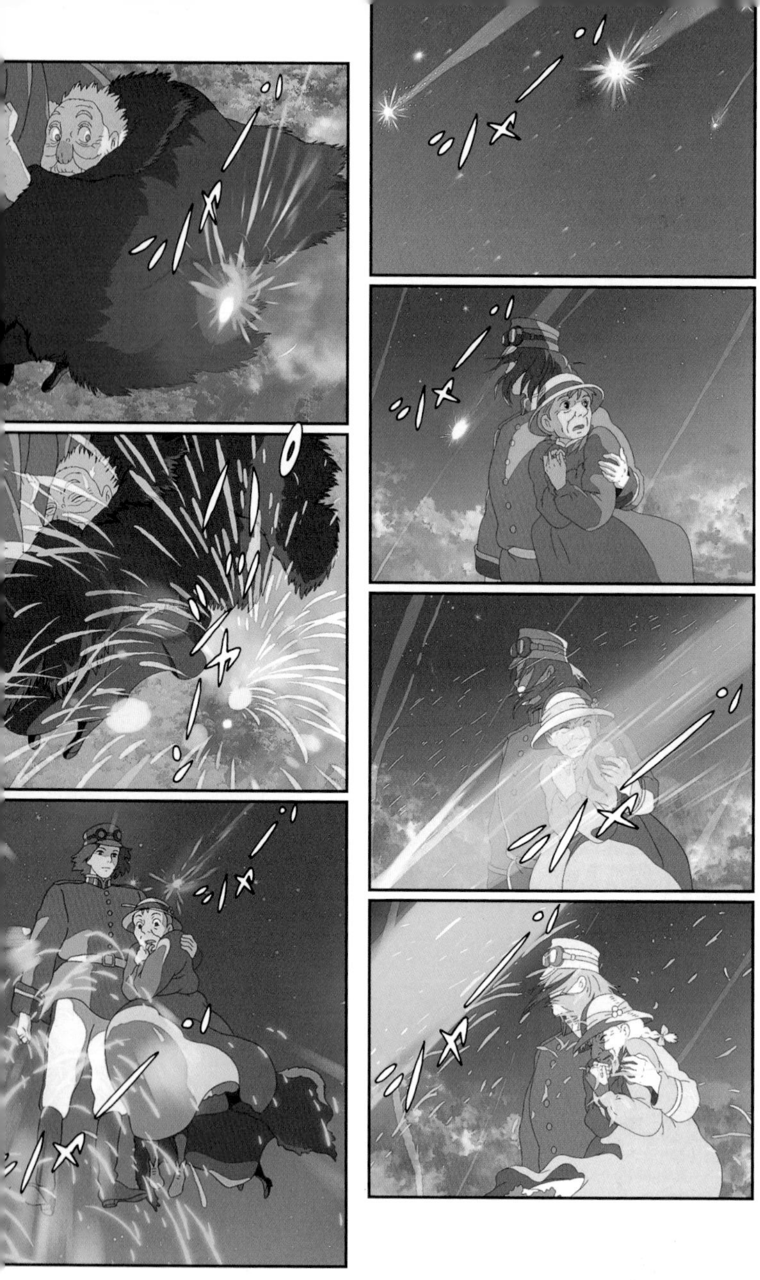

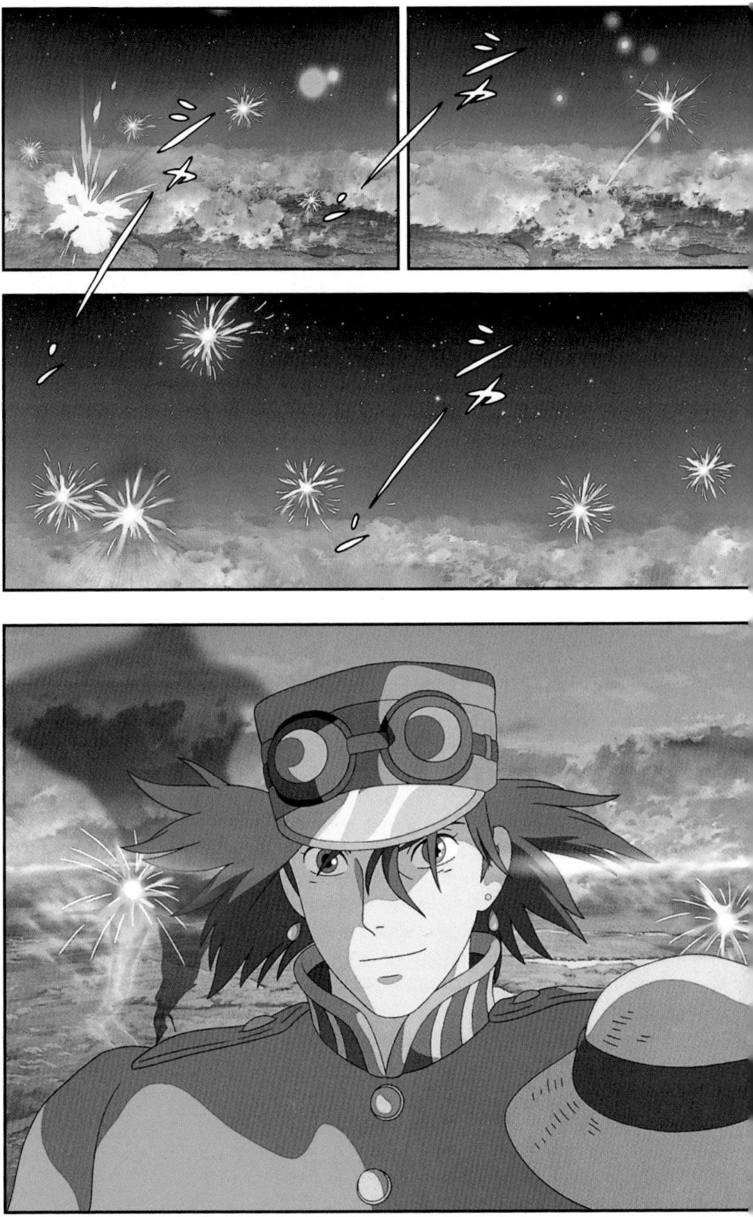

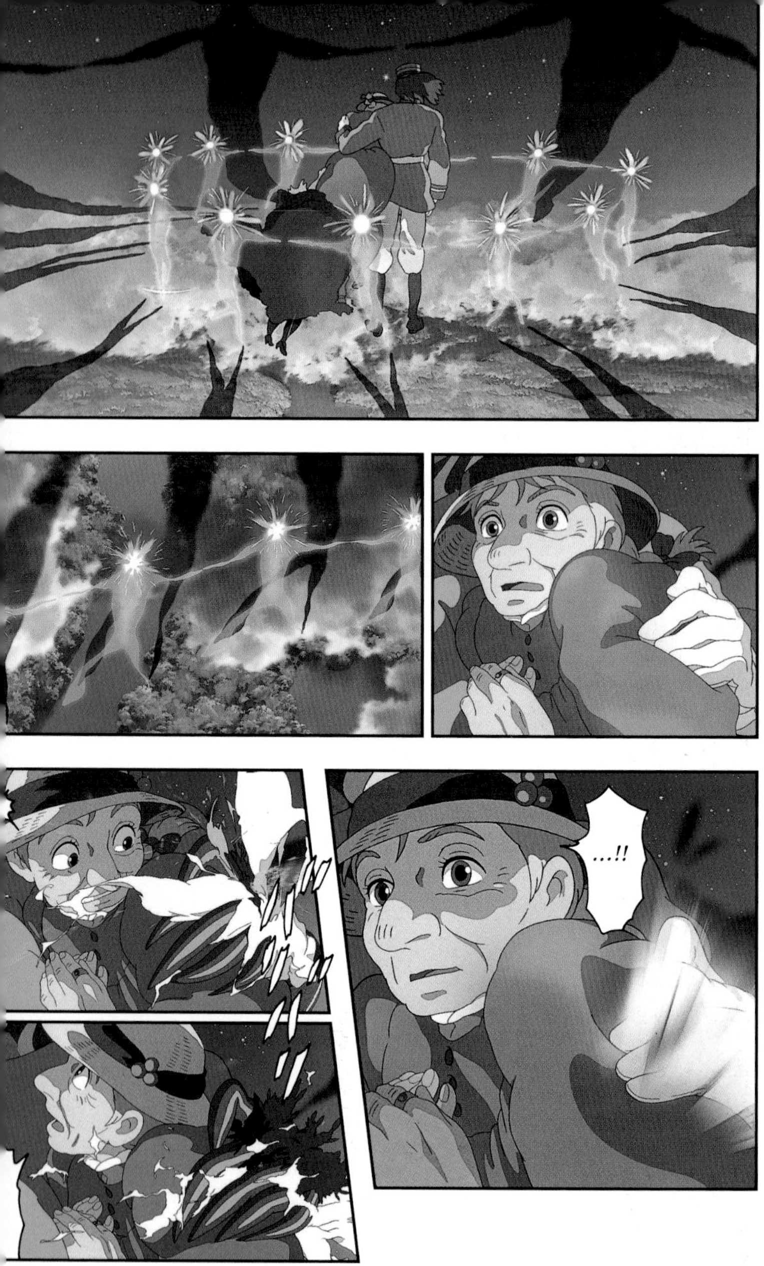
...!!

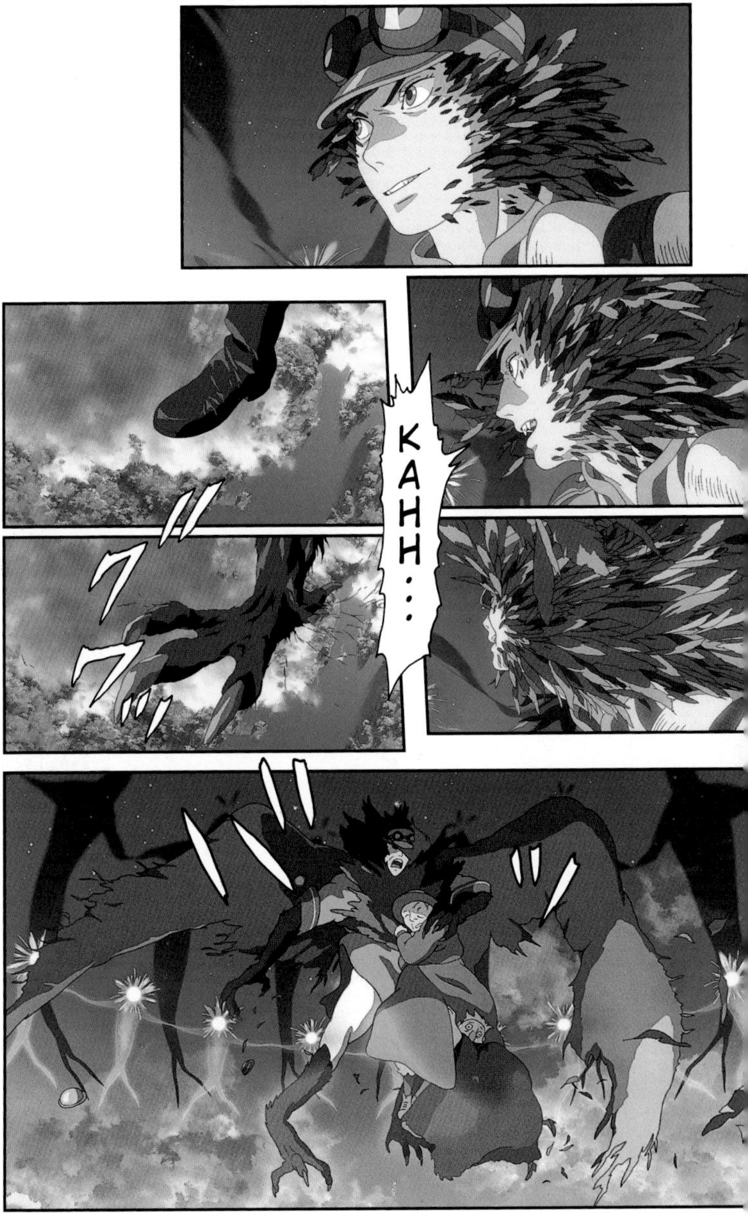
KAHH...

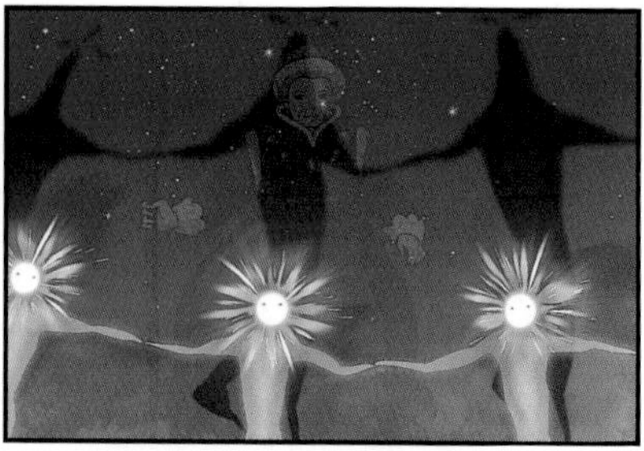
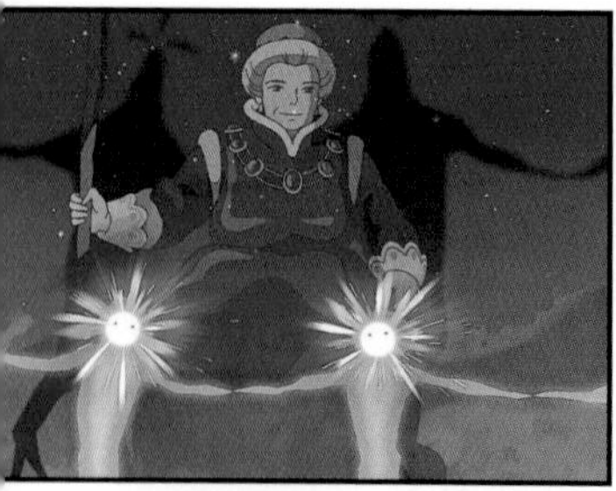
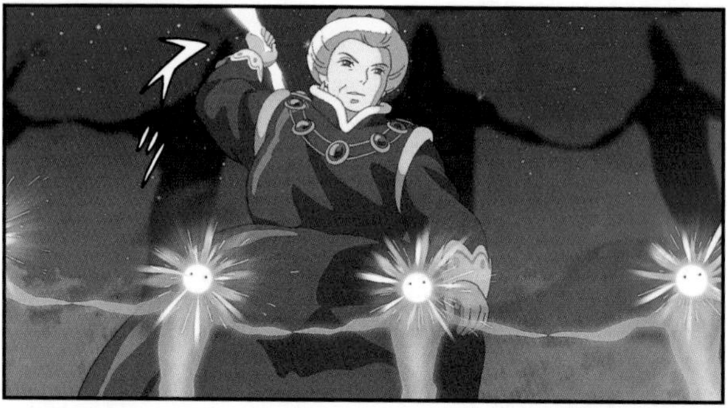
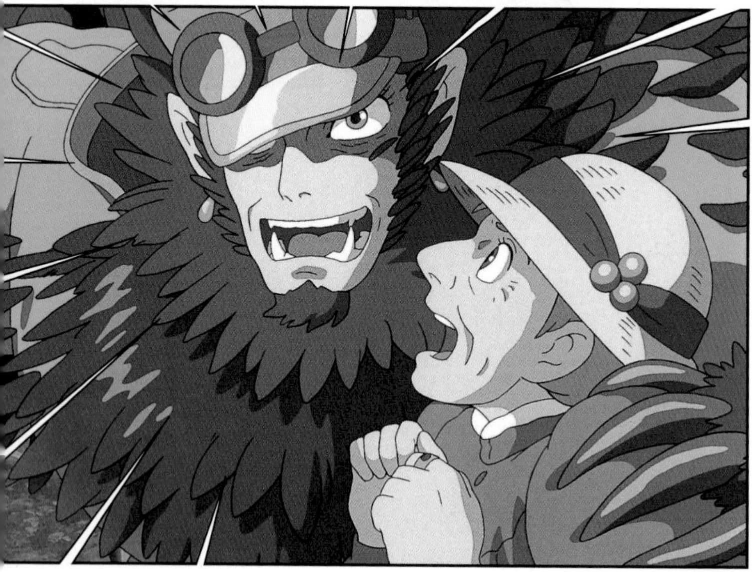

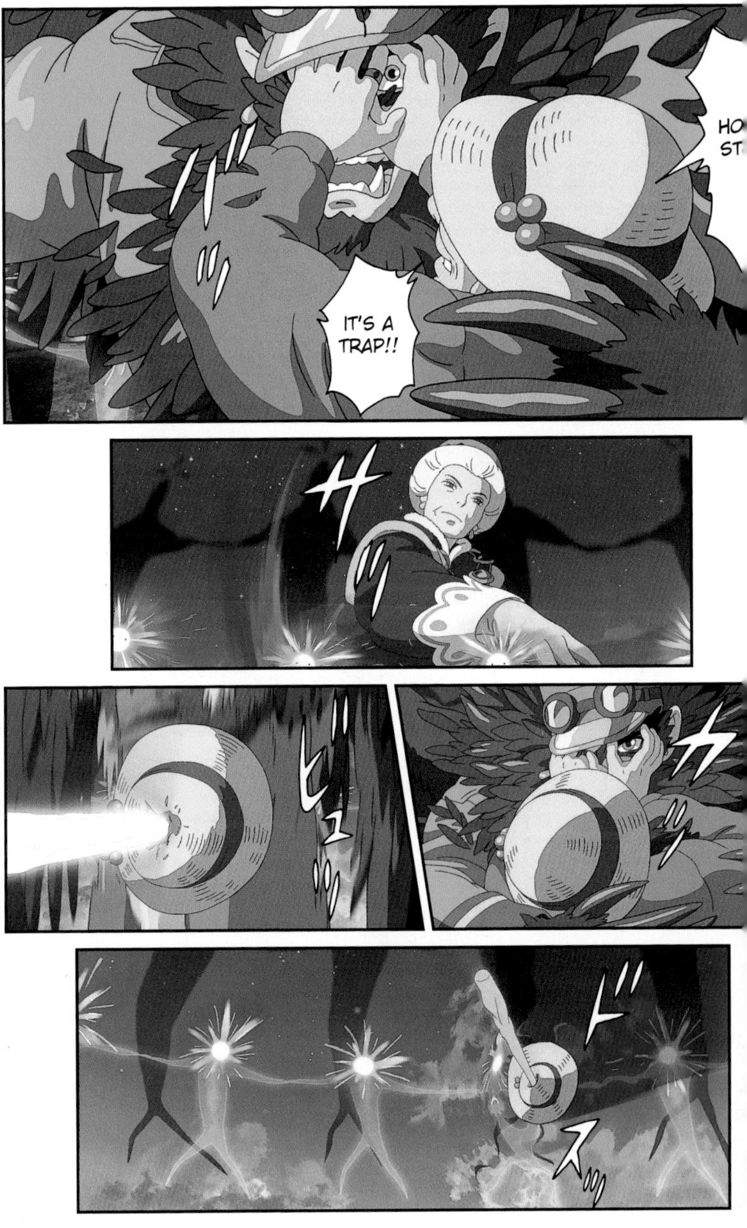
IT'S A TRAP!!

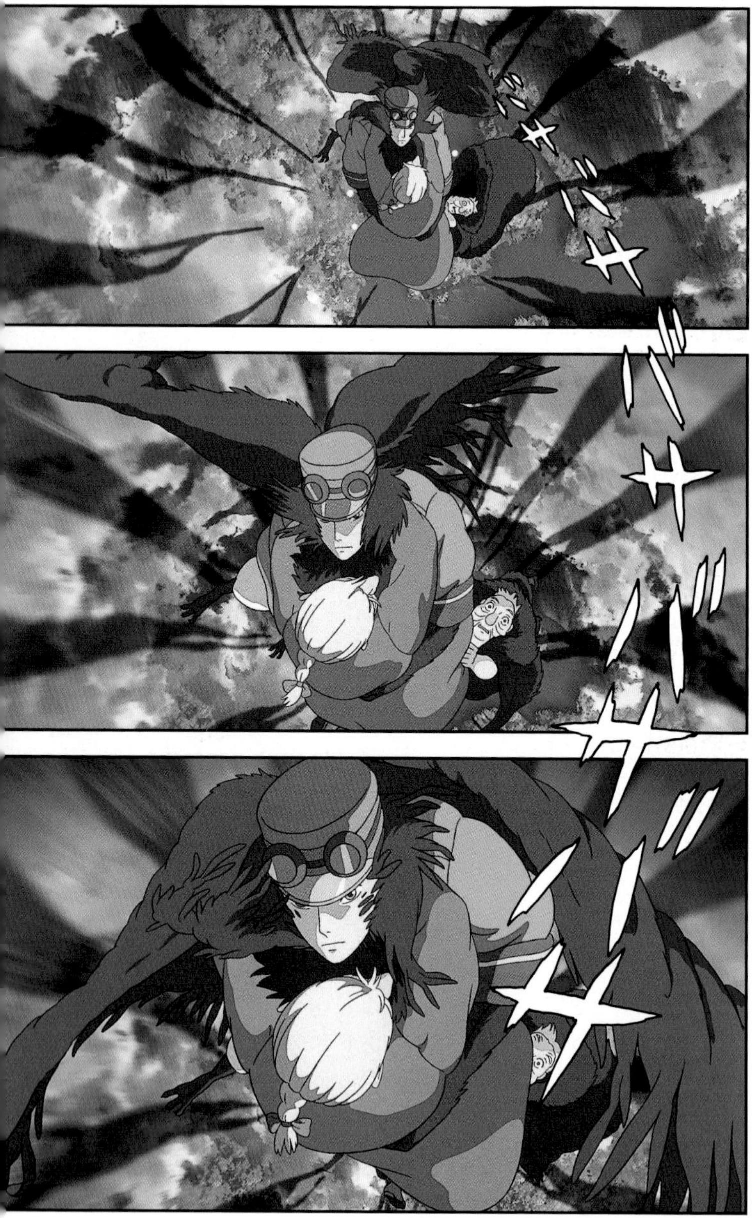

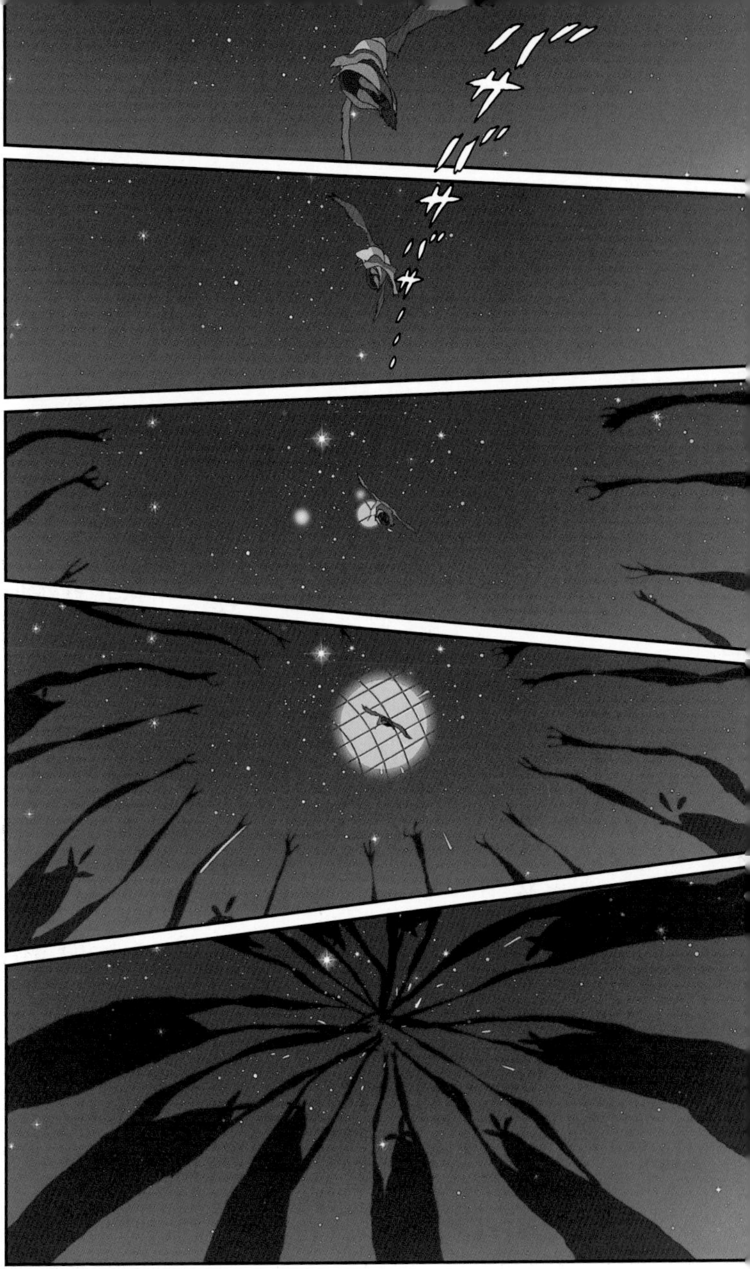
バサ
バサ
バサ

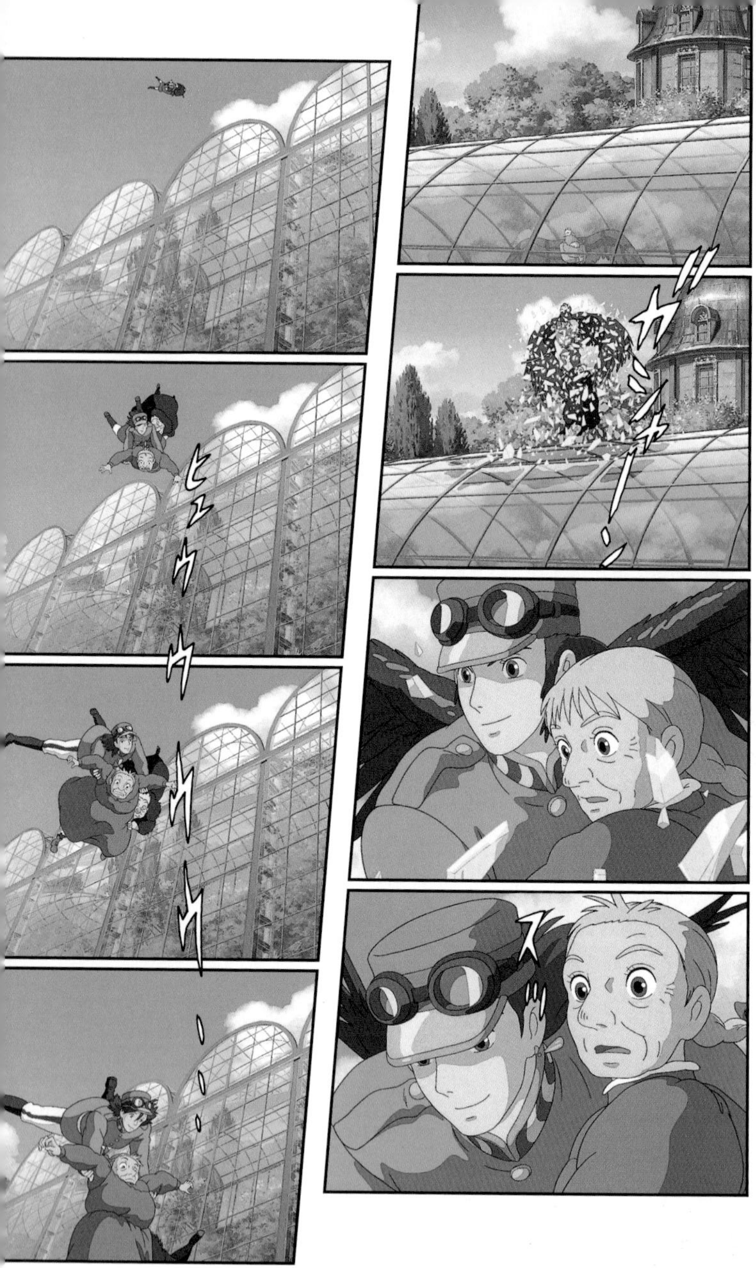
ガシャーン
ス
ヒュウウウウ…

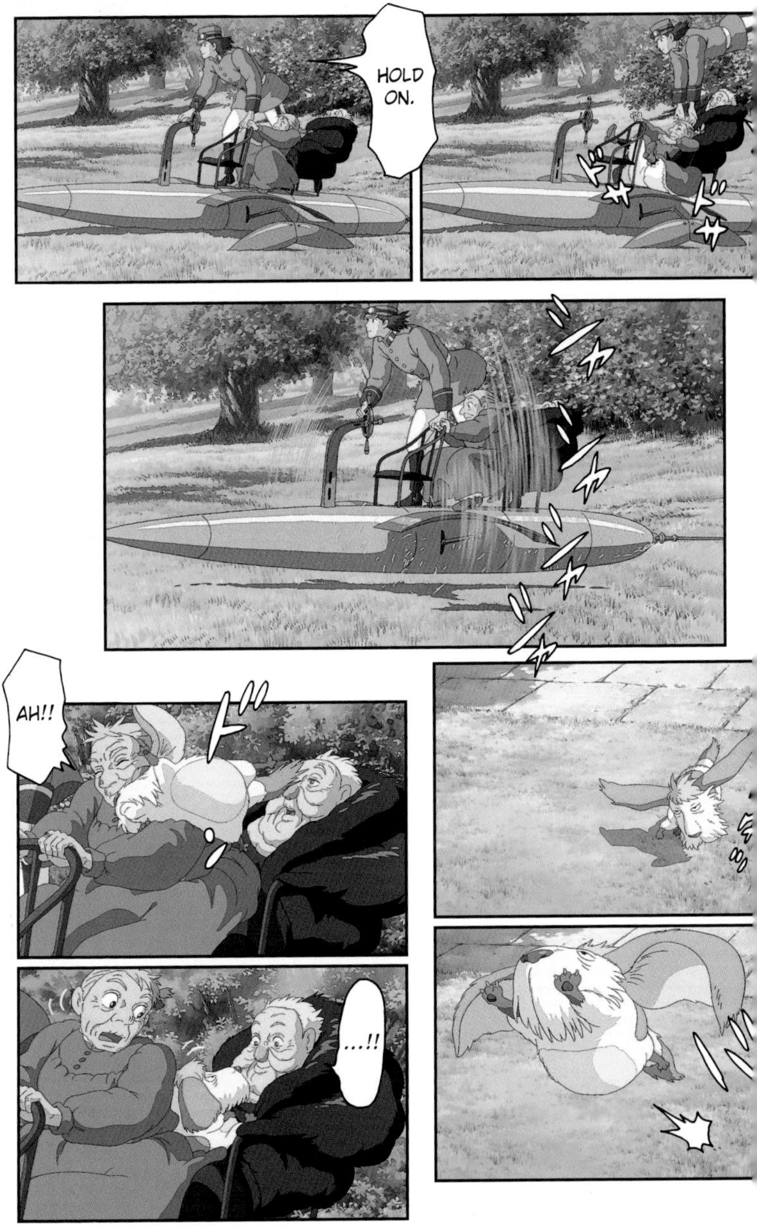
HOLD ON.
AH!!
...!!

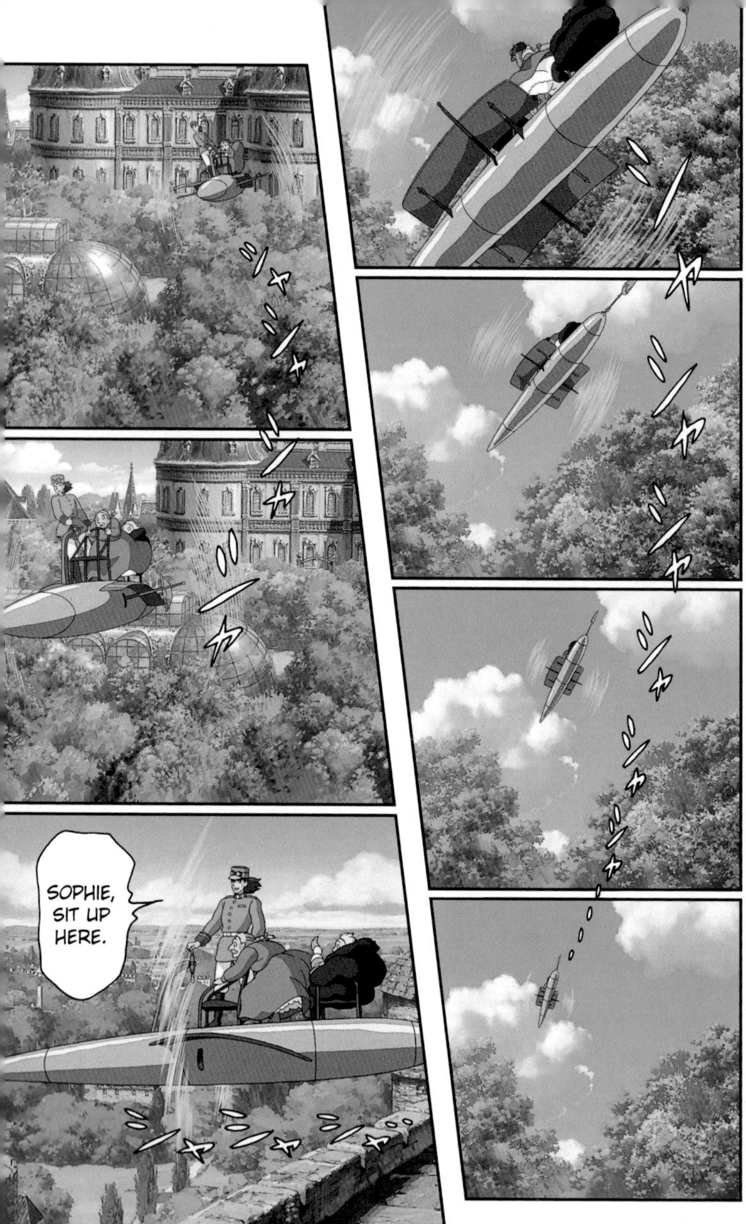
SOPHIE, SIT UP HERE.

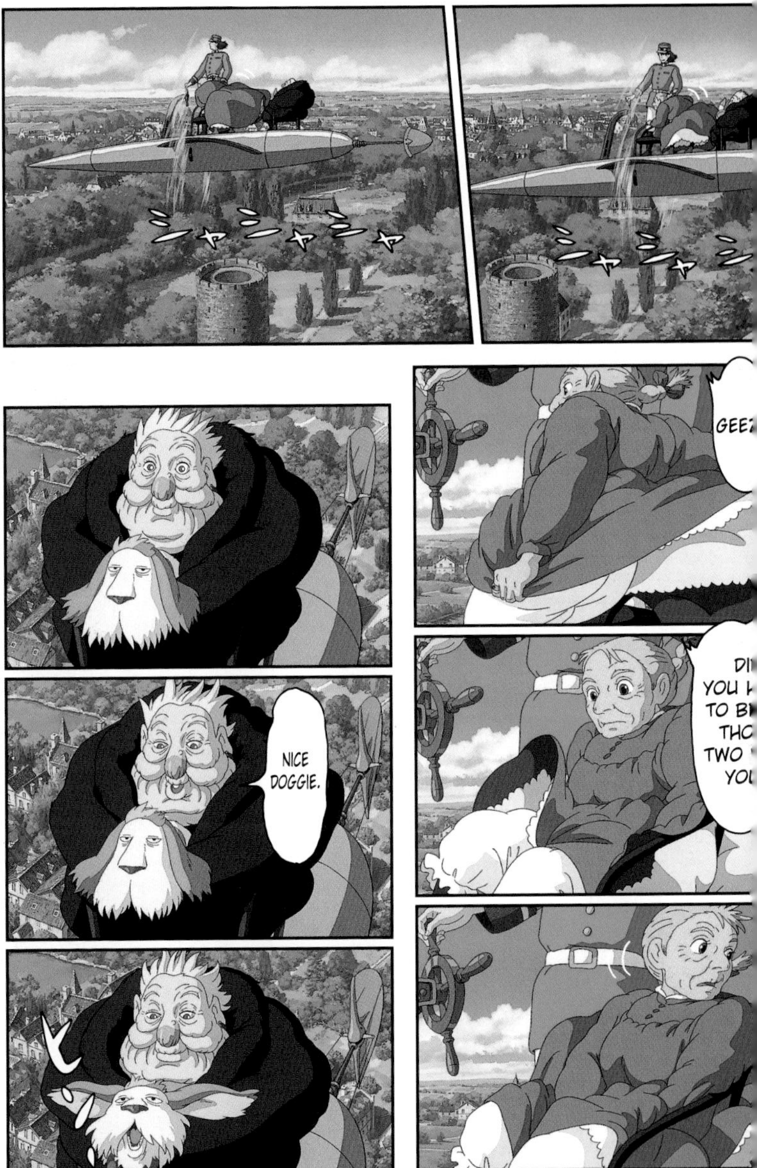
NICE DOGGIE.

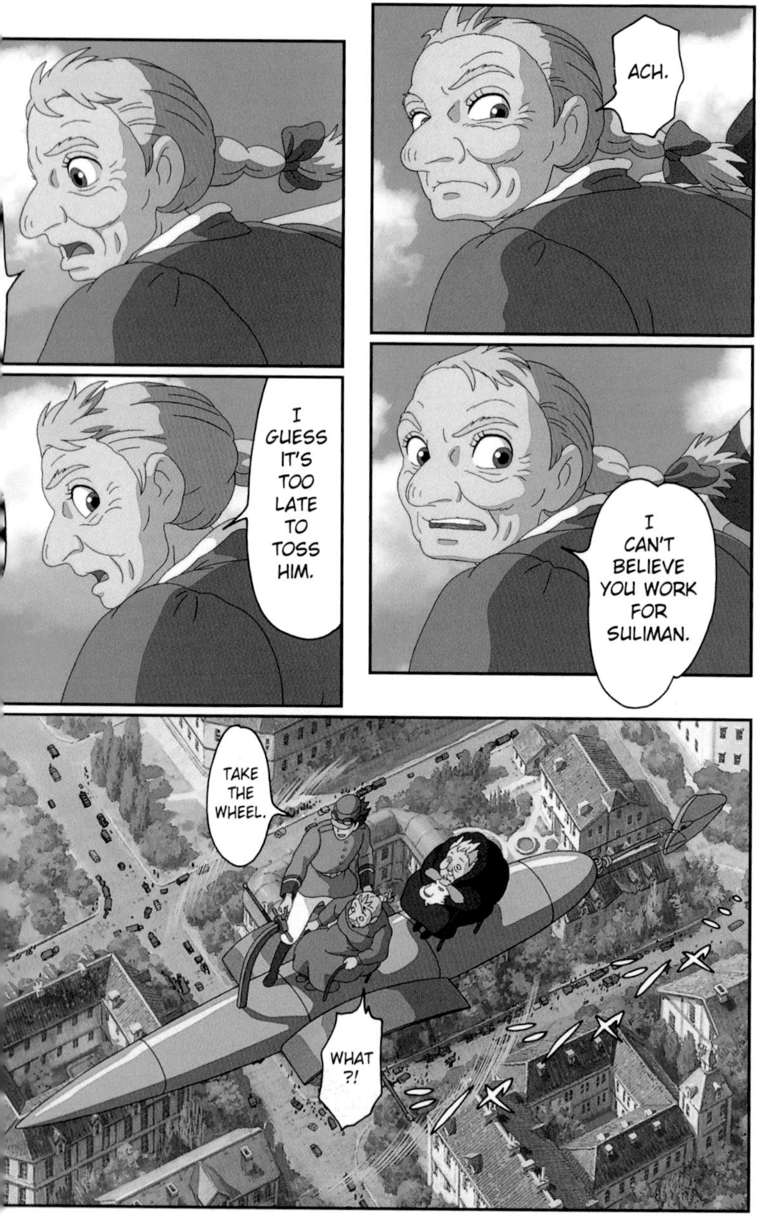
ACH.
I CAN'T BELIEVE YOU WORK FOR SULIMAN.
I GUESS IT'S TOO LATE TO TOSS HIM.
TAKE THE WHEEL.
WHAT?!

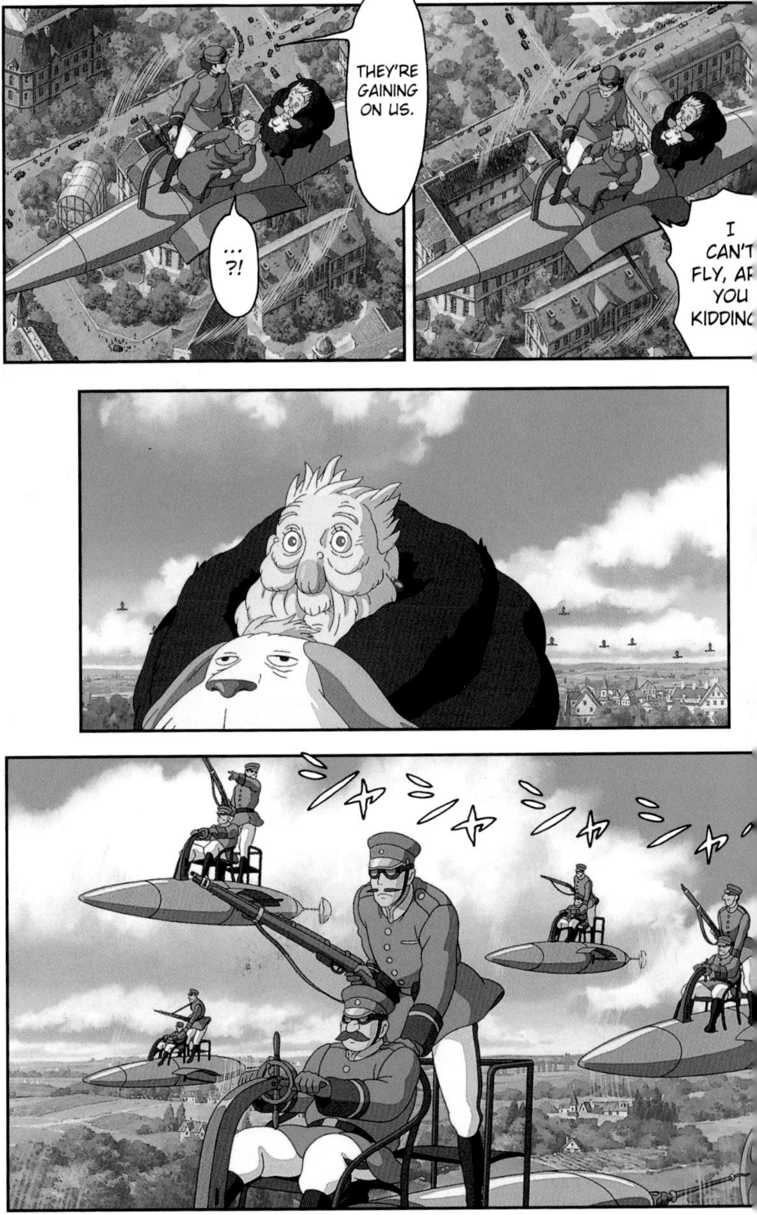
I CAN'T FLY, A
YOU KIDDIN
THEY'RE GAINING ON US.
...?!

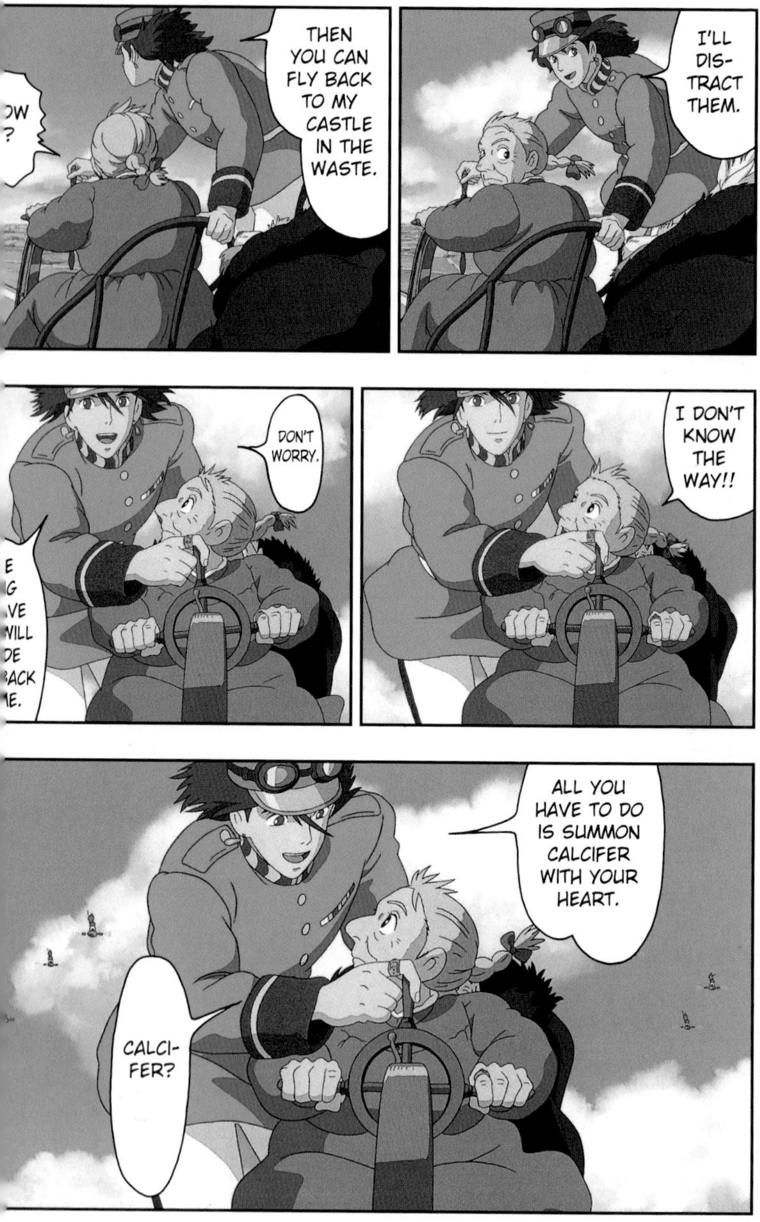
I'LL DIS-TRACT THEM.
THEN YOU CAN FLY BACK TO MY CASTLE IN THE WASTE.
I DON'T KNOW THE WAY!!
DON'T WORRY.
ALL YOU HAVE TO DO IS SUMMON CALCIFER WITH YOUR HEART.
CALCI-FER?

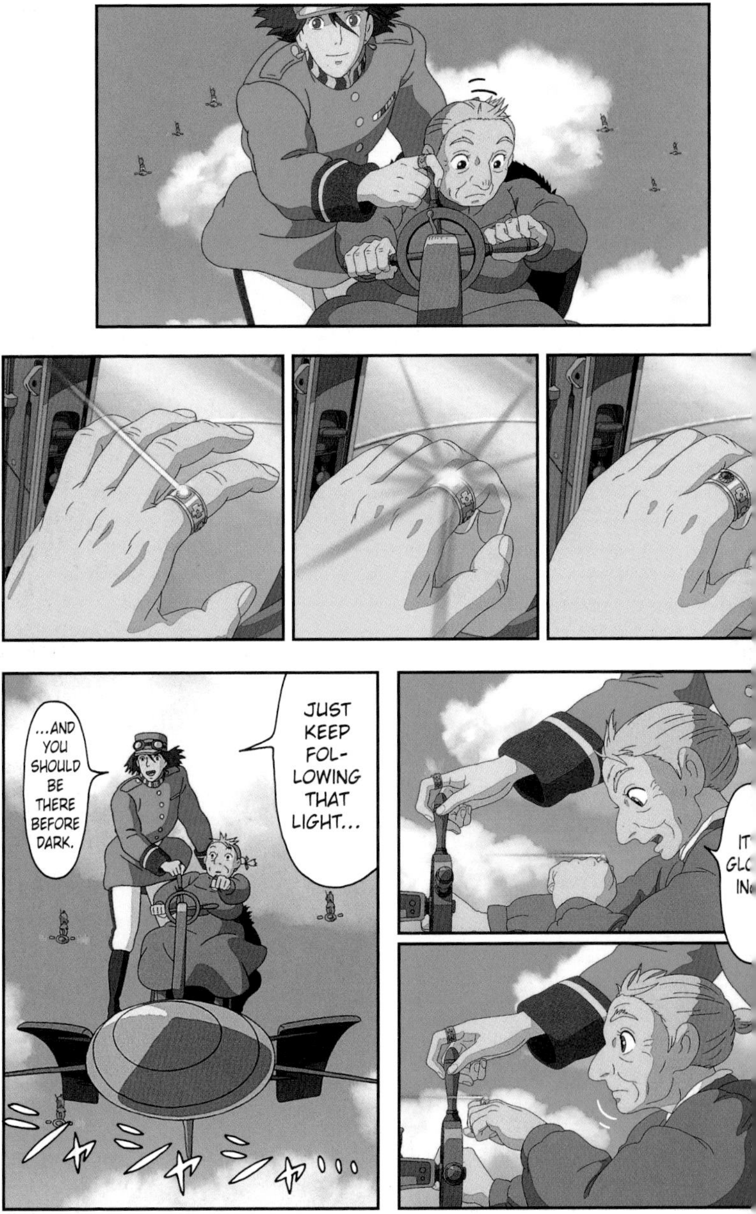
JUST KEEP FOL-LOWING THAT LIGHT...
...AND YOU SHOULD BE THERE BEFORE DARK.

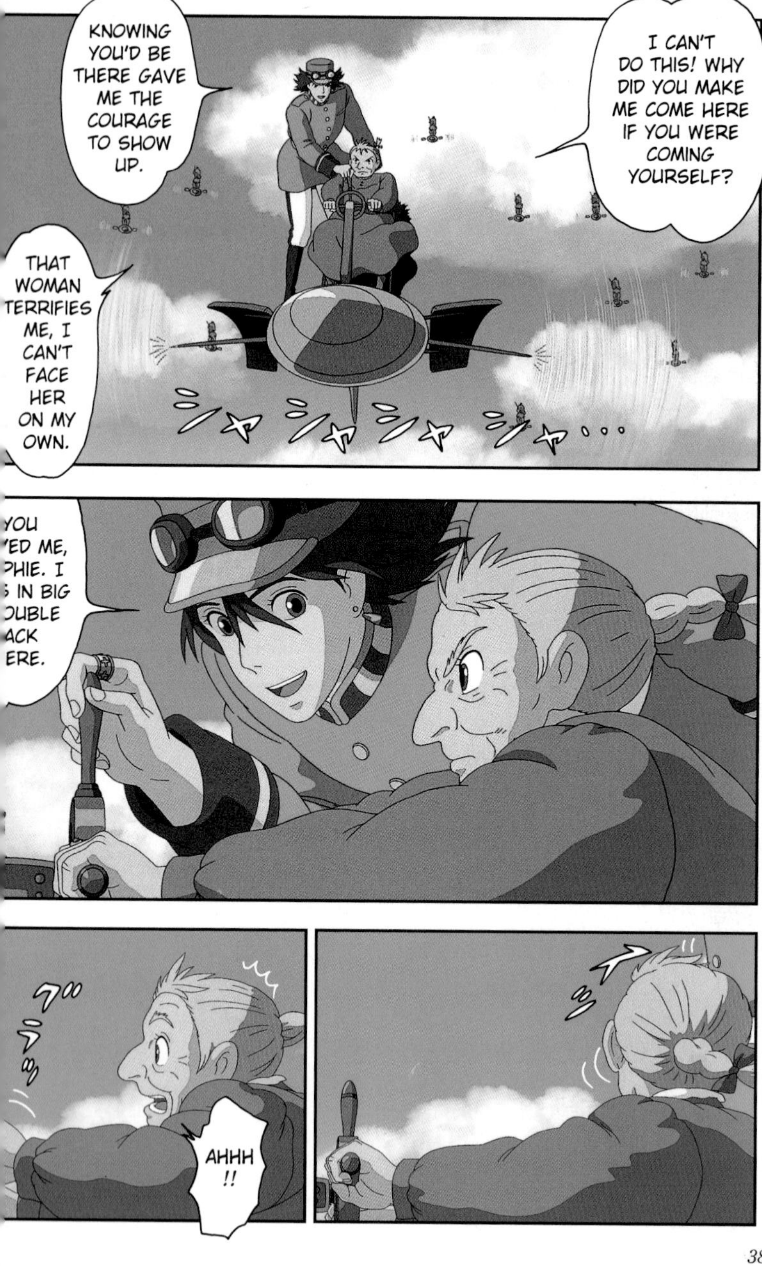
I CAN'T DO THIS! WHY DID YOU MAKE ME COME HERE IF YOU WERE COMING YOURSELF?
KNOWING YOU'D BE THERE GAVE ME THE COURAGE TO SHOW UP.
THAT WOMAN TERRIFIES ME, I CAN'T FACE HER ON MY OWN.
YOU 'ED ME, PHIE. I S IN BIG OUBLE ACK ERE.
AHHH !!

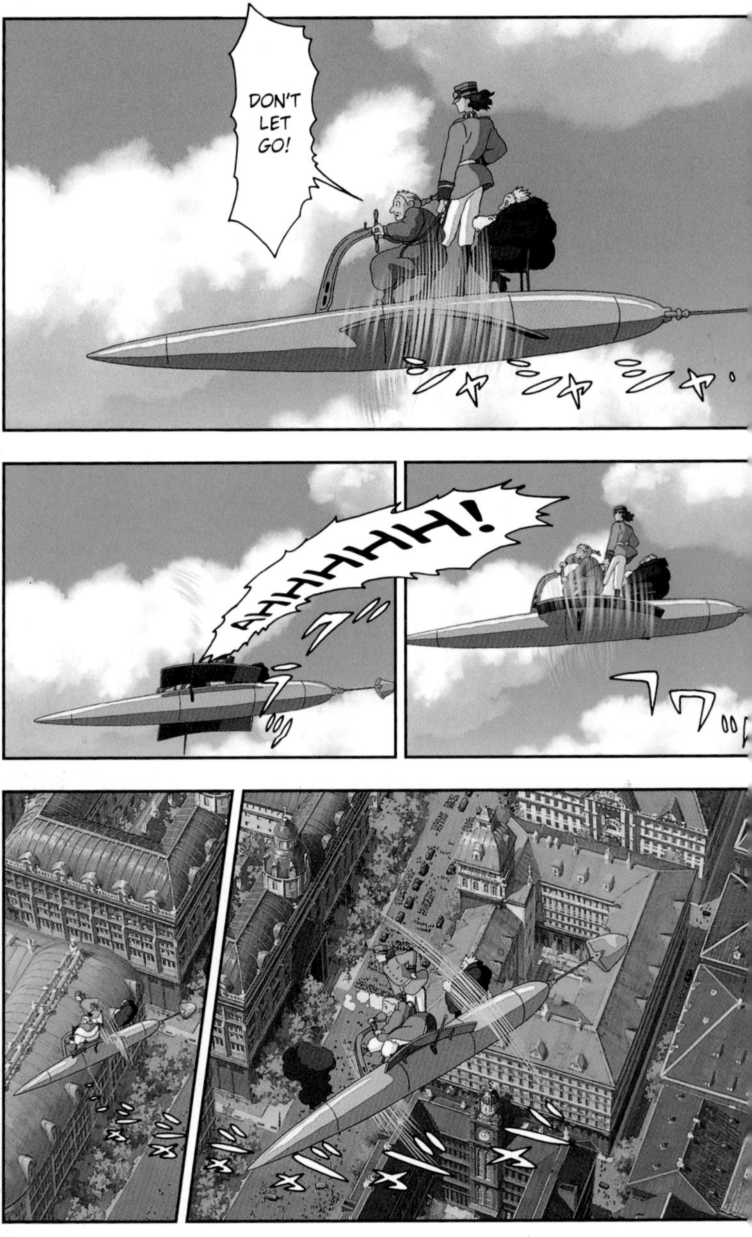
DON'T LET GO!
AHHHHHH!

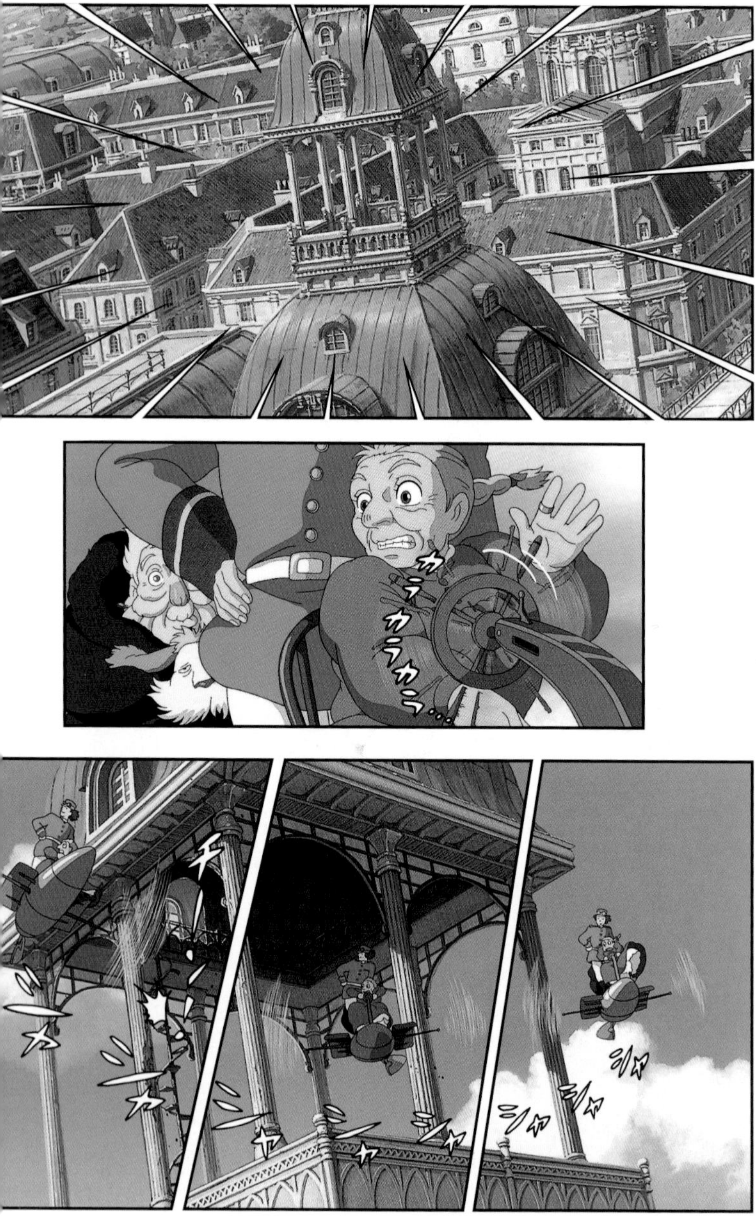
カラカラカラ…

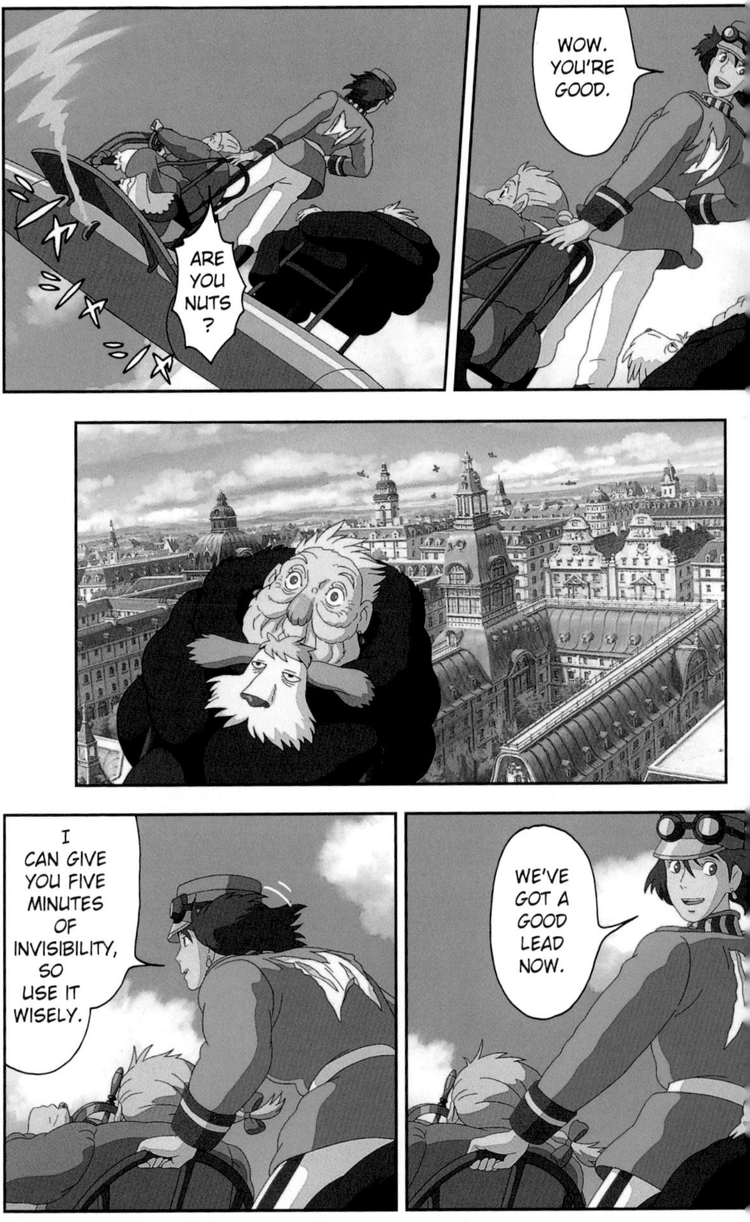
ARE YOU NUTS?
WOW. YOU'RE GOOD.
I CAN GIVE YOU FIVE MINUTES OF INVISIBILITY, SO USE IT WISELY.
WE'VE GOT A GOOD LEAD NOW.

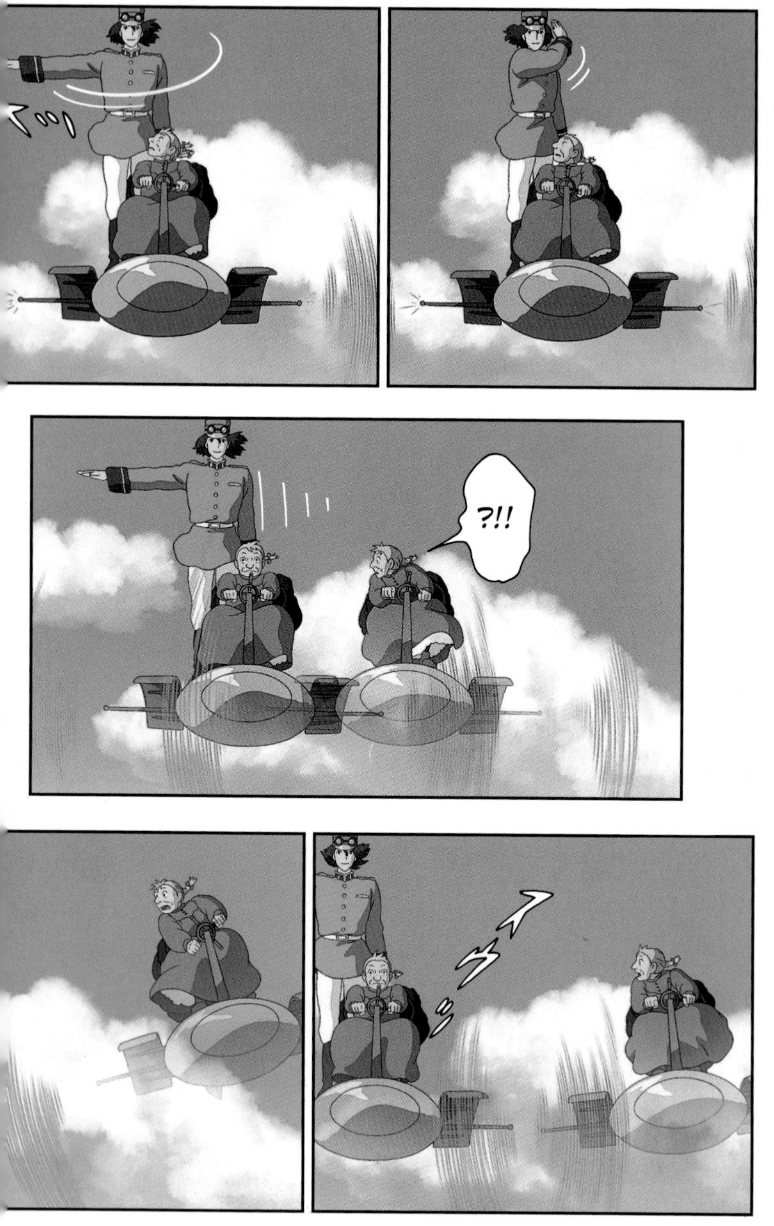
?!!

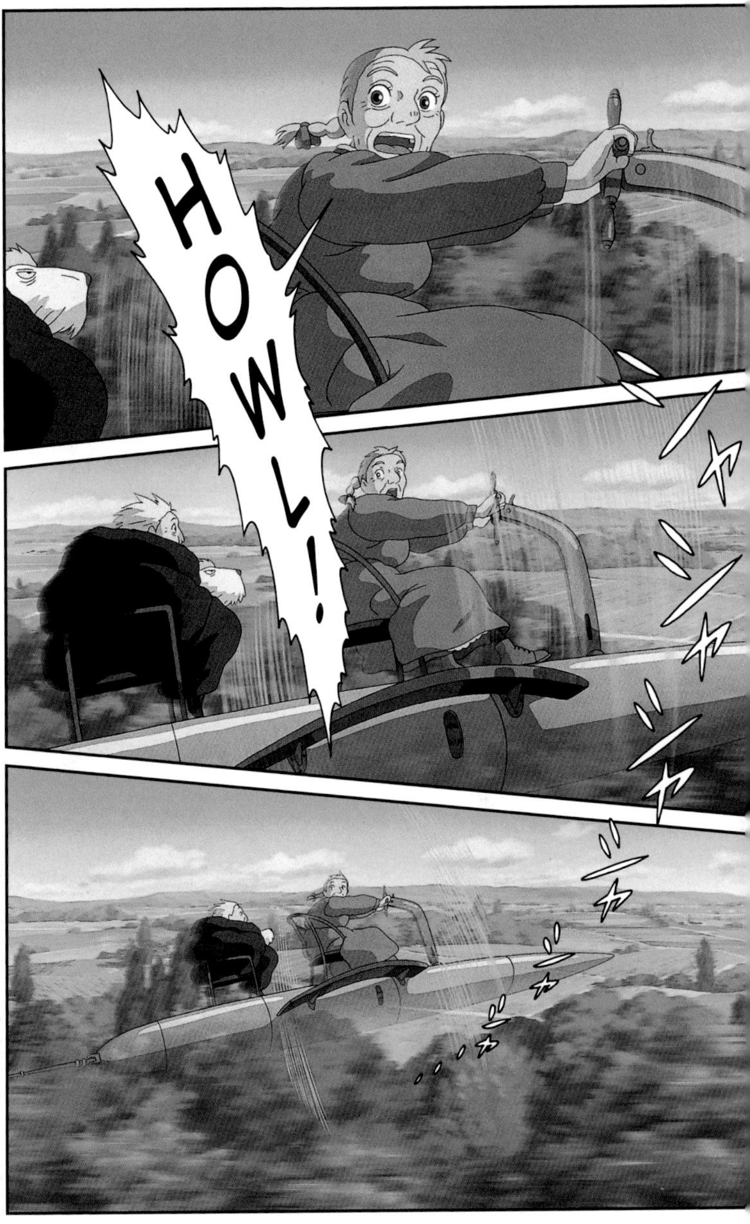
HOWL!

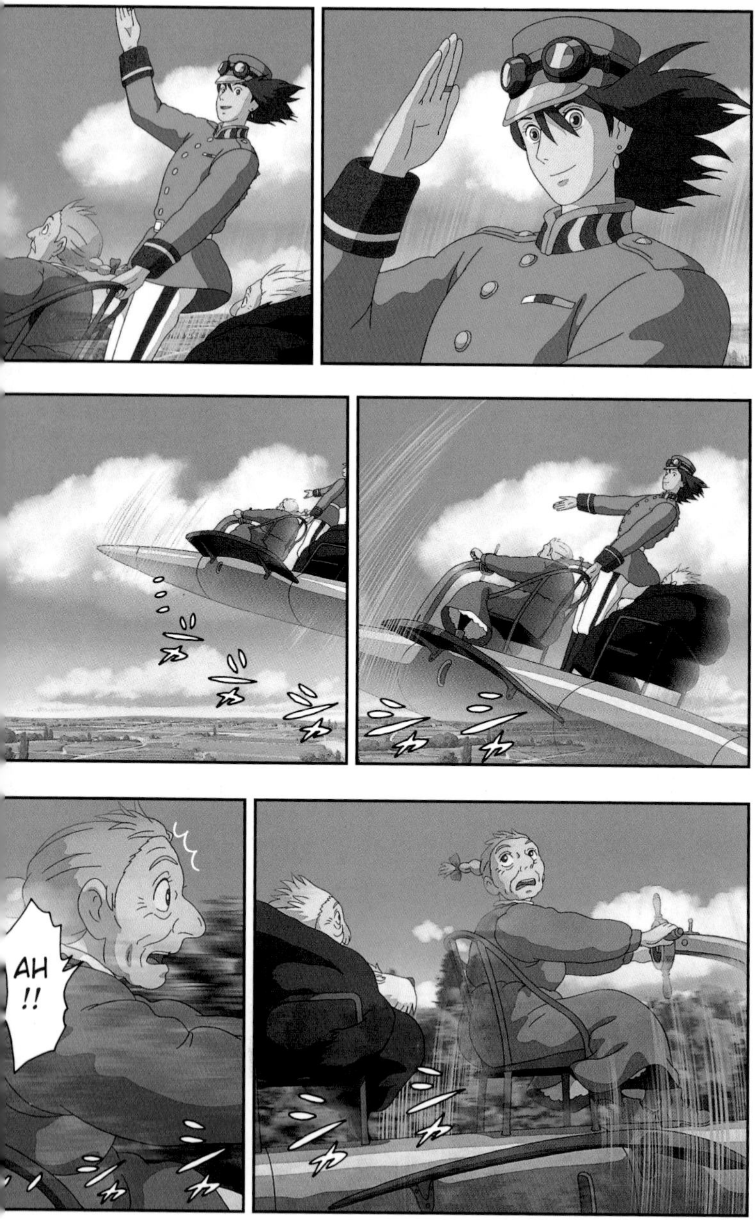
AH !!

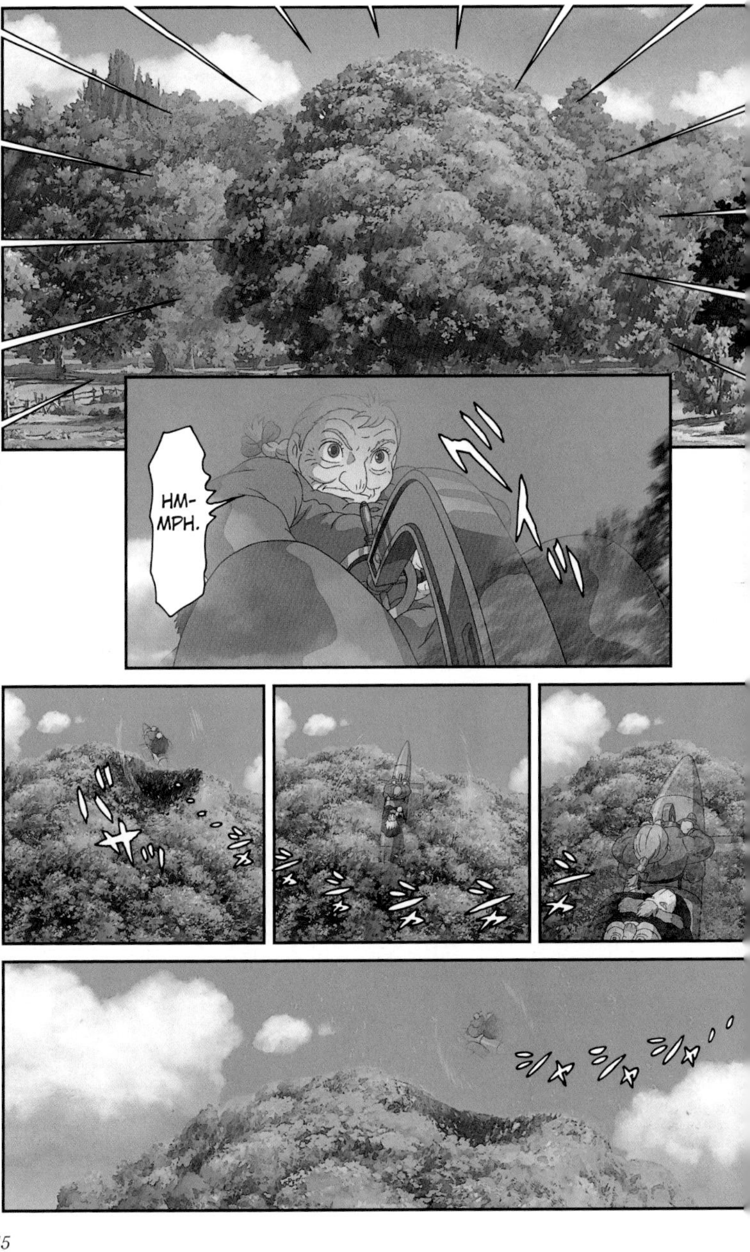
HM-
MPH.

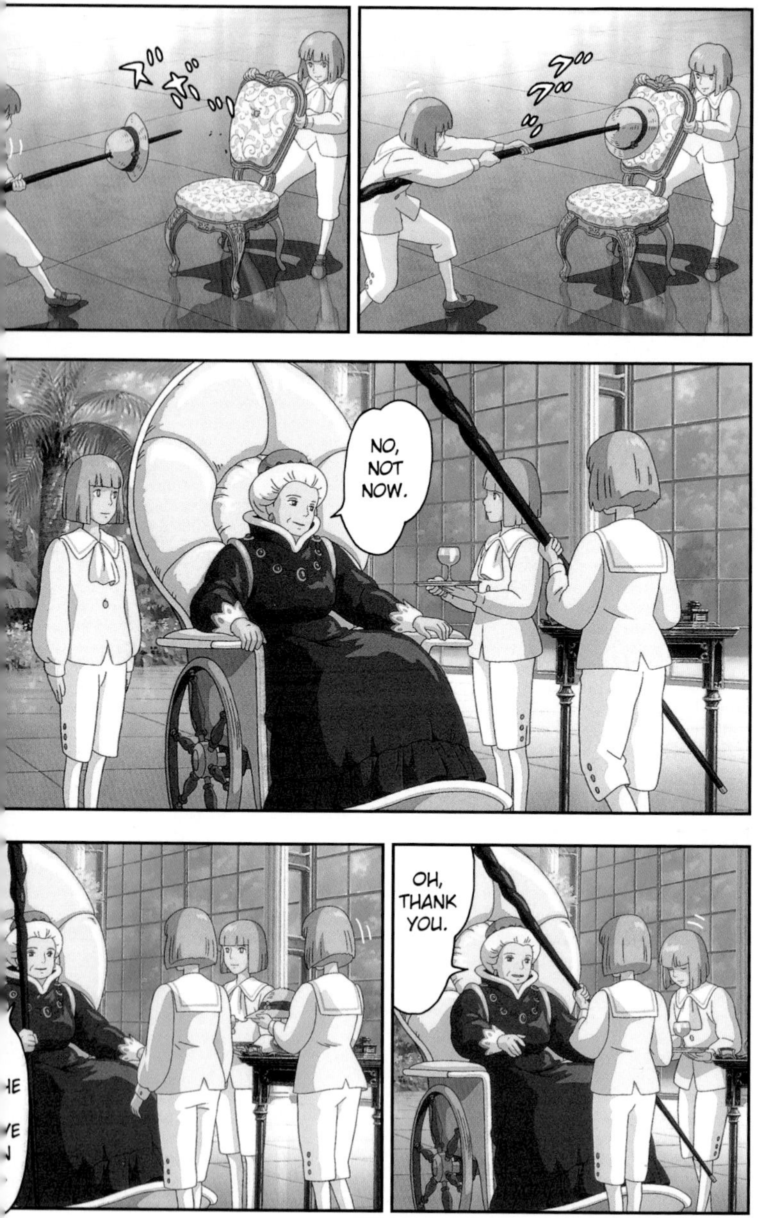
NO, NOT NOW.
OH, THANK YOU.

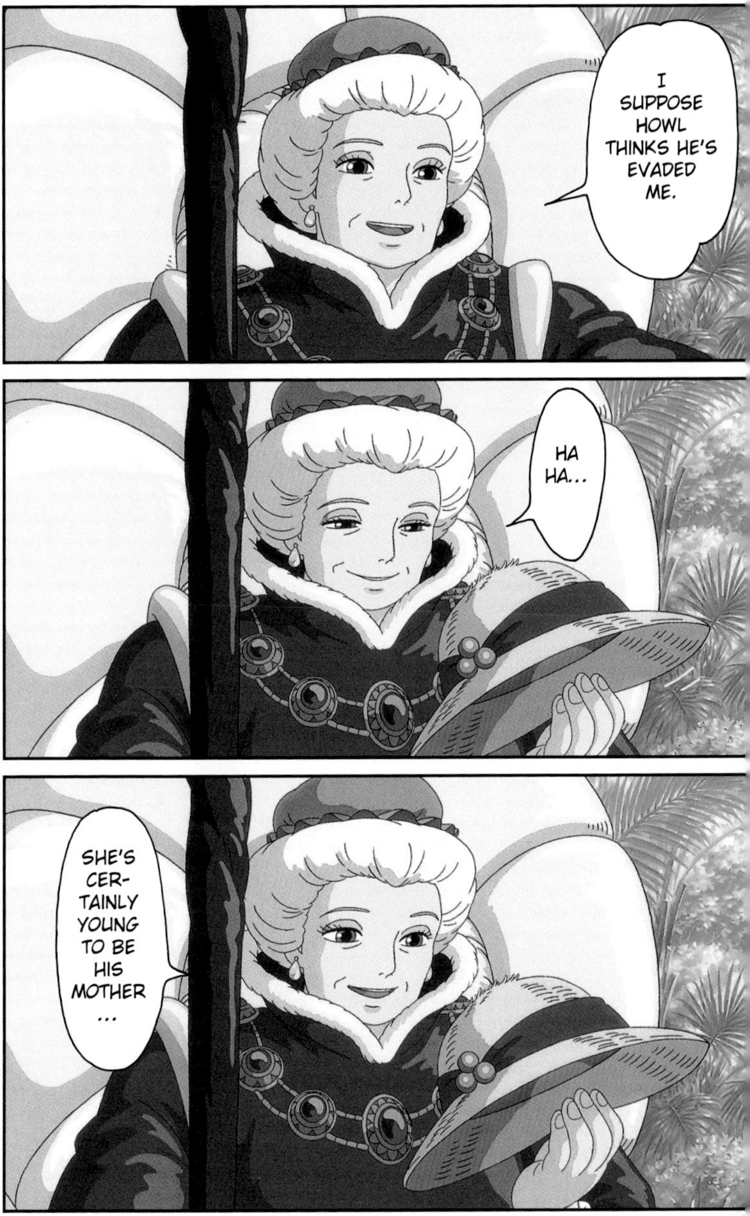
I SUPPOSE HOWL THINKS HE'S EVADED ME.
HA HA...
SHE'S CER-TAINLY YOUNG TO BE HIS MOTHER ...

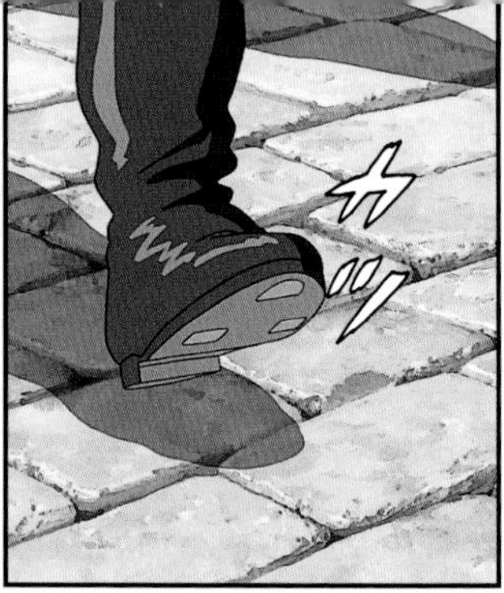
カッ

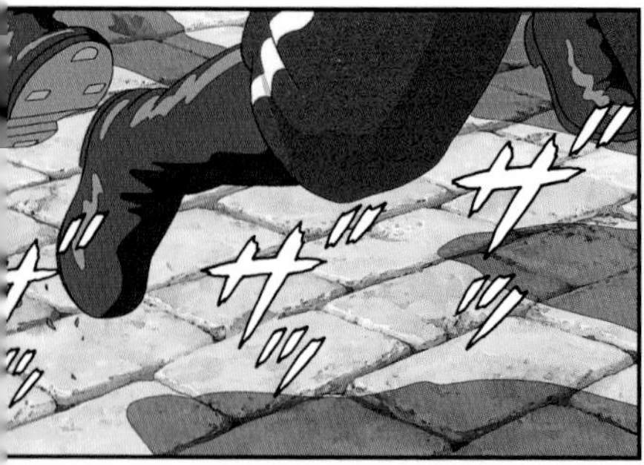
ザッ
ザッ
ザッ

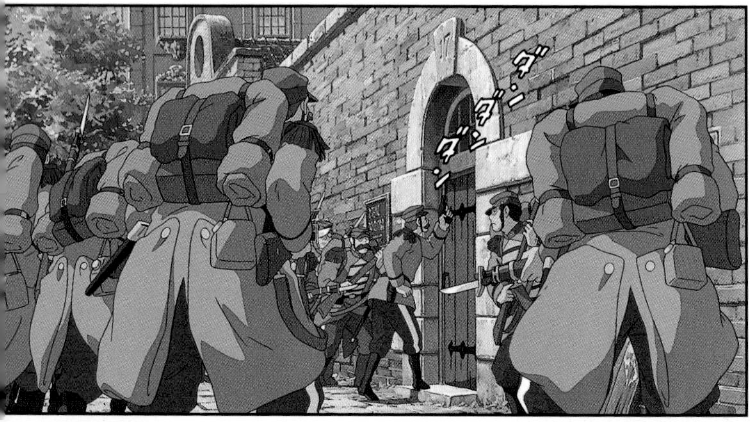
ダン
ダン
ダン

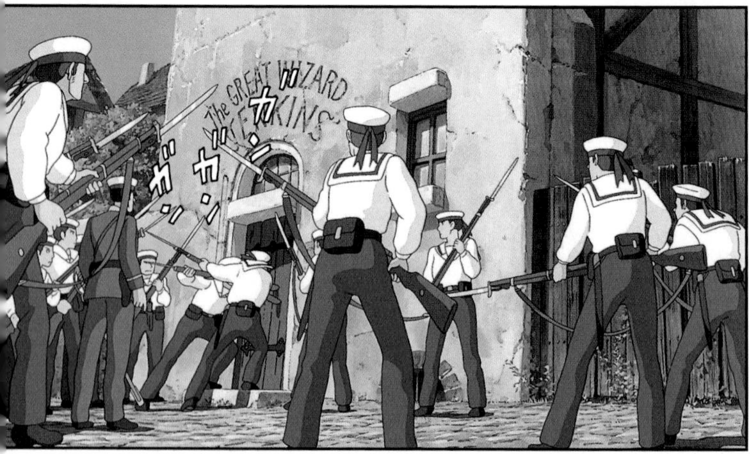
The GREAT WIZARD
カッ
ガッ
ガッ

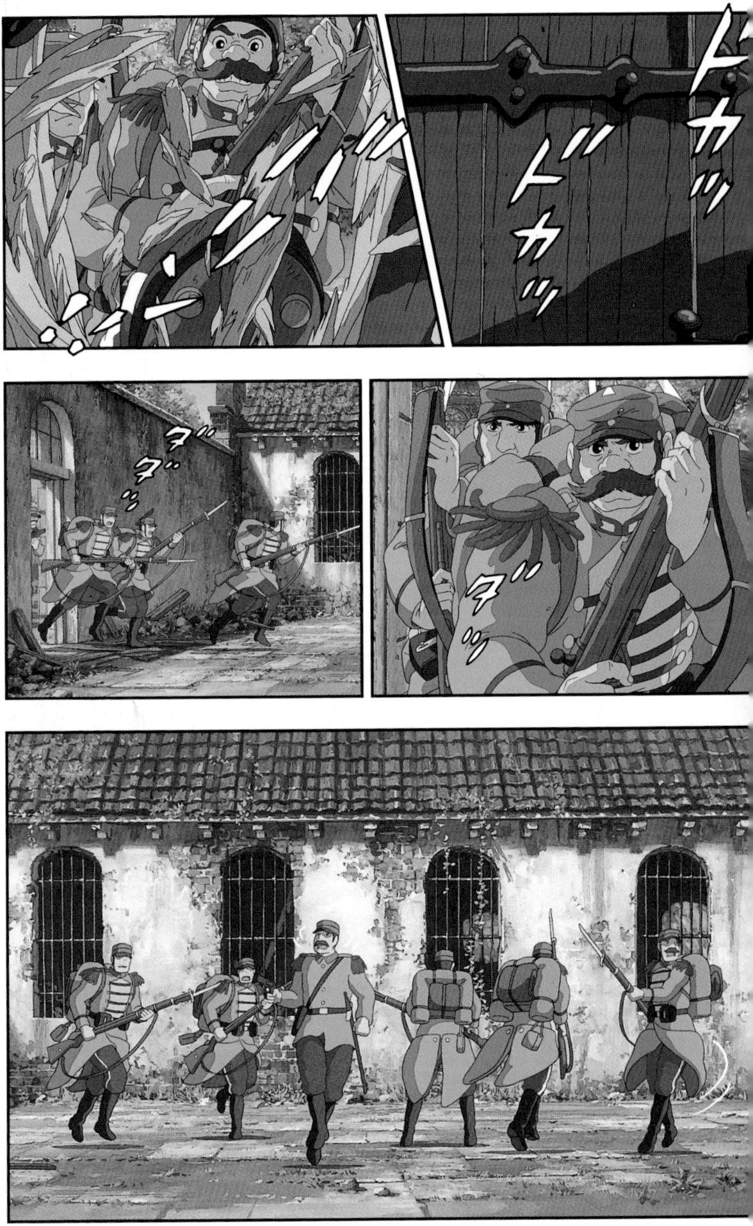

ドカッ
ドカッ
バリ
ダダッ
ダダッ

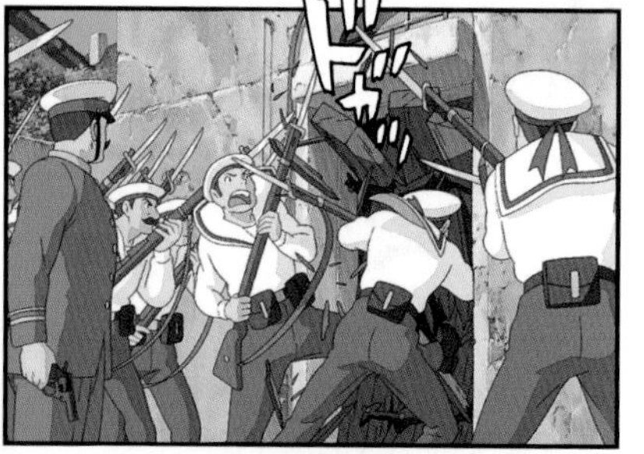

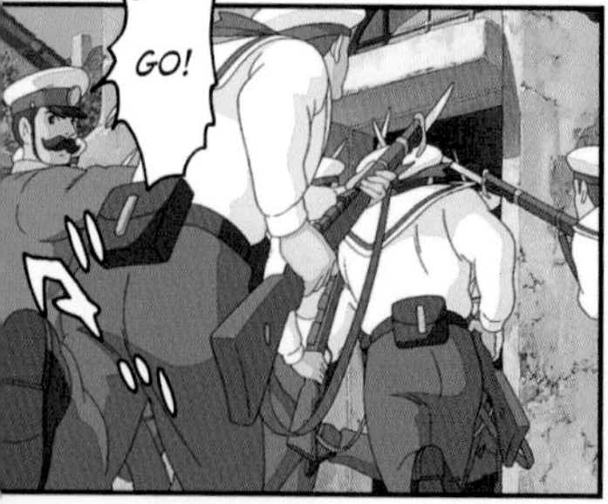
GO!

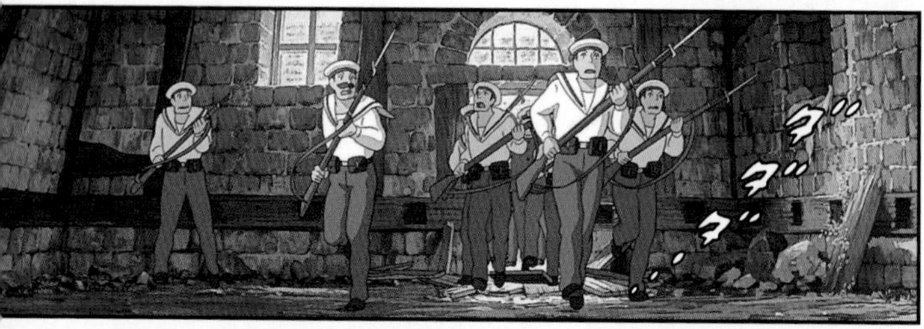

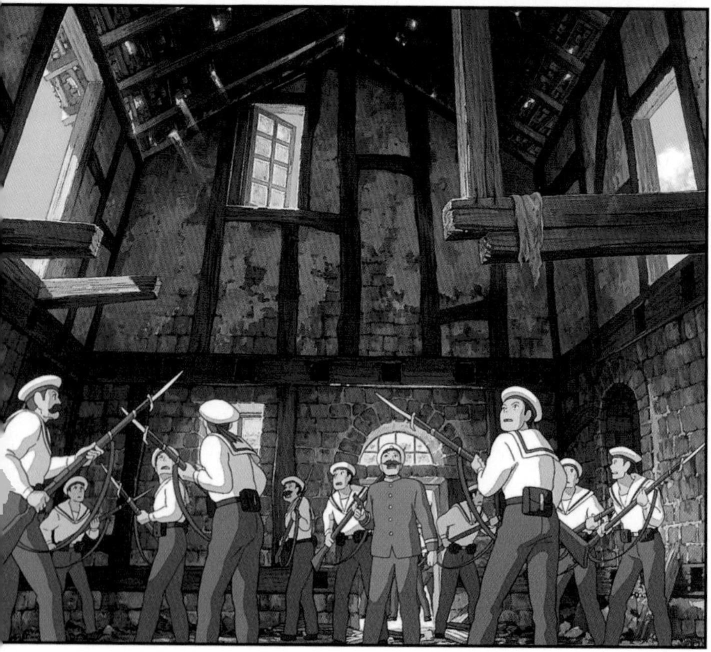

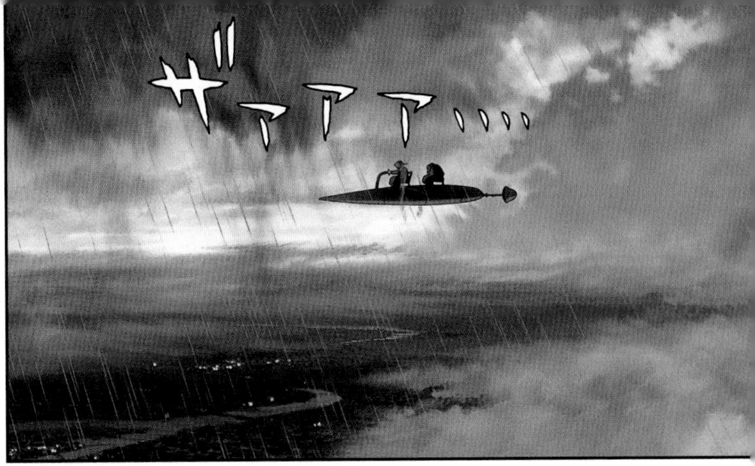
ザァアア・・・・
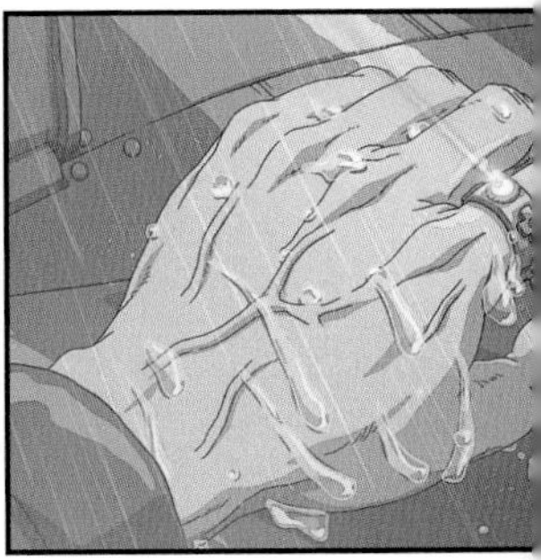
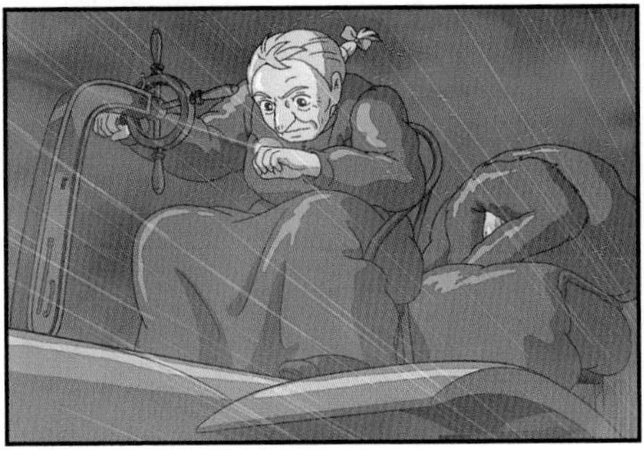
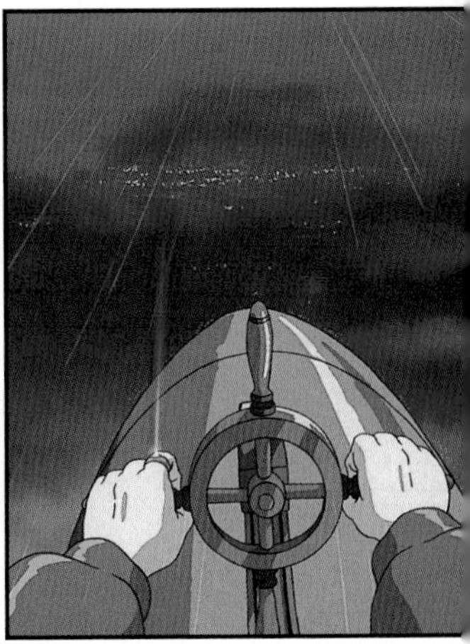
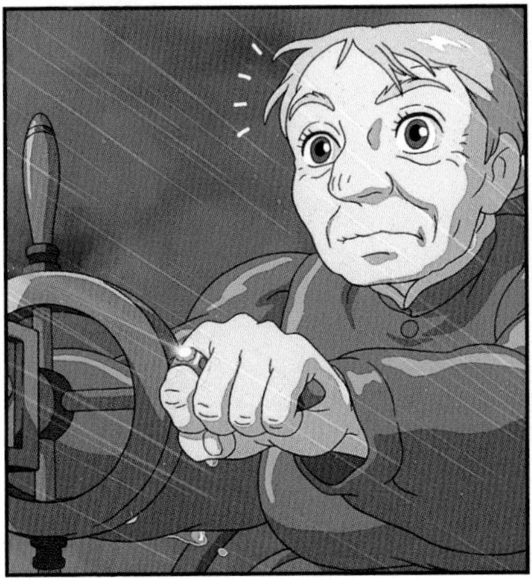

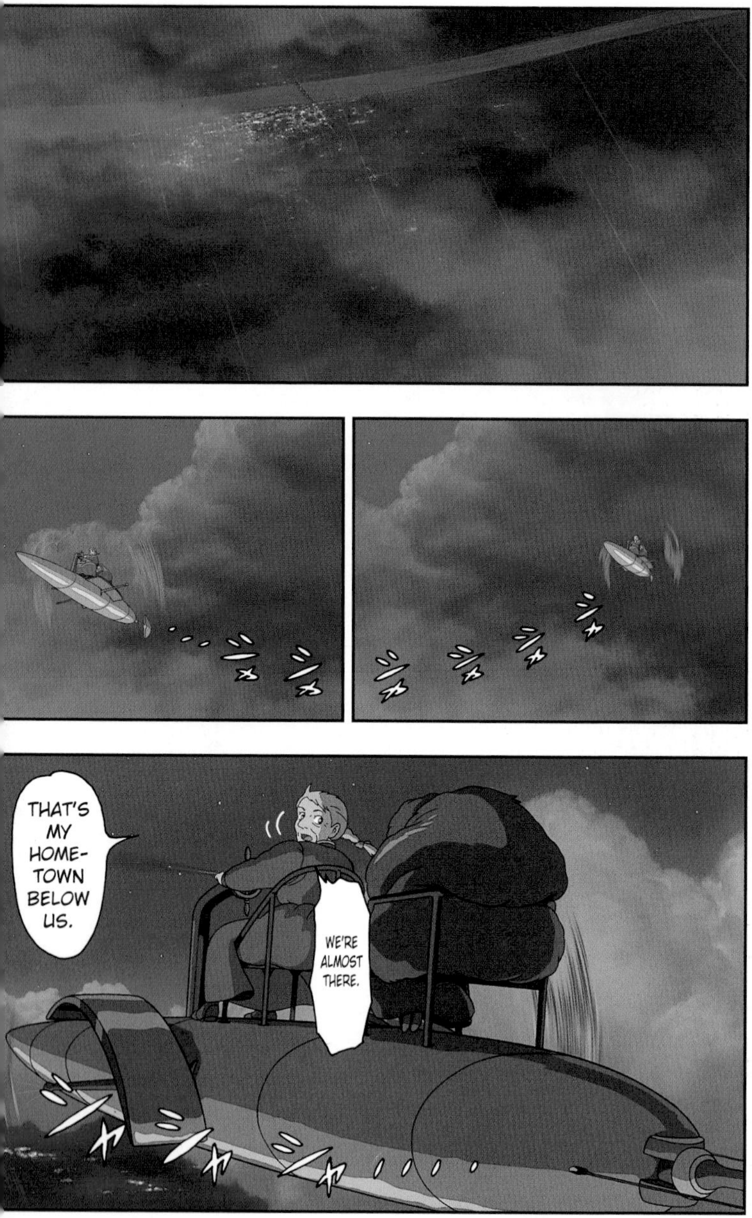
WE'RE ALMOST THERE.
THAT'S MY HOME-TOWN BELOW US.

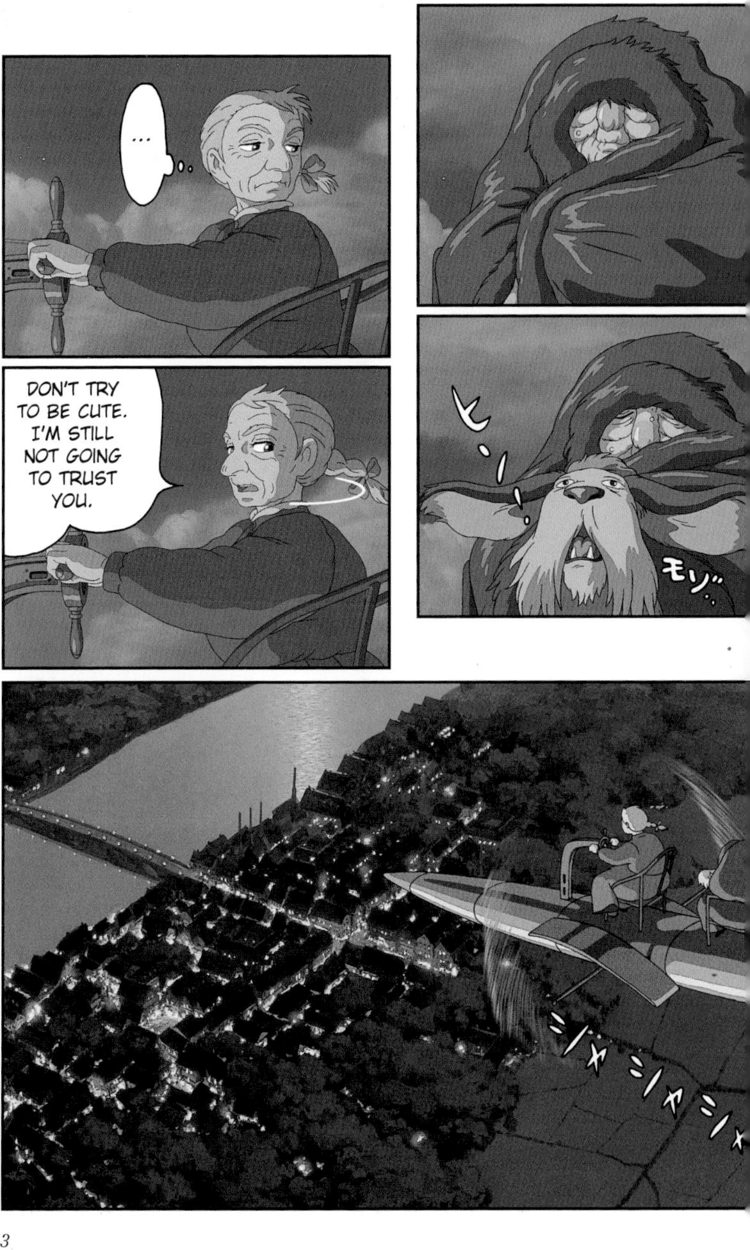
ヒ・!!
モゾ..
...
DON'T TRY TO BE CUTE. I'M STILL NOT GOING TO TRUST YOU.
シャシャシャ

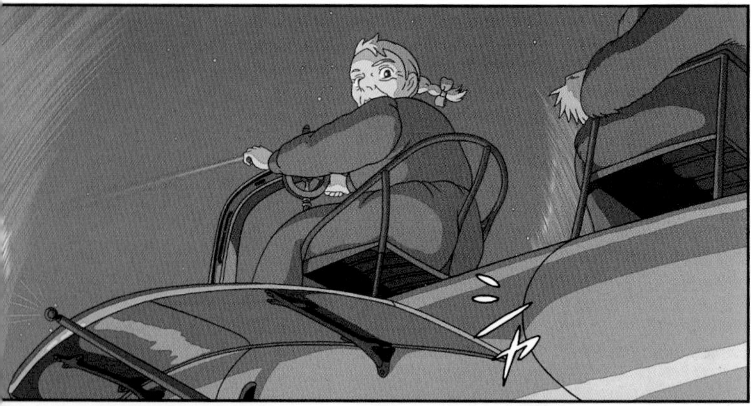
ジャ

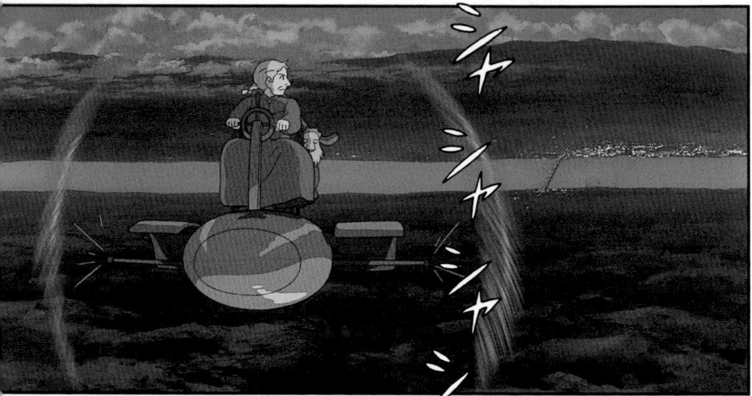
ジャ
ジャ
ジャ
ジャ

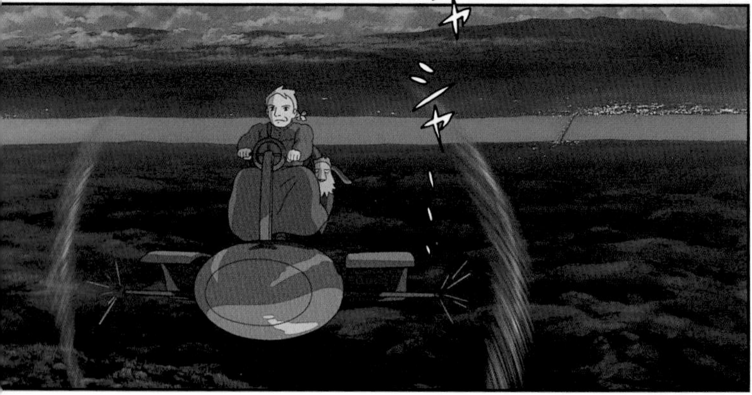
ジャー

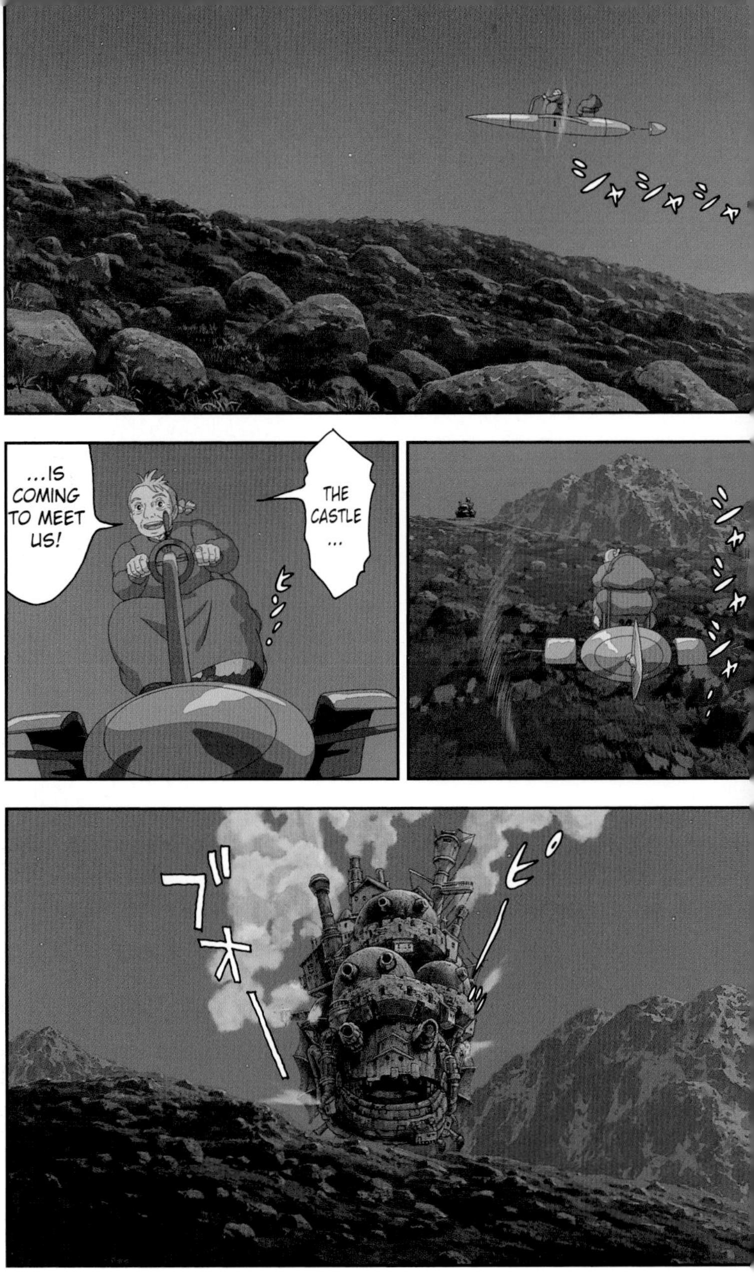
シャシャシャ
シャシャシャ…
THE CASTLE…
…IS COMING TO MEET US!
ピー
ブオー

SOPHIE! HI!

OW
M I
POSED
AND
HIS
NG?

MARKL, HELP ME!

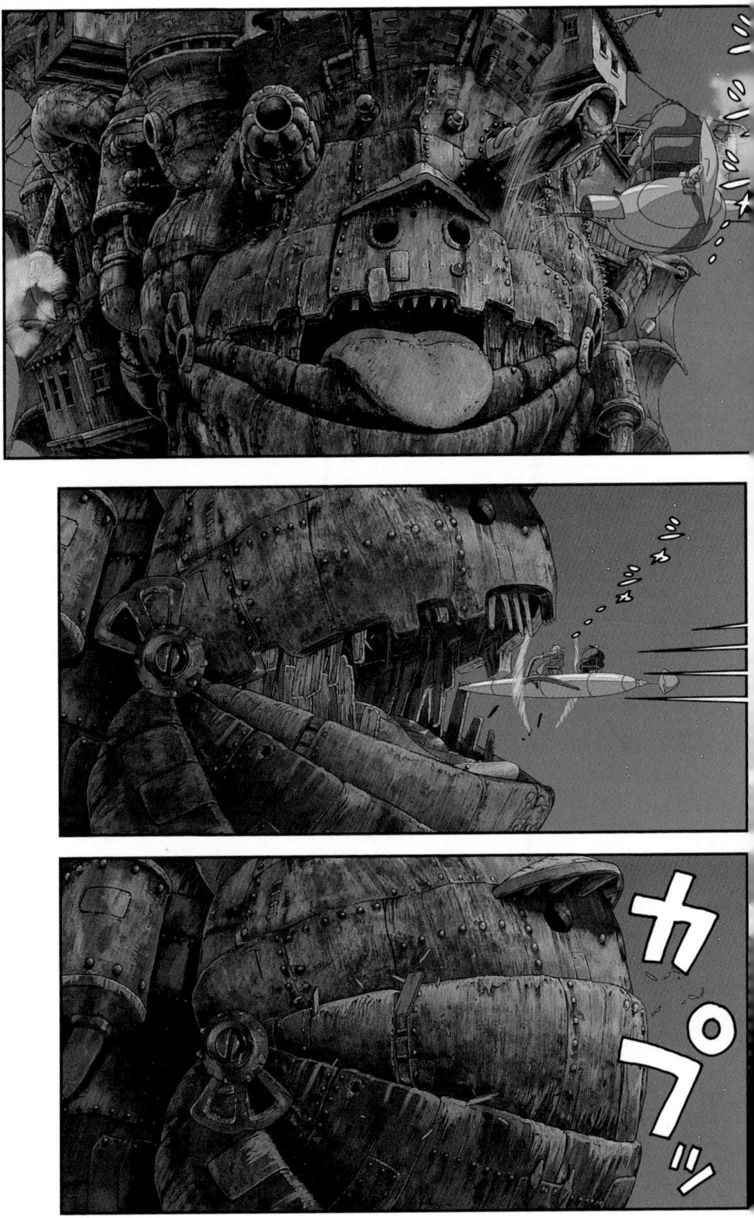
カプッ

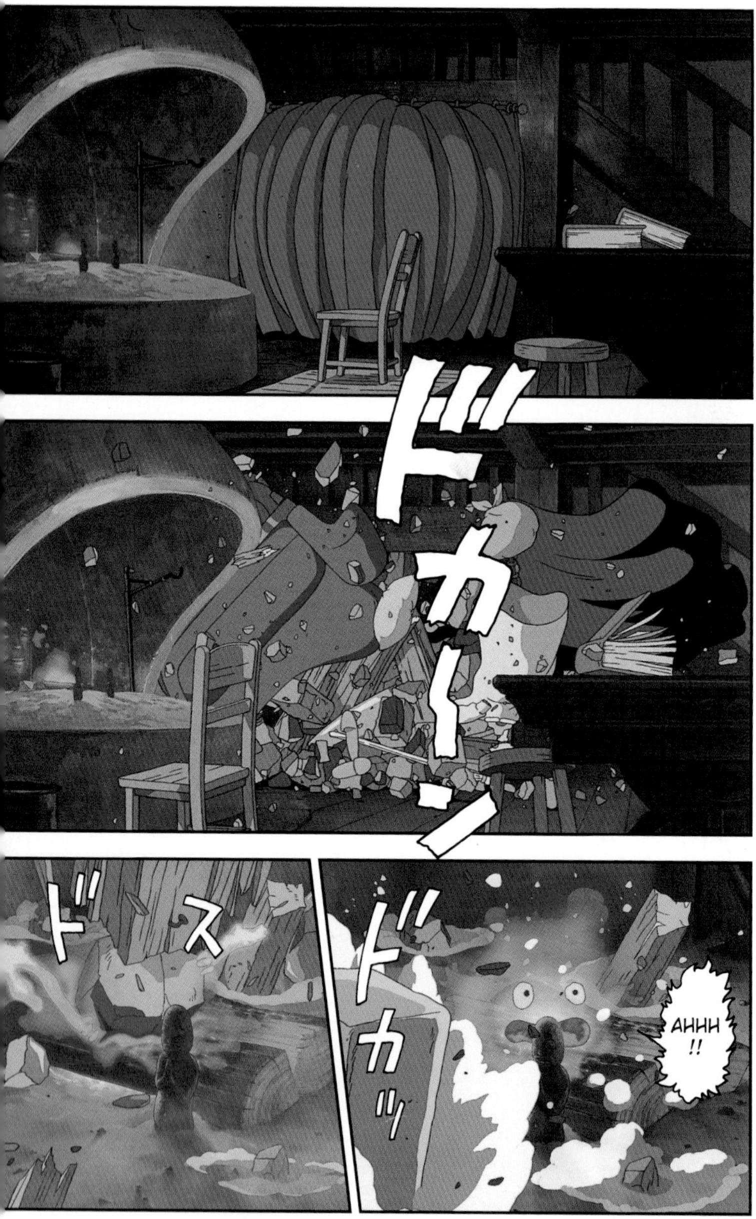
ドカ〜ン
ドカッ
AHHH!!
ドス

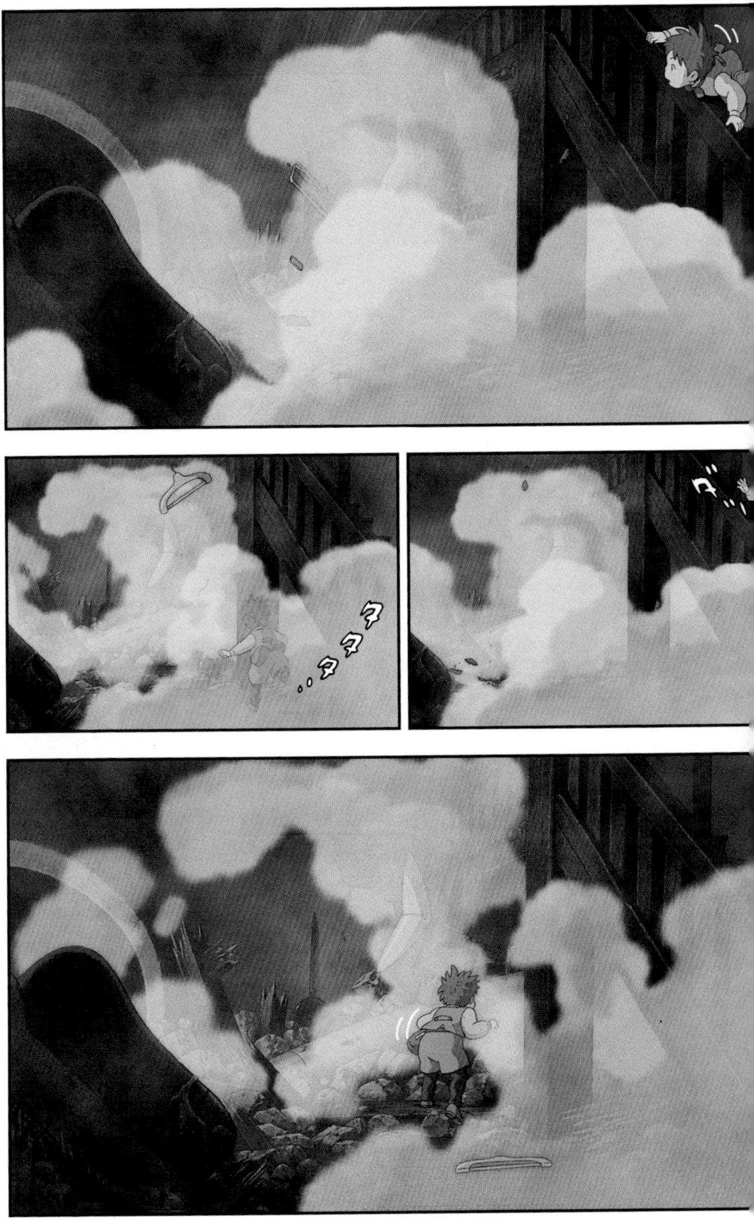
タタタ

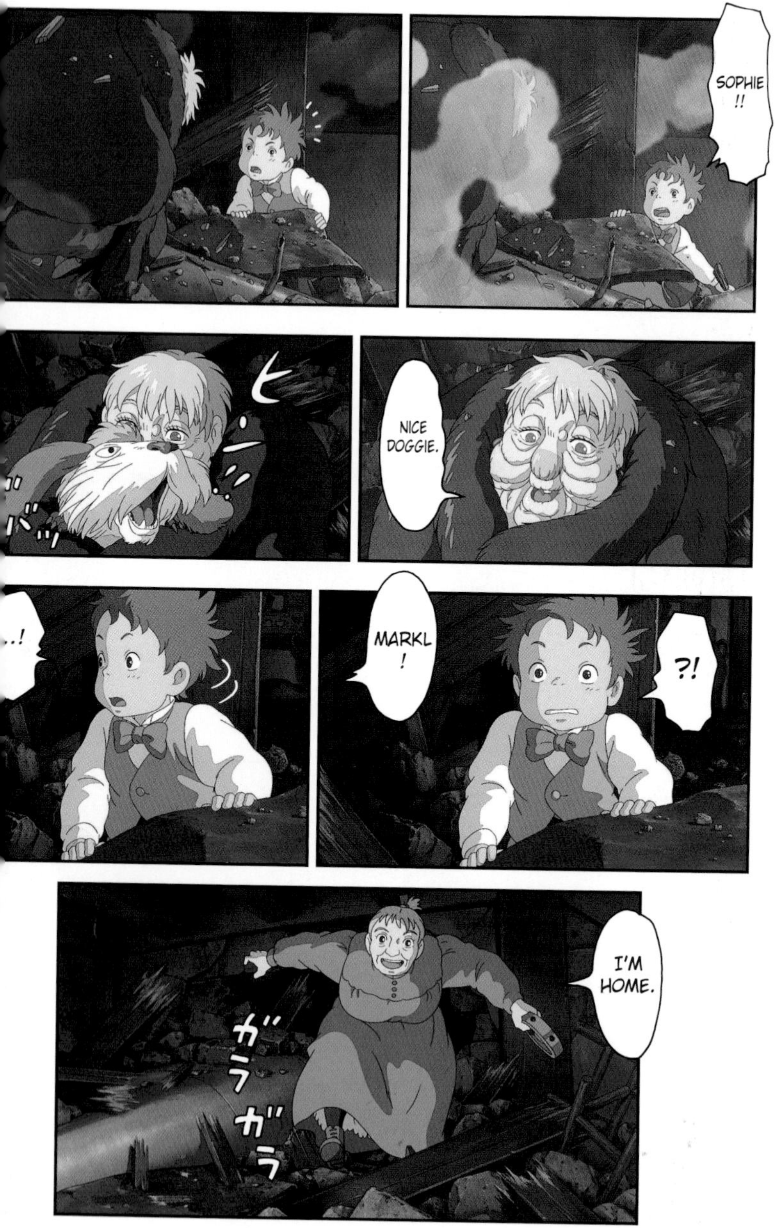
SOPHIE !!
NICE DOGGIE.
MARKL !
?!
...!
I'M HOME.
ガラガラ

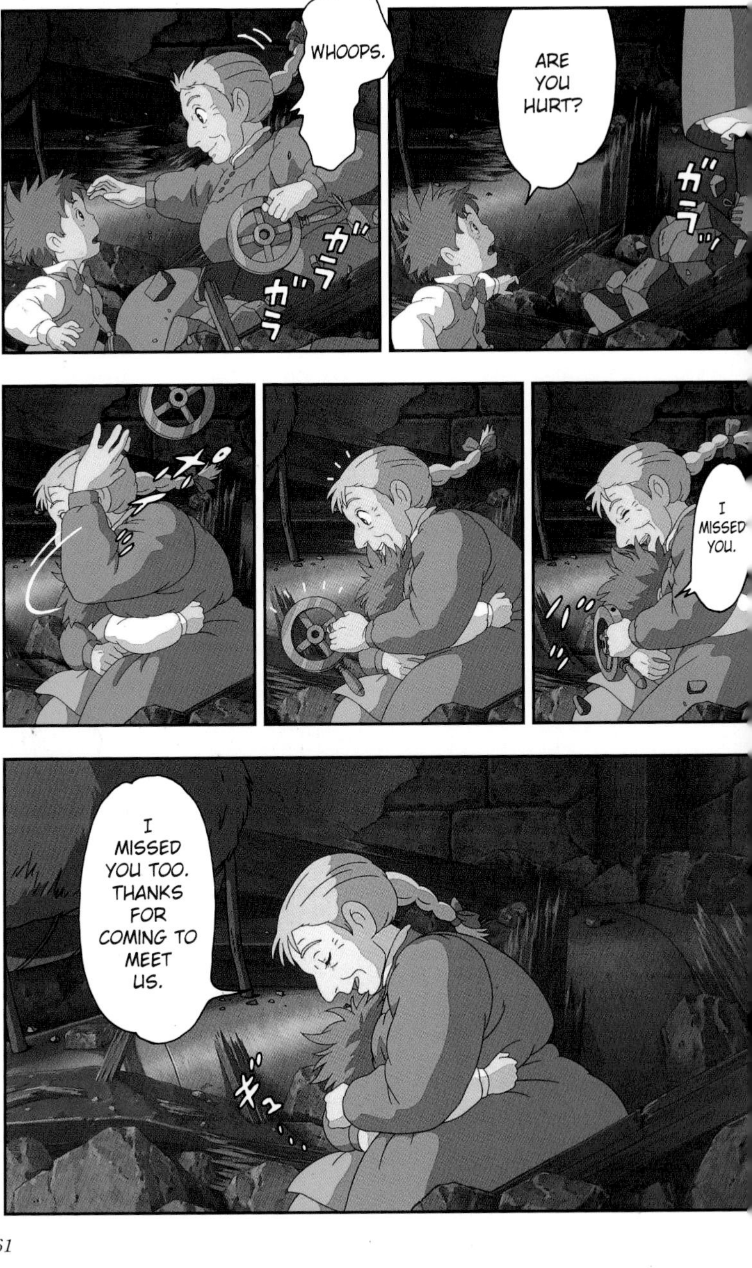
ARE YOU HURT?
WHOOPS.
I MISSED YOU.
I MISSED YOU TOO. THANKS FOR COMING TO MEET US.

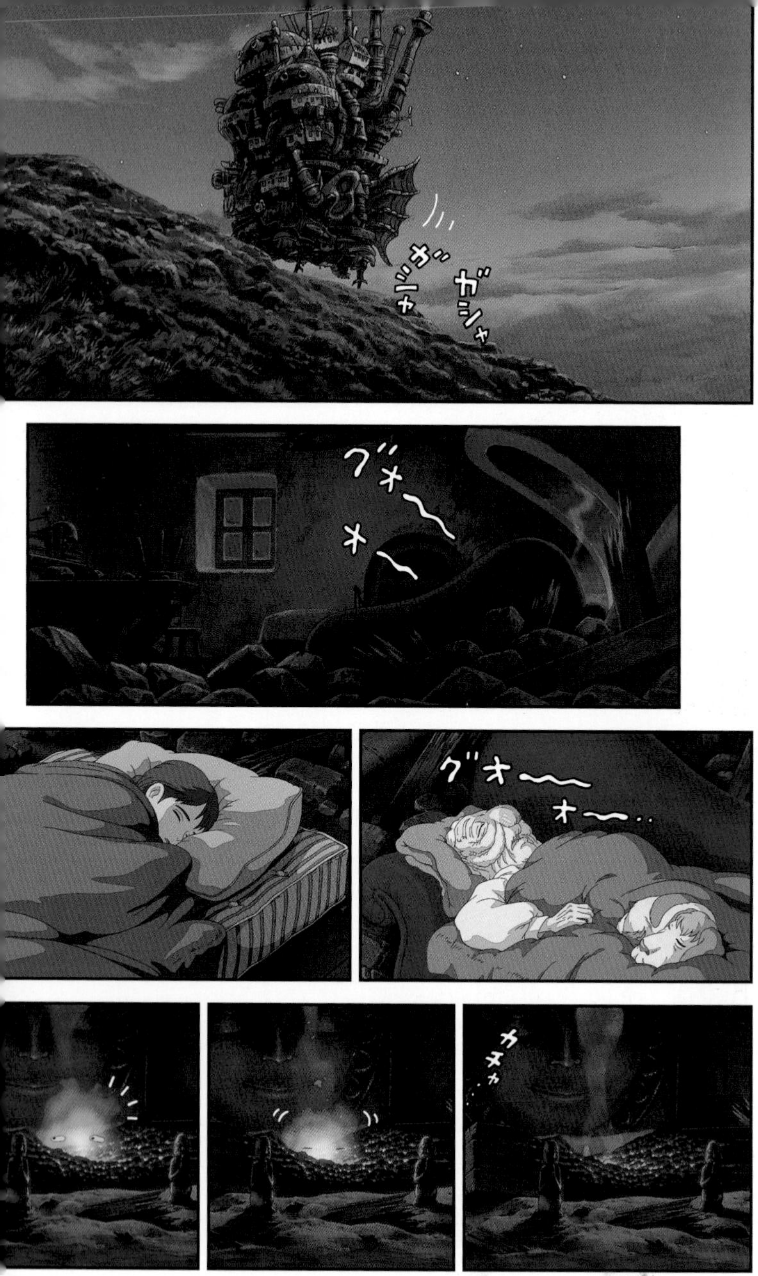
ガシャ
ガシャ
グオ〜〜
オ〜
グオ〜〜
オ〜..
カヌャ...

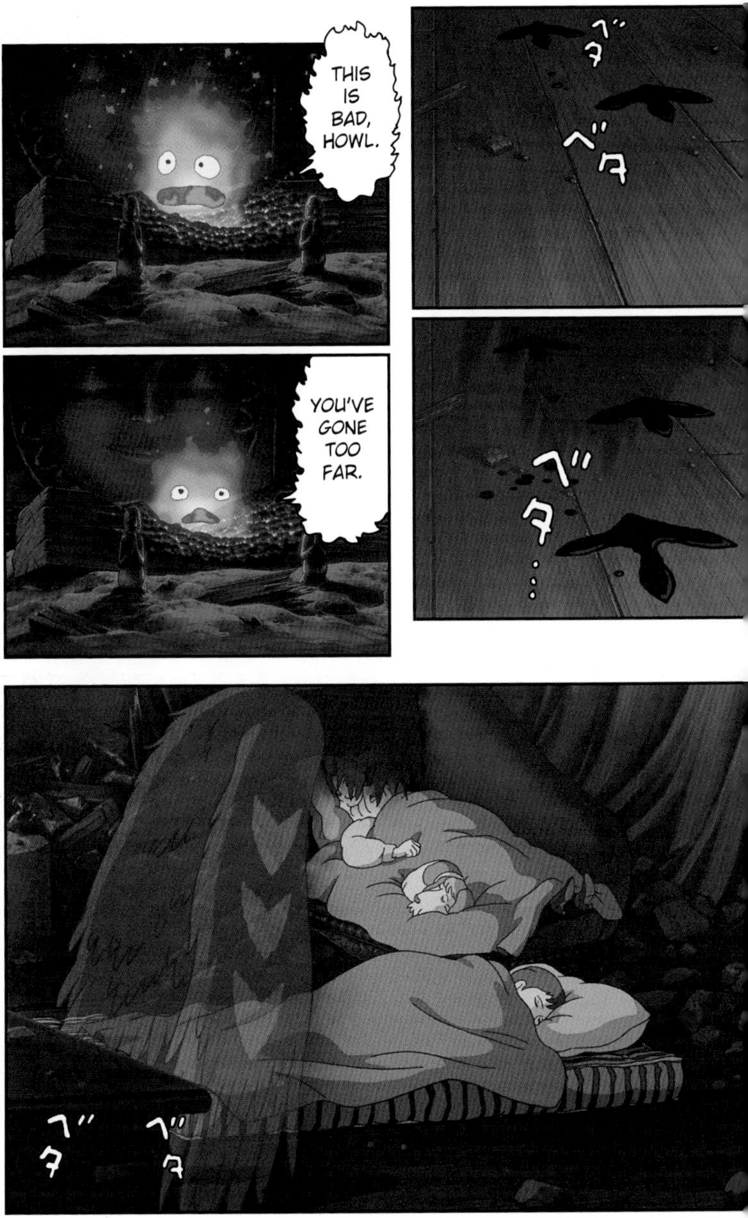
ベタ
ベタ
THIS IS BAD, HOWL.
ベタ...
YOU'VE GONE TOO FAR.
ベタ
ベタ

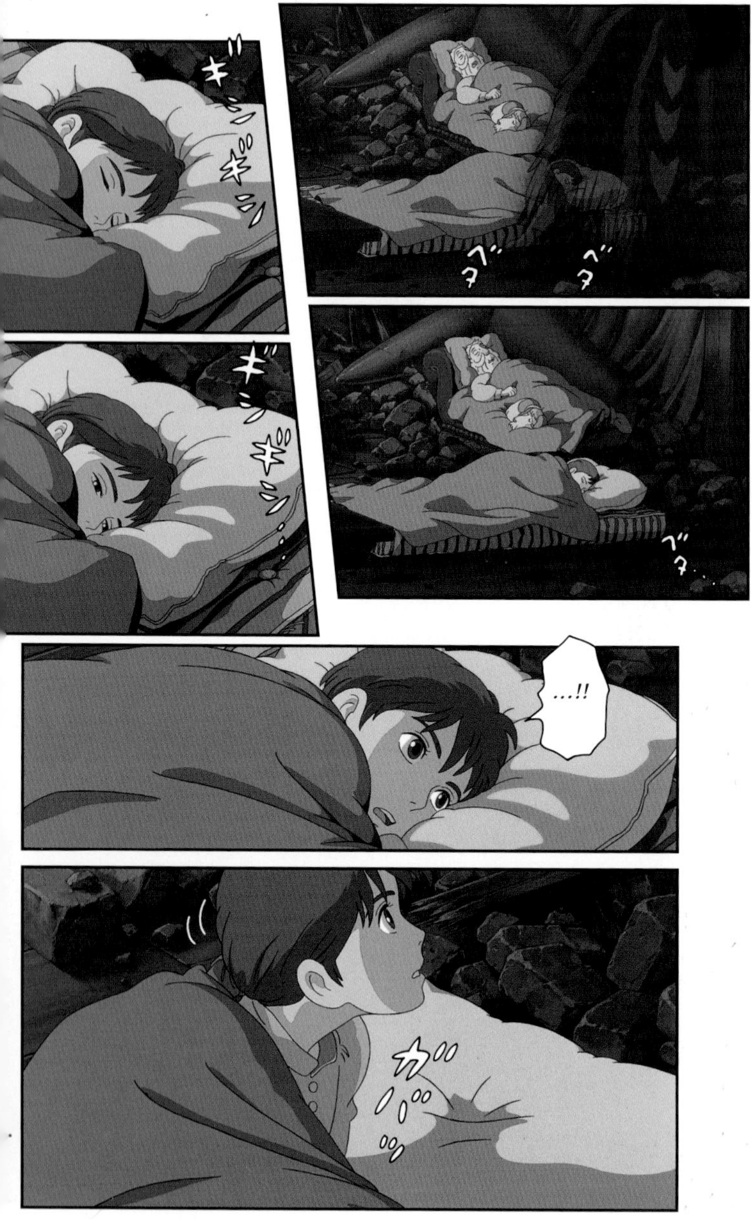
ベタ
ベタ
ベタ...
ギシ
ギシ
ギシ
ギシ...
...!!
ガバ

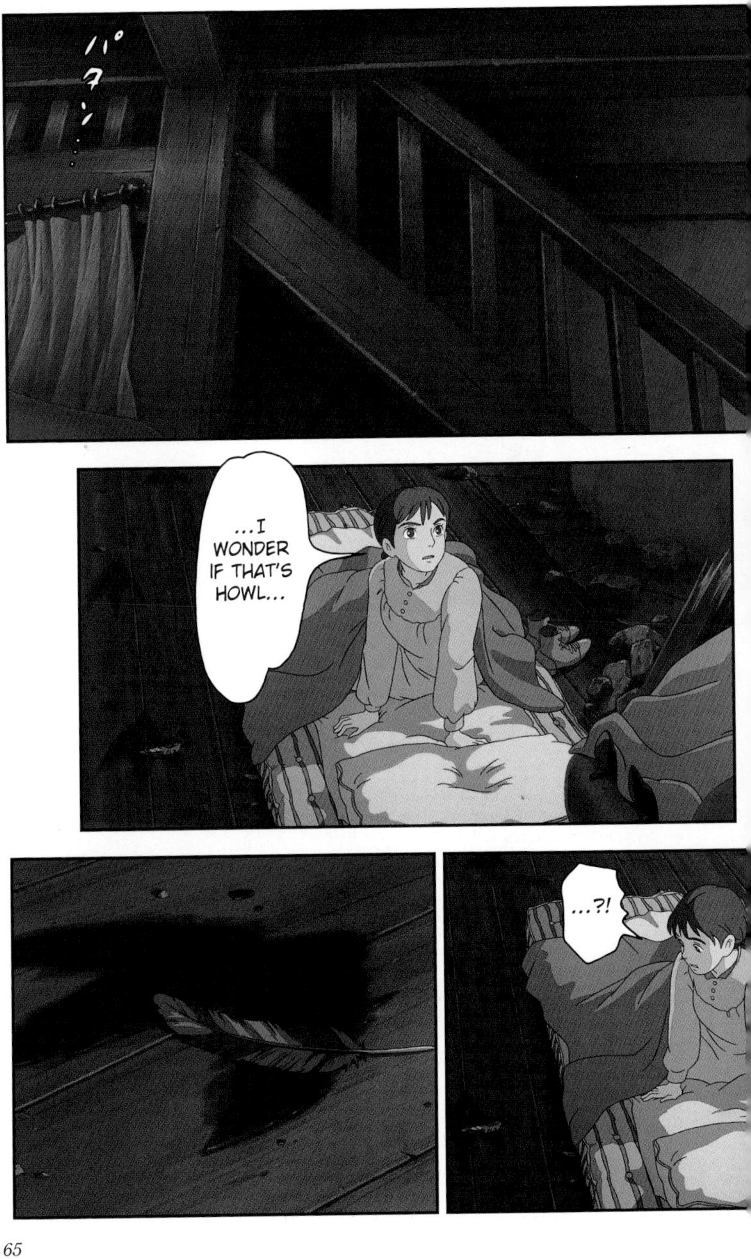
パタン…
...I WONDER IF THAT'S HOWL...
...?!

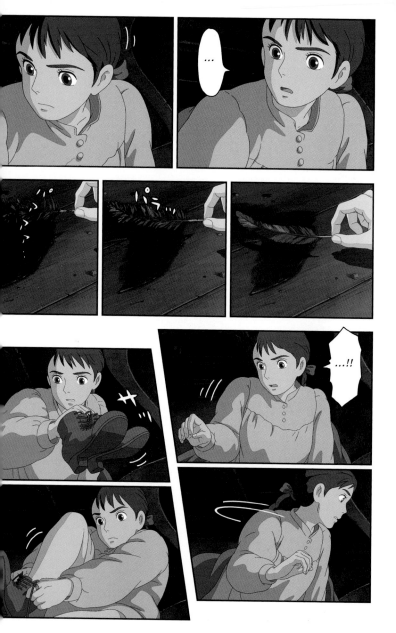

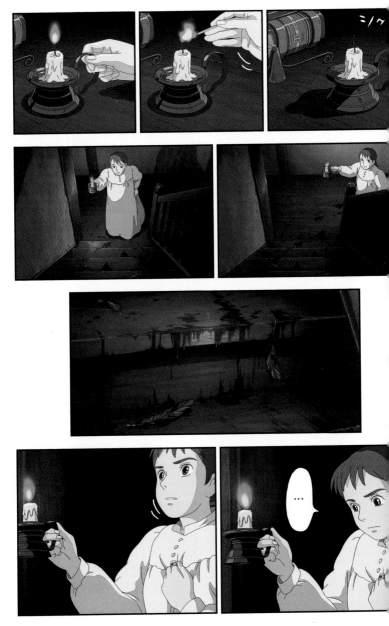

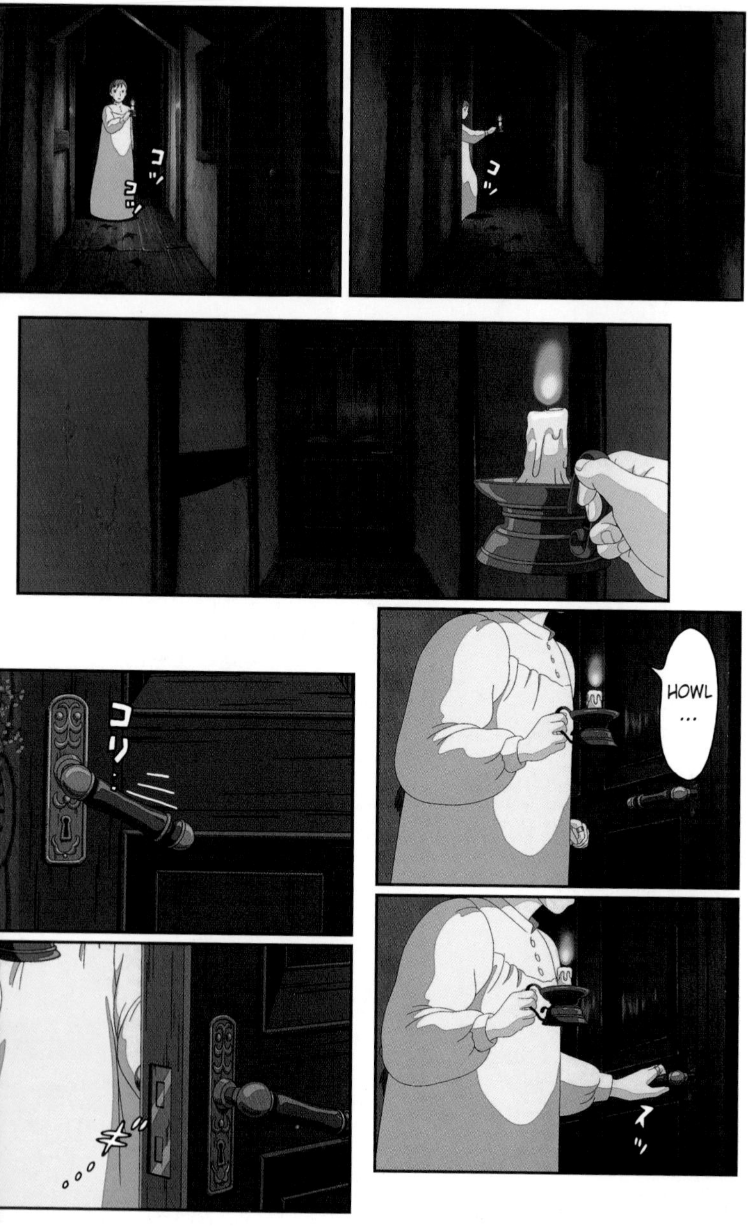
コツ
コツ
コツ
HOWL ...
スッ
コリ
ギ

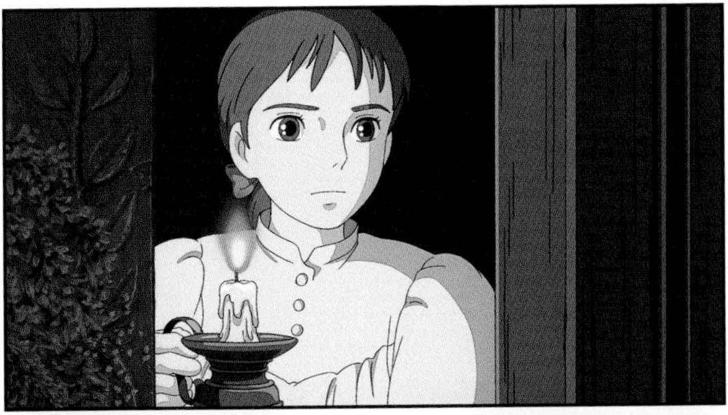

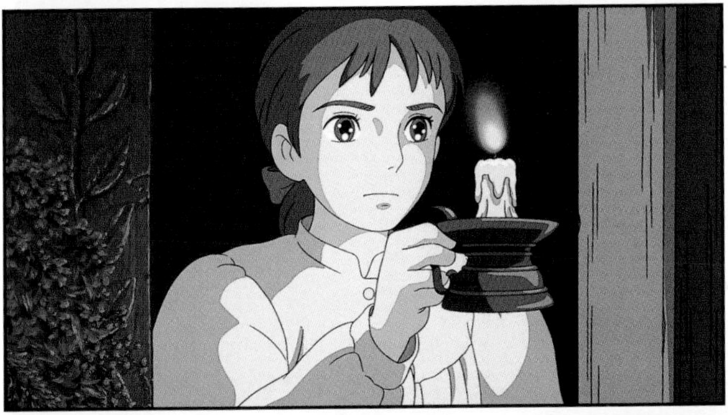

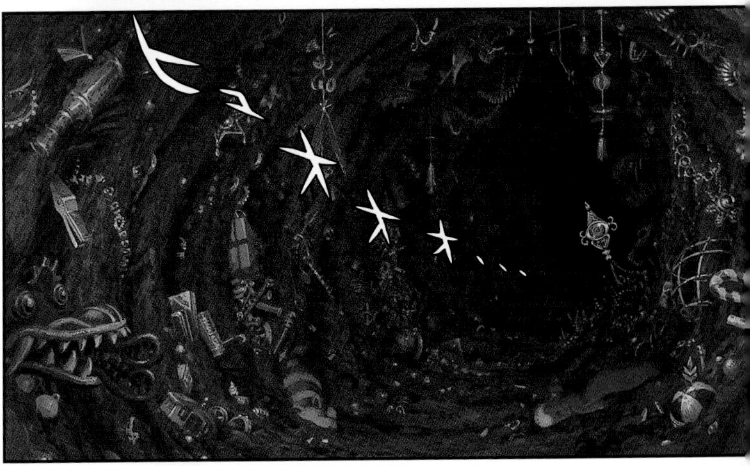
ヒュ

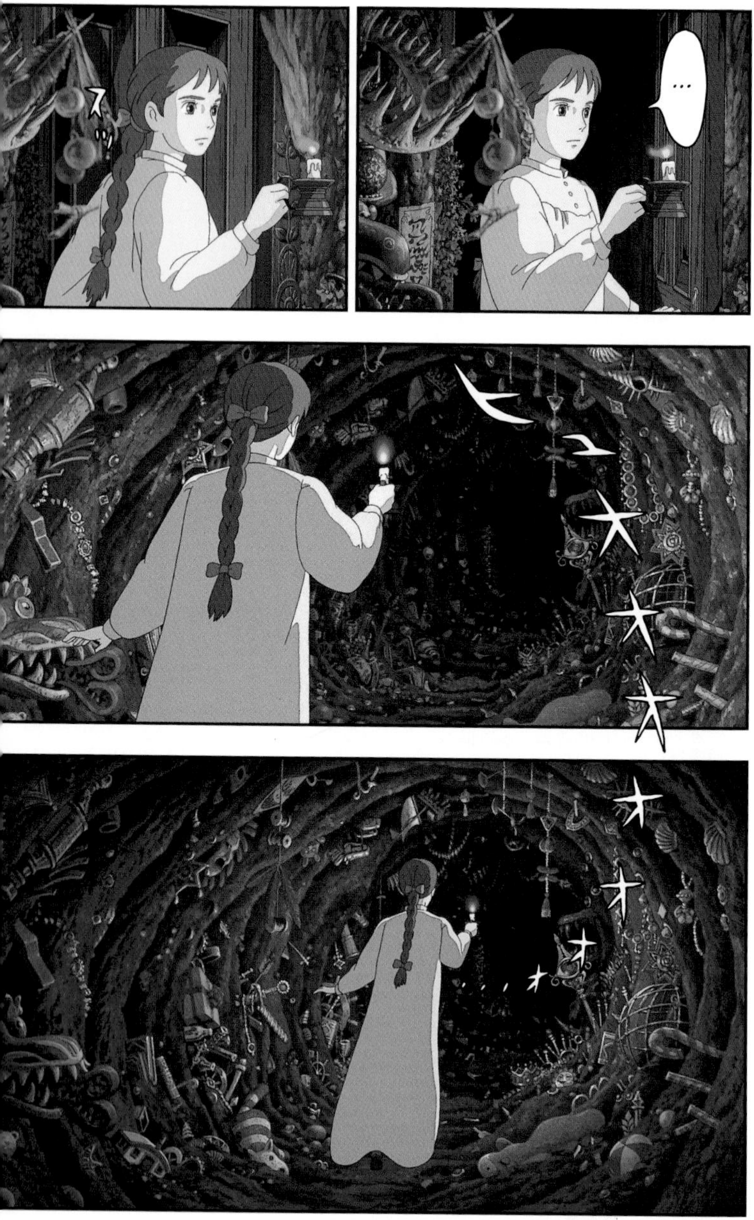
...
スッ
ヒュ

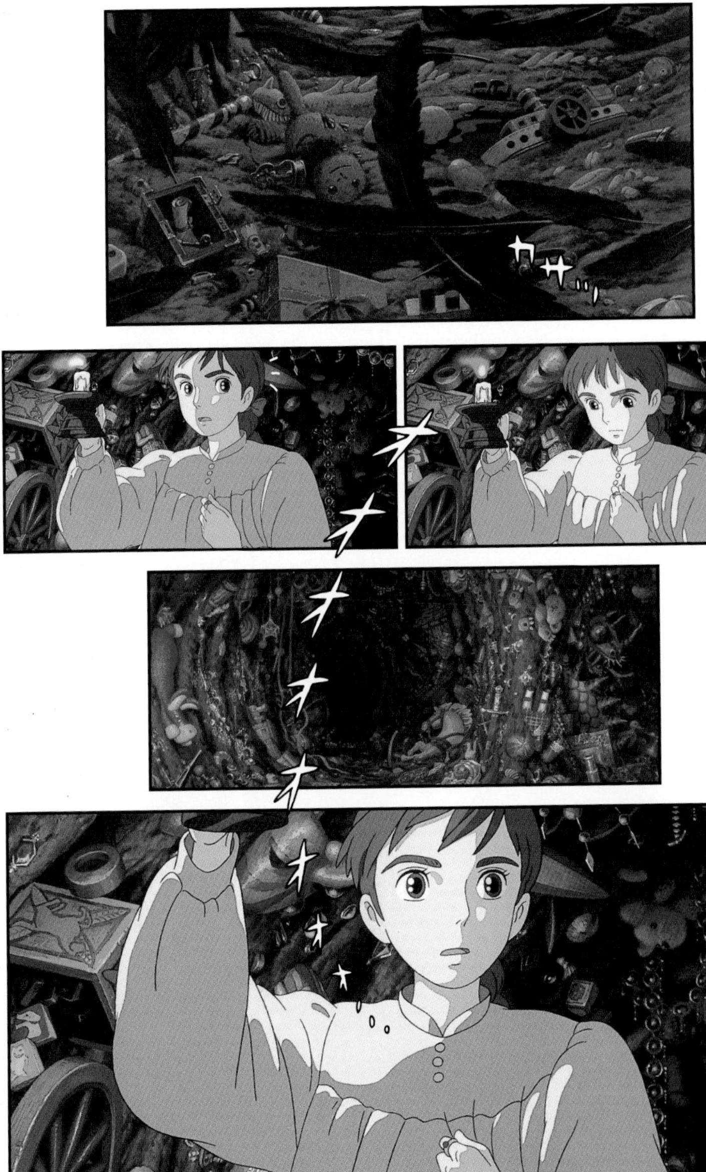

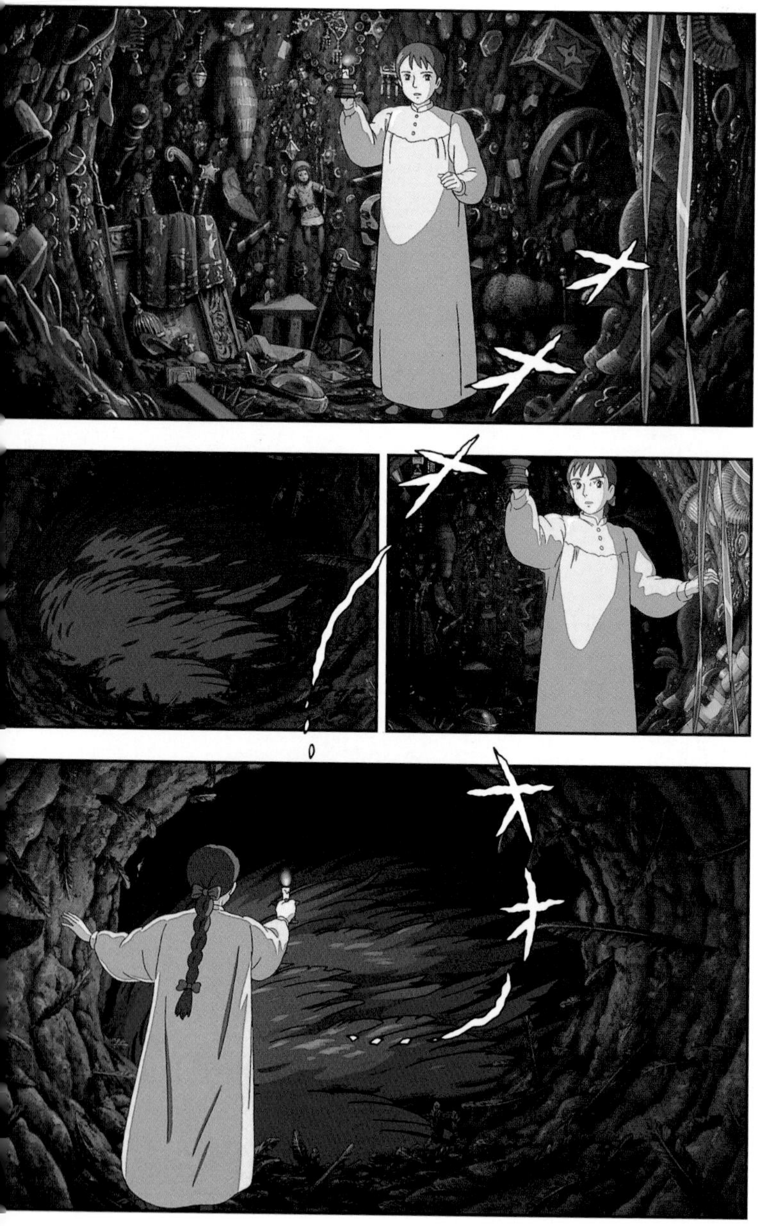

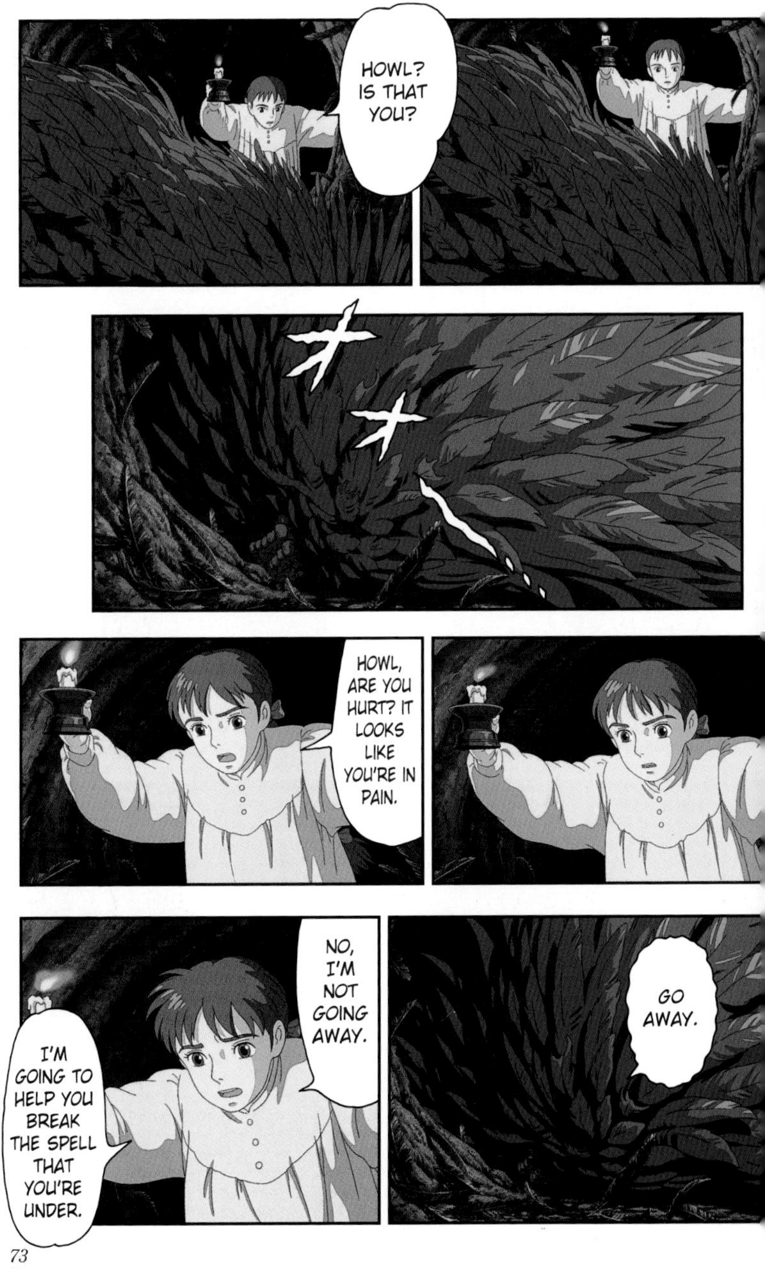
HOWL? IS THAT YOU?
HOWL, ARE YOU HURT? IT LOOKS LIKE YOU'RE IN PAIN.
GO AWAY.
NO, I'M NOT GOING AWAY.
I'M GOING TO HELP YOU BREAK THE SPELL THAT YOU'RE UNDER.

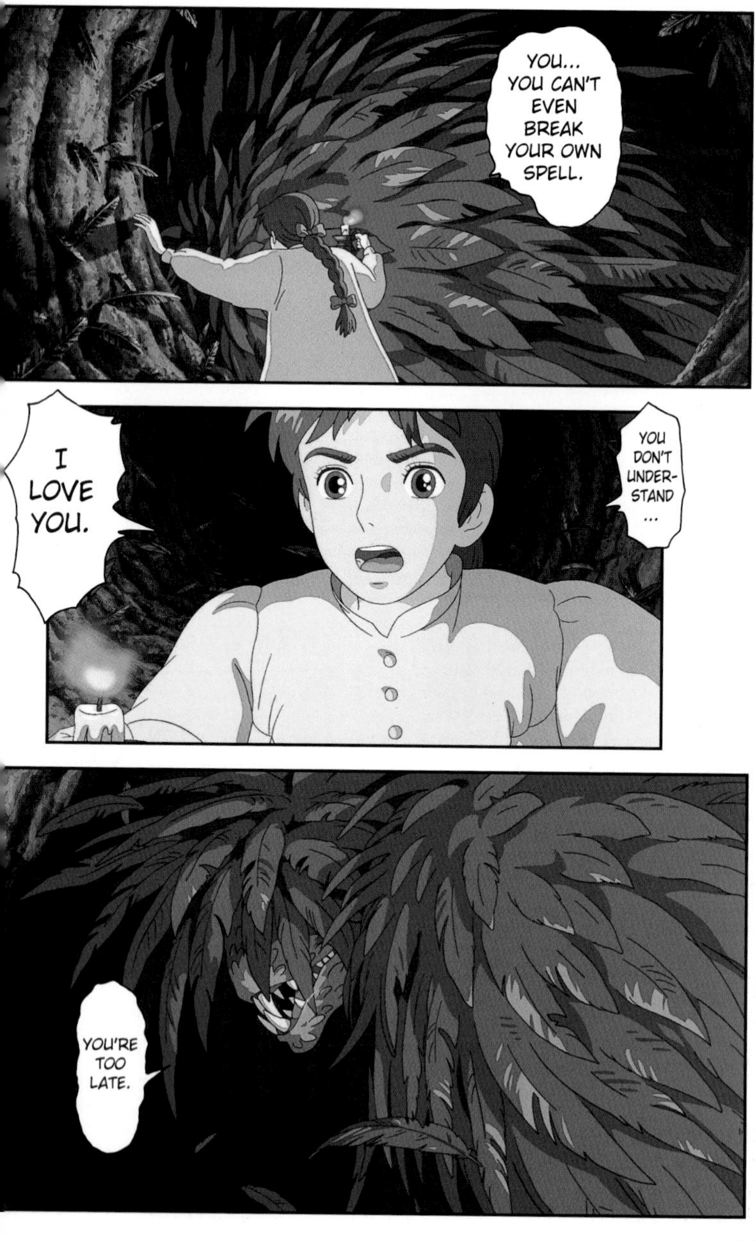
YOU... YOU CAN'T EVEN BREAK YOUR OWN SPELL.
YOU DON'T UNDER-STAND...
I LOVE YOU.
YOU'RE TOO LATE.

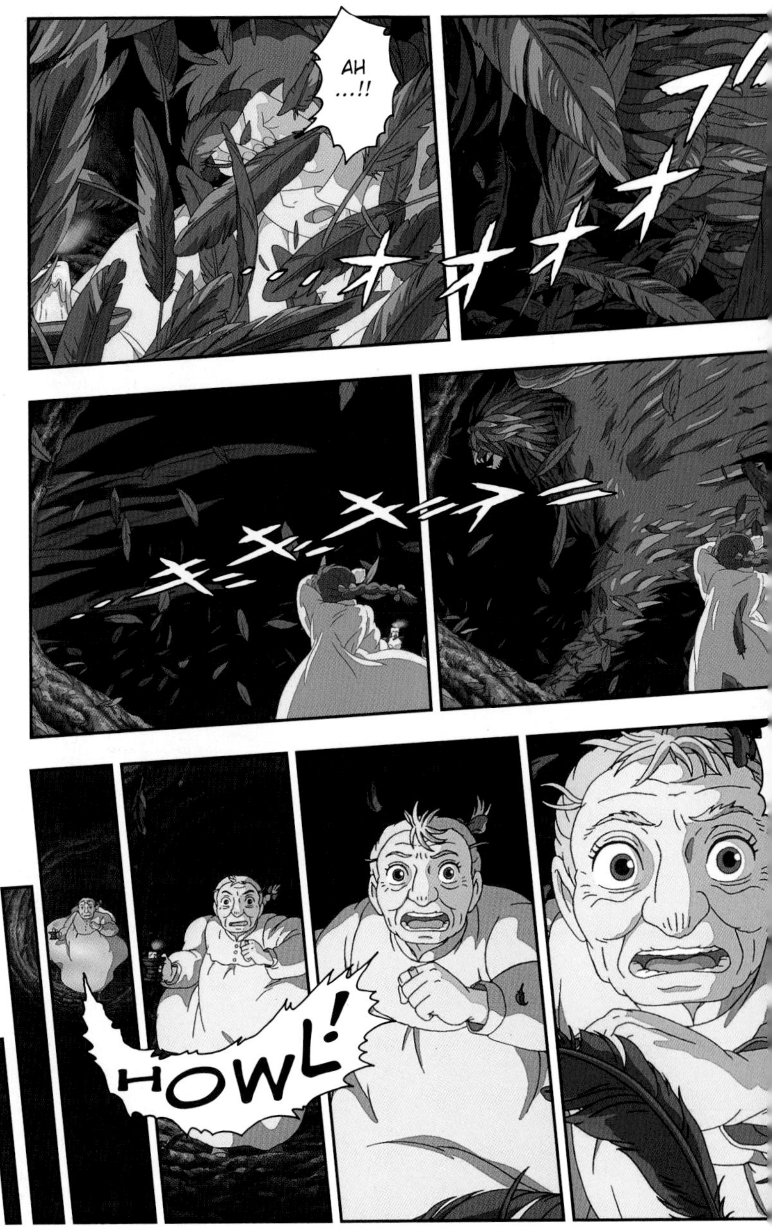
AH ...!!
HOWL!

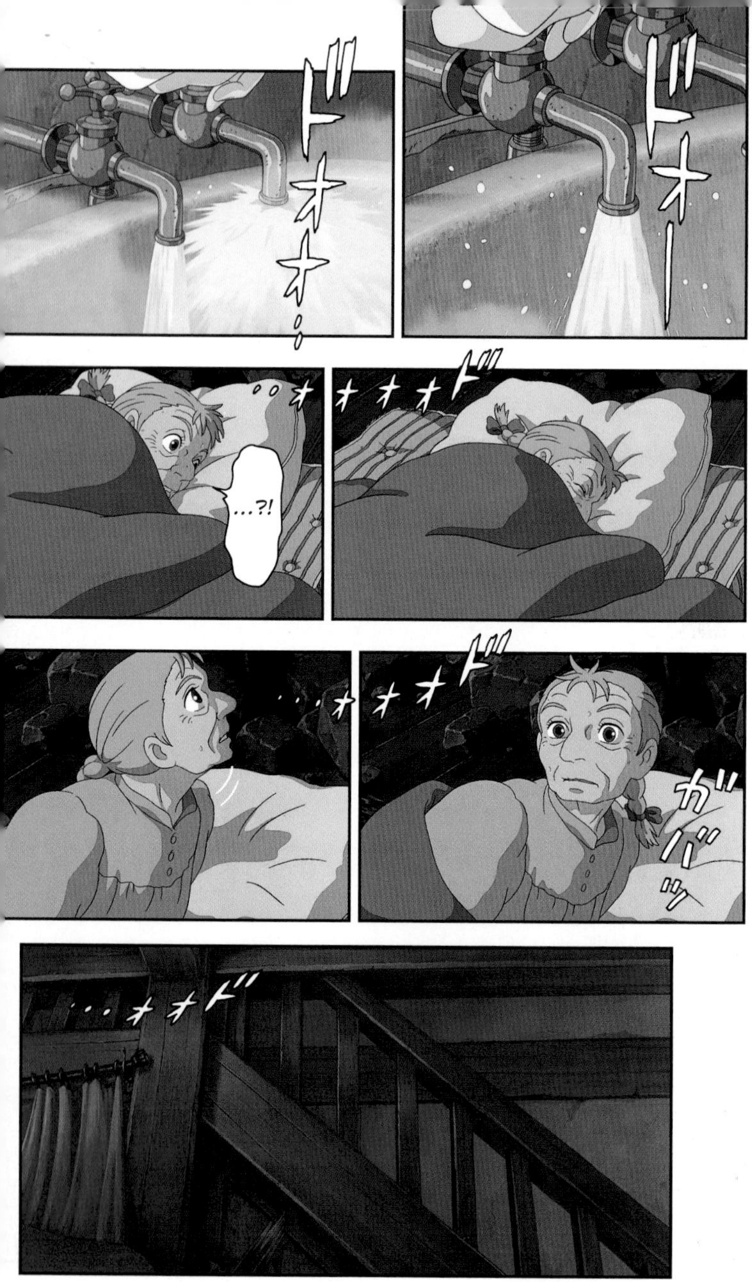
ドドオーー
ドドオオオ…
…オオオオドド
…?!
…オオオドド
ガバッ
…オオドド

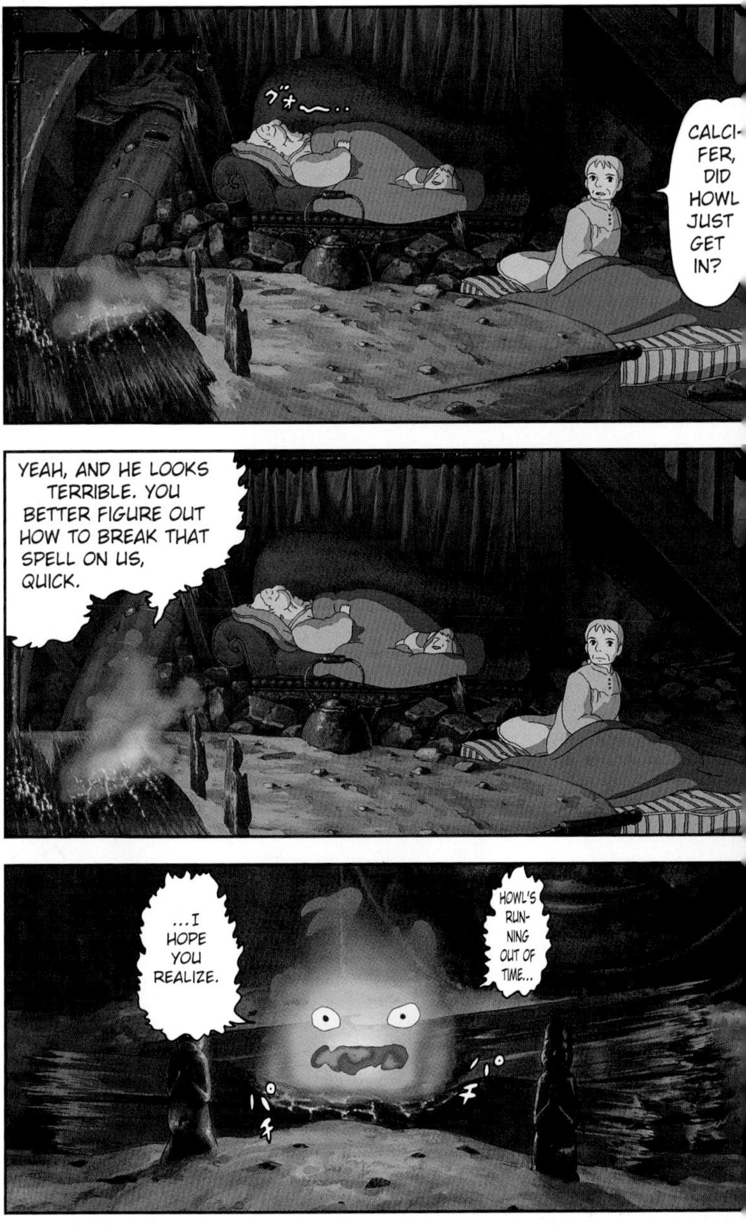
CALCI-FER, DID HOWL JUST GET IN?
グォ〜‥
YEAH, AND HE LOOKS TERRIBLE. YOU BETTER FIGURE OUT HOW TO BREAK THAT SPELL ON US, QUICK.
HOWL'S RUN-NING OUT OF TIME...
...I HOPE YOU REALIZE.
パチ
パチ

N'T
YOU
LS
HE
SE,
YOU
LD
W BY
N.

IS
THAT
IT?

YOU
MEAN
HE'LL
BECOME
A
MON-
STER.

SHE SAID
THAT HOWL'S
HEART WAS
STOLEN BY A
DEMON.

DO YOU
KNOW
WHAT
MADAME
SULIMAN
SAID?

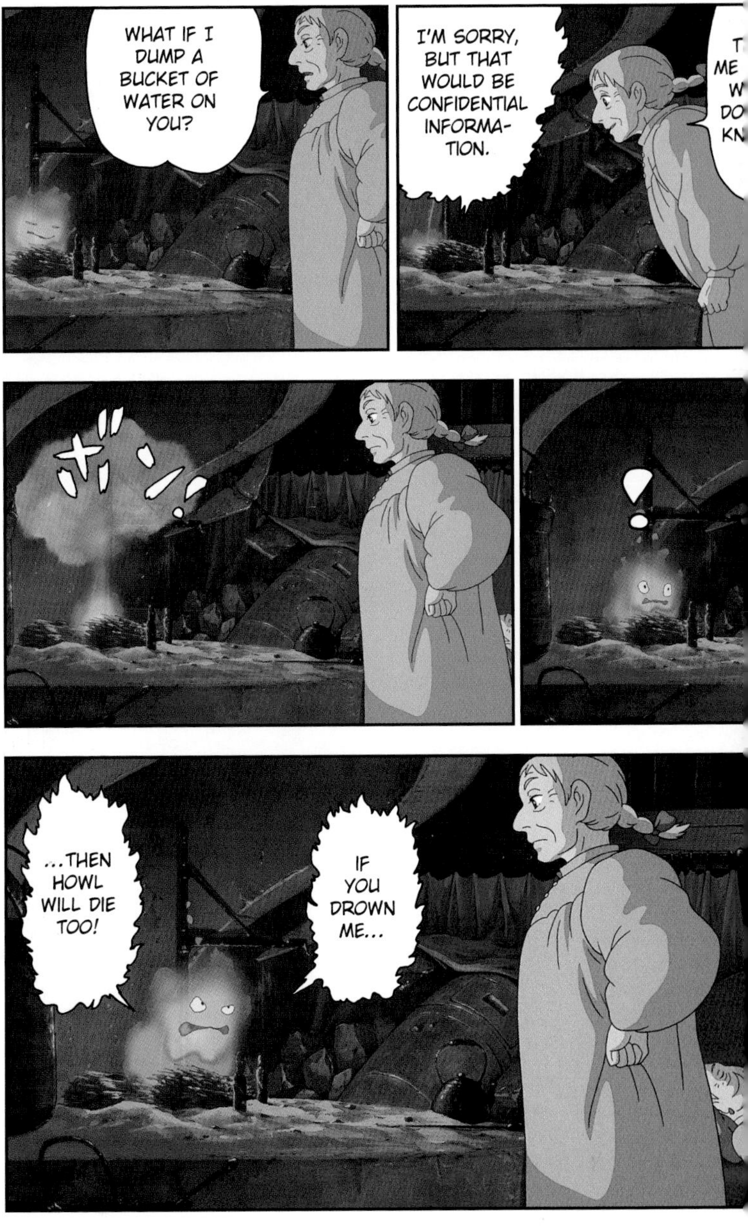
I'M SORRY, BUT THAT WOULD BE CONFIDENTIAL INFORMATION.
WHAT IF I DUMP A BUCKET OF WATER ON YOU?
IF YOU DROWN ME...
...THEN HOWL WILL DIE TOO!

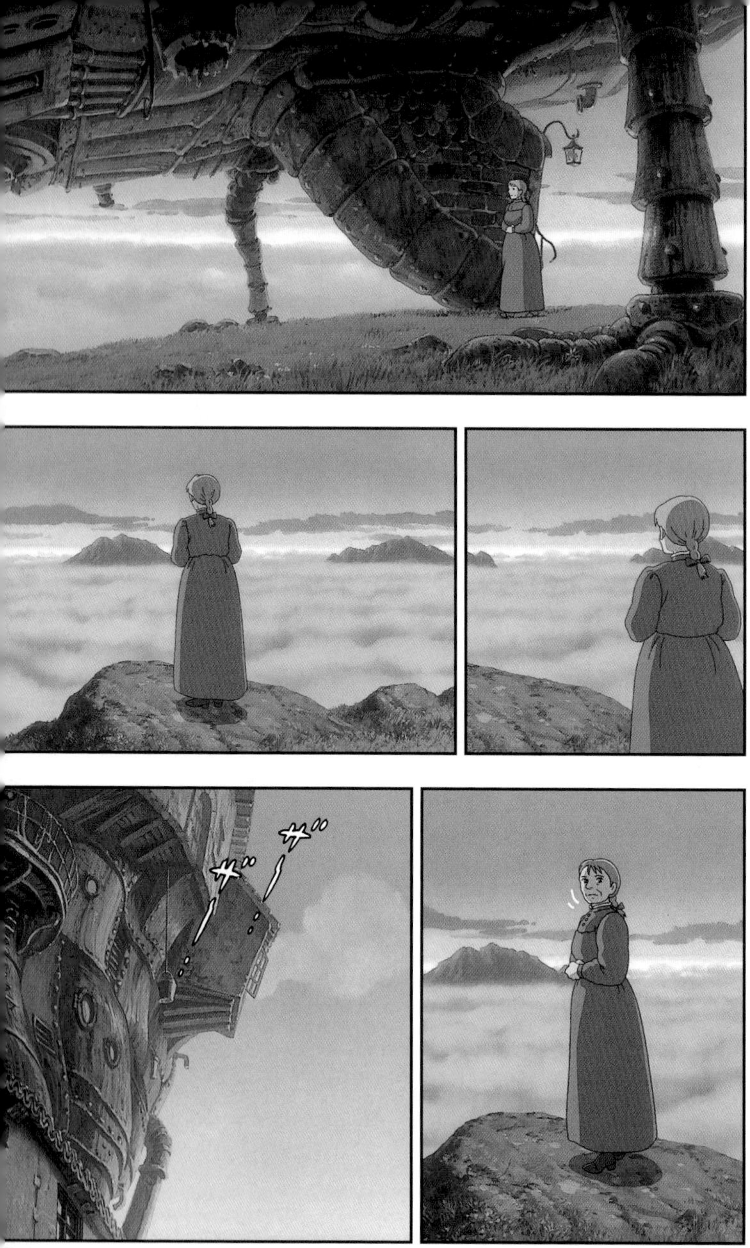

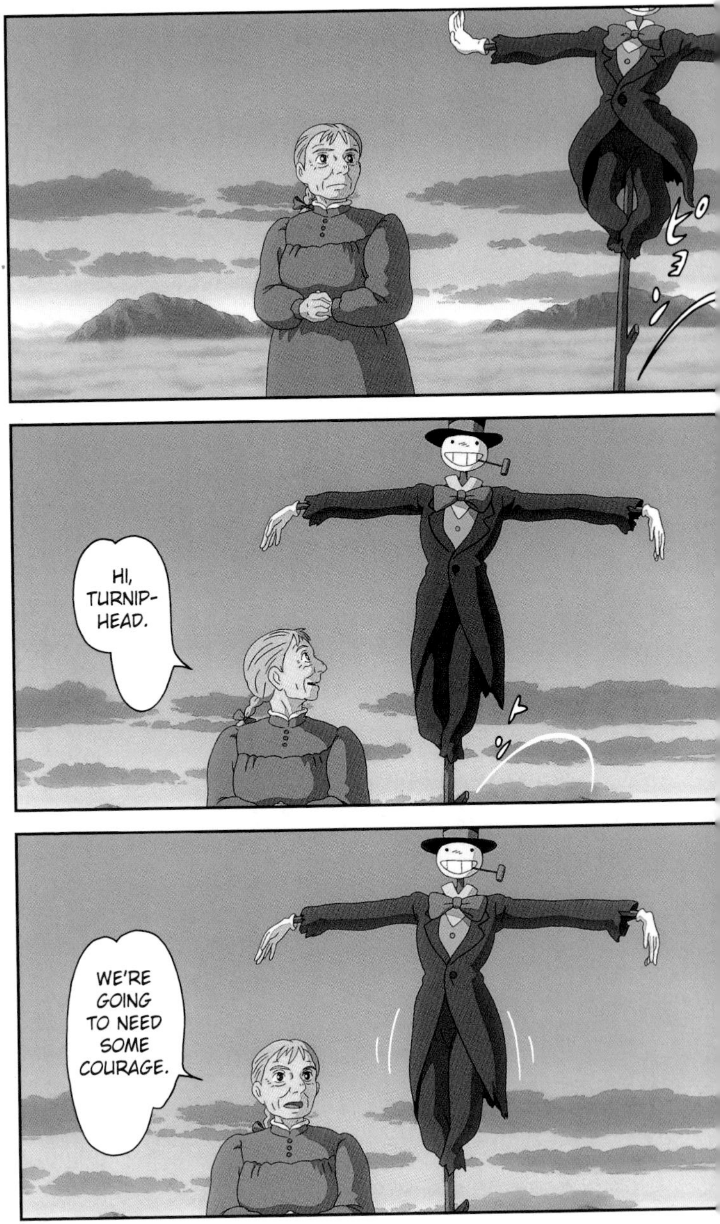
ピョン
HI, TURNIP-HEAD.
トン
WE'RE GOING TO NEED SOME COURAGE.

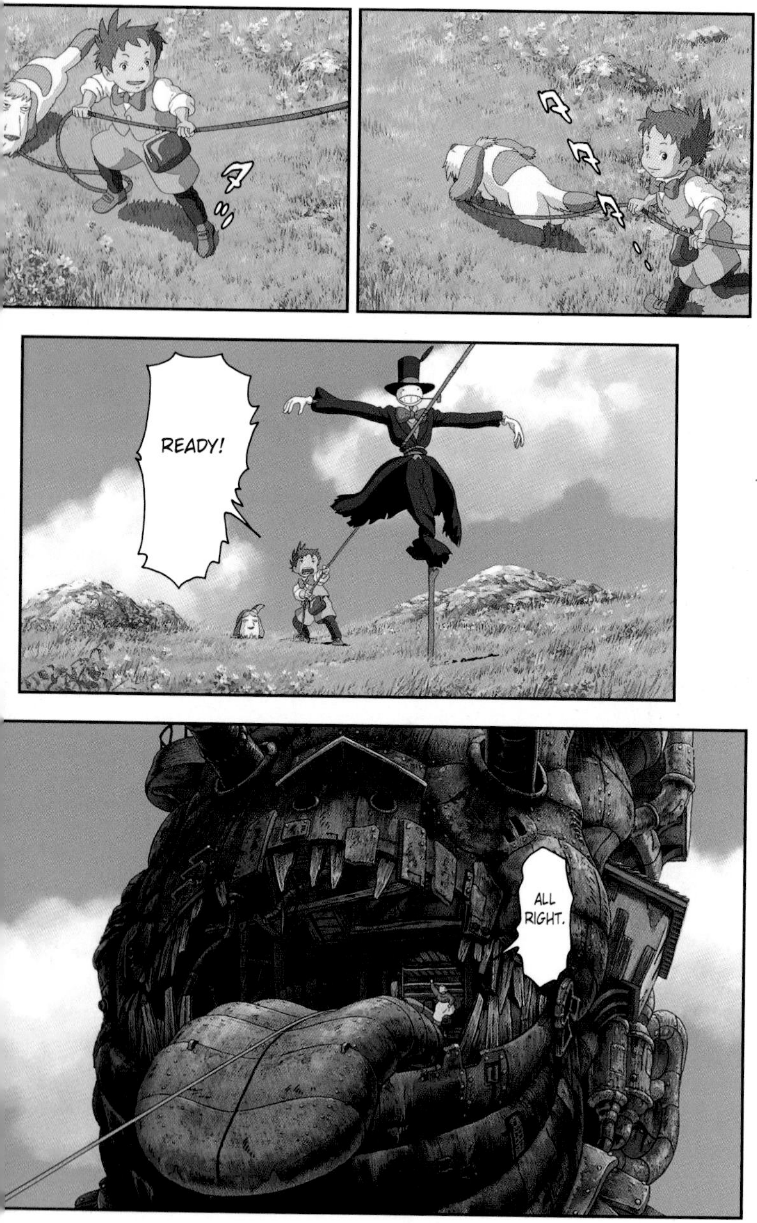
READY!
ALL RIGHT.

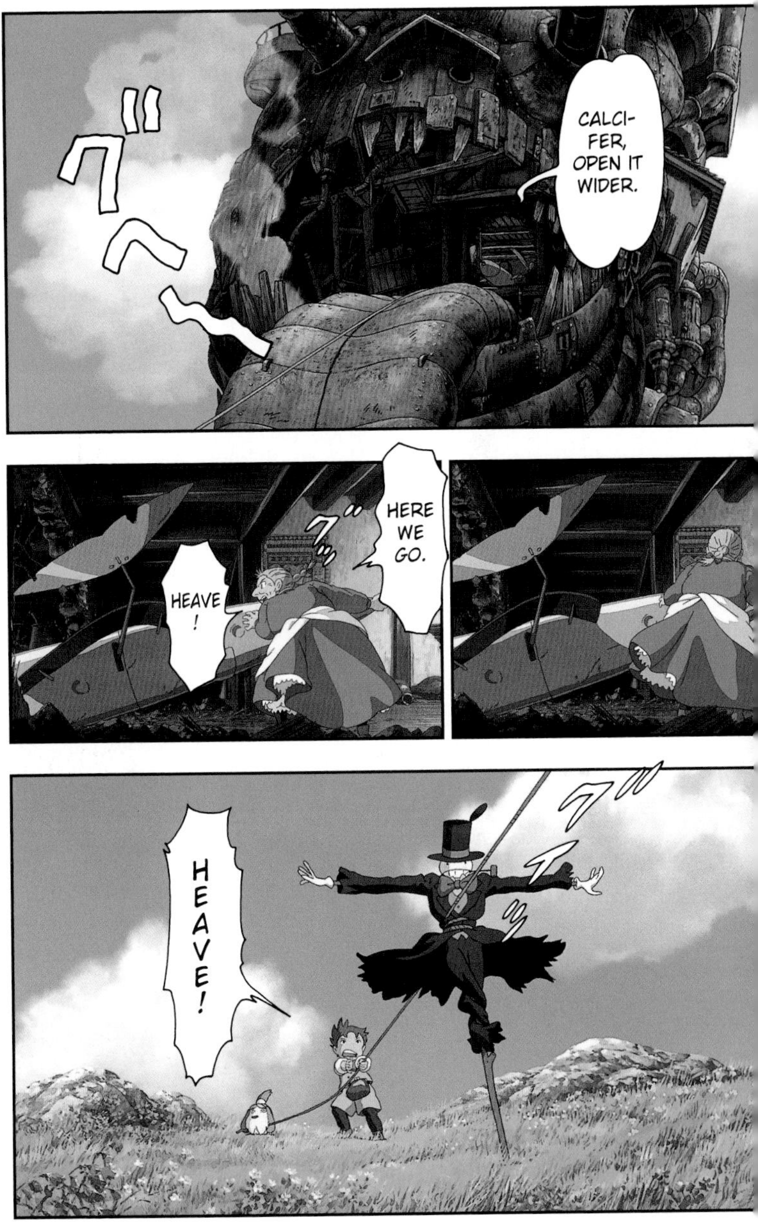
CALCI-FER, OPEN IT WIDER.
HERE WE GO.
HEAVE!
HEAVE!

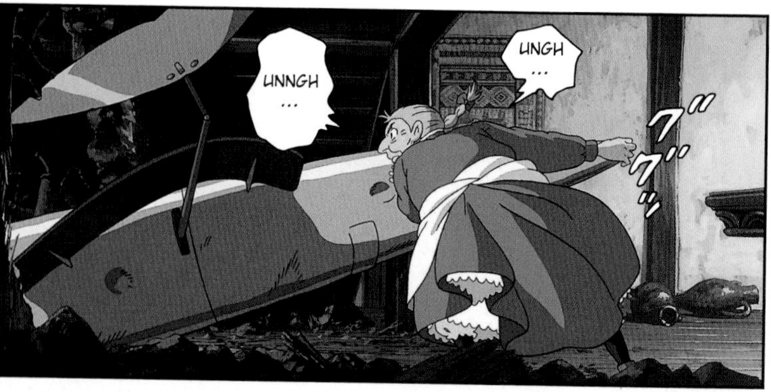
UNGH ...
UNNGH ...

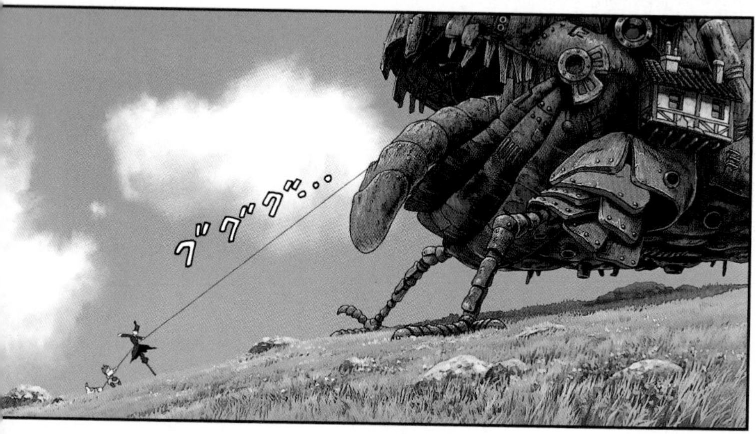

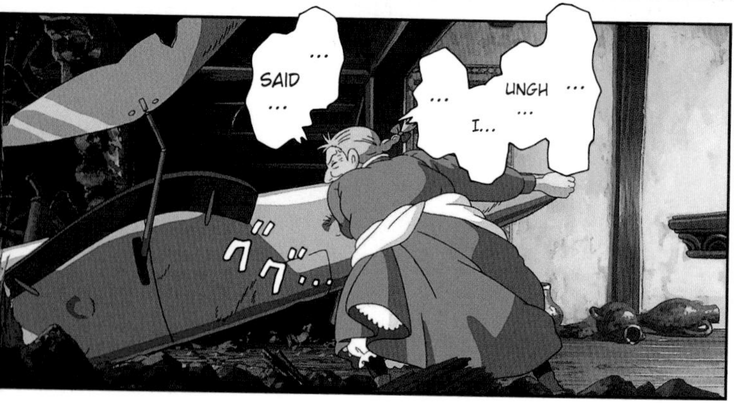
... UNGH ... ... I...
... SAID ...

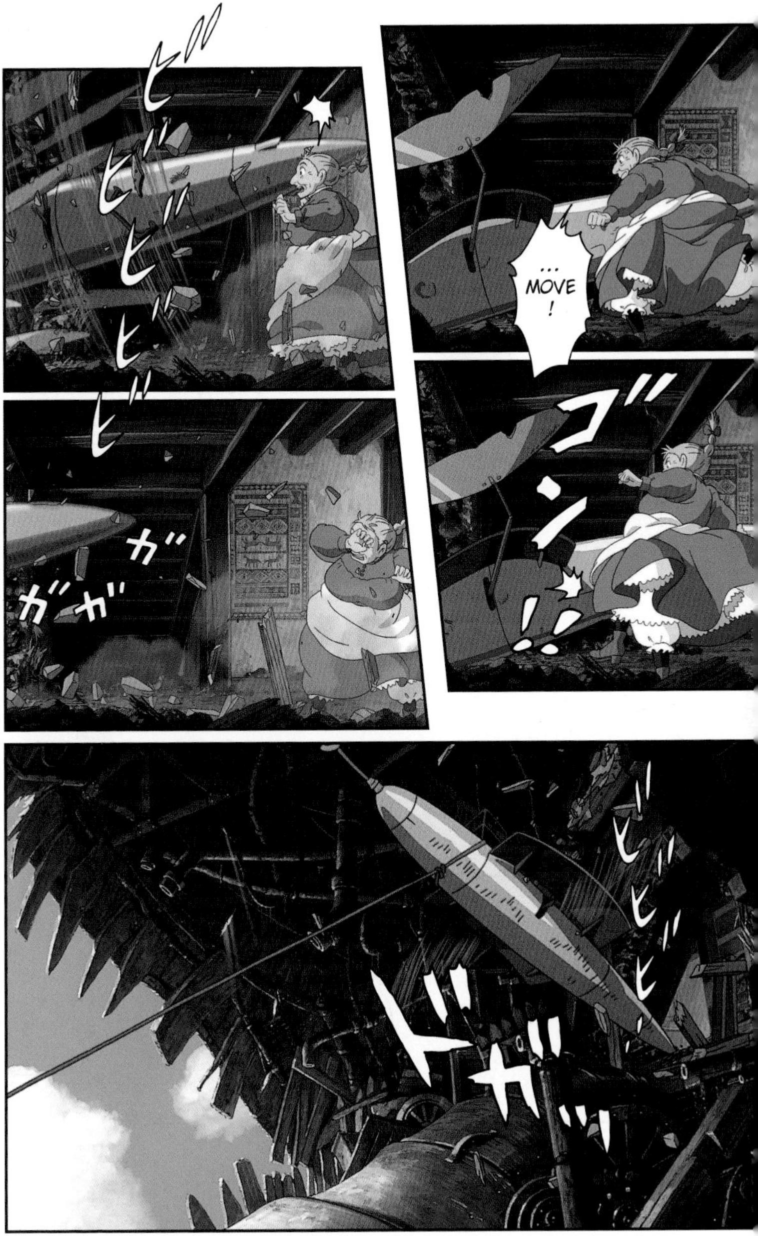
...MOVE!
ビビビビビビビ
ゴン!!
ガガガ
ビビビビ
ドガッ

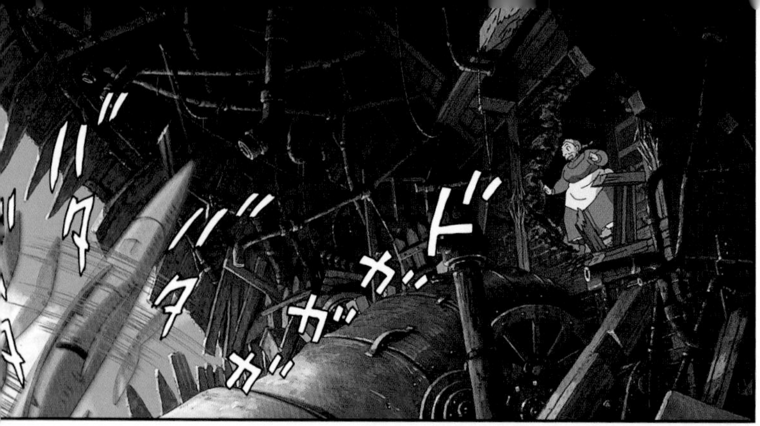

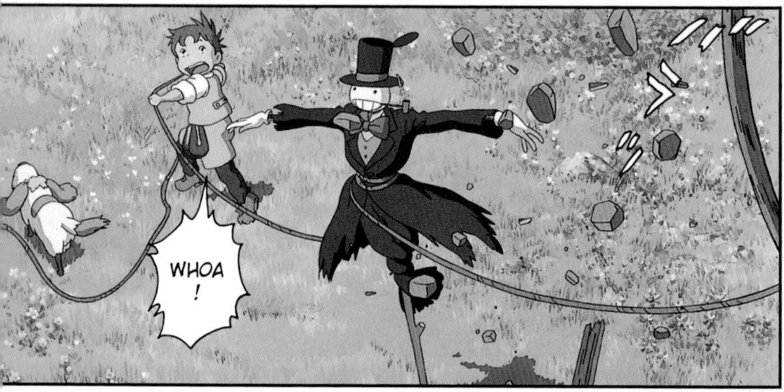
WHOA
!

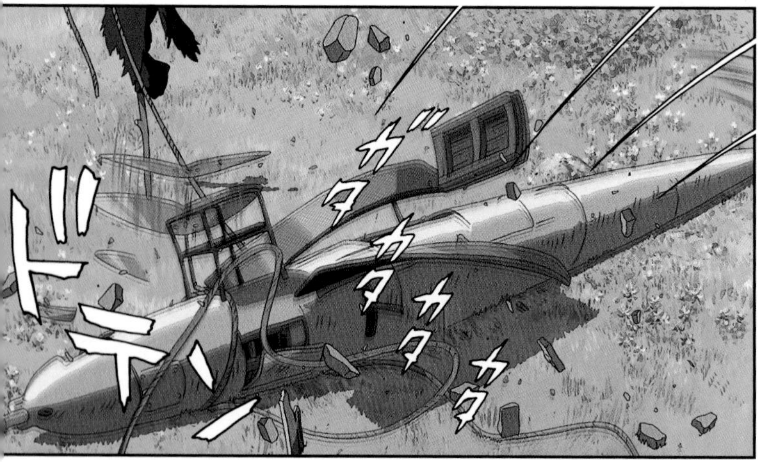

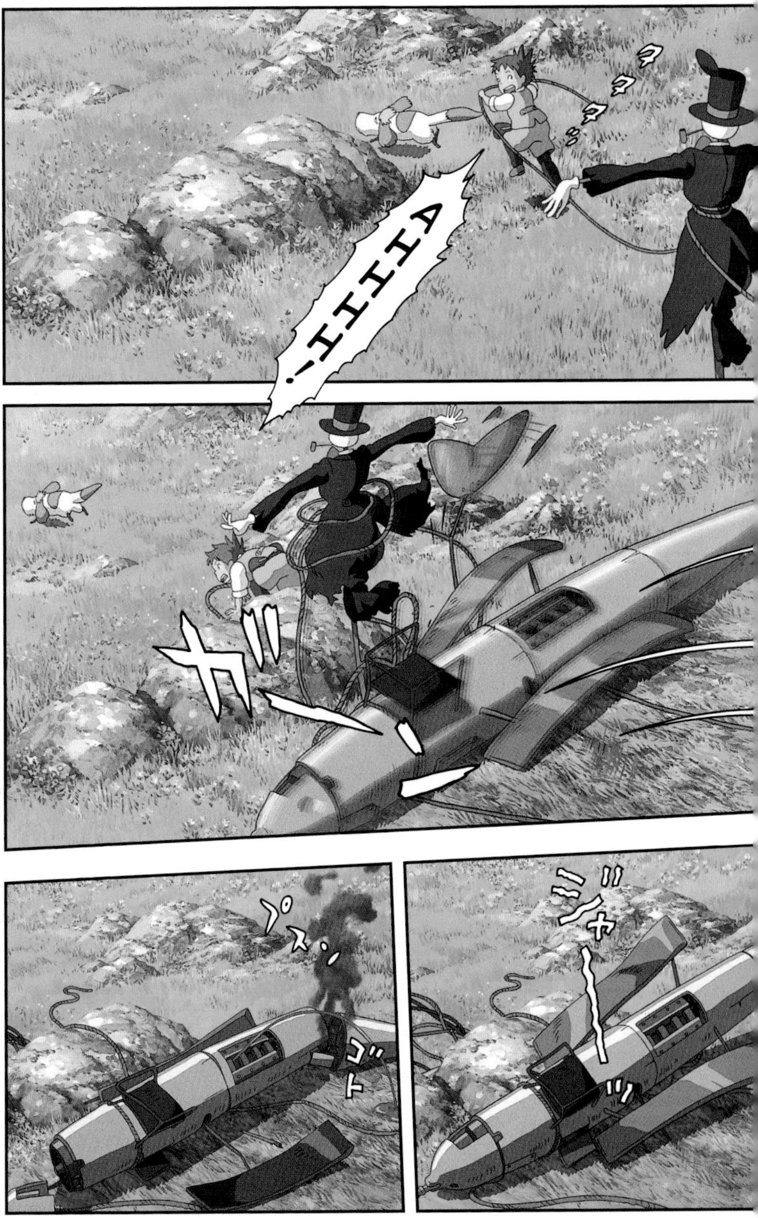
タタタッ
AHHHH!
ガッ
ジャーッ
ッ
プスッ
ゴトッ

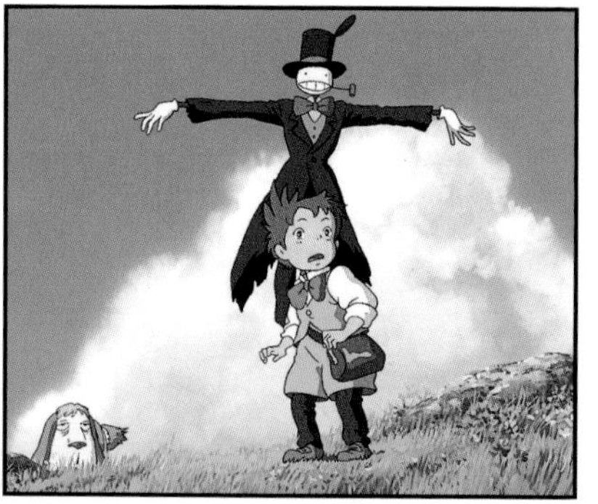

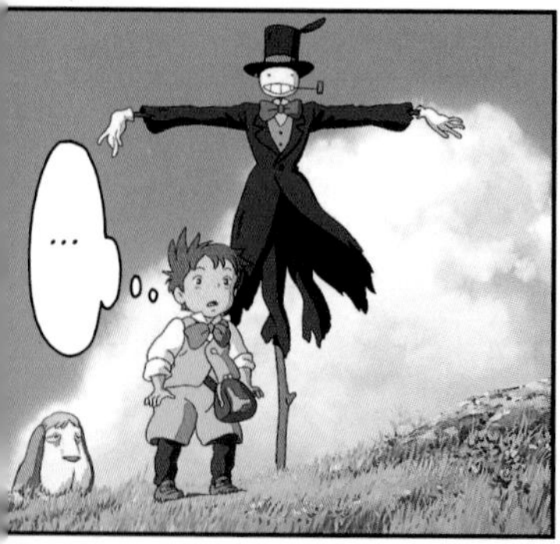
...

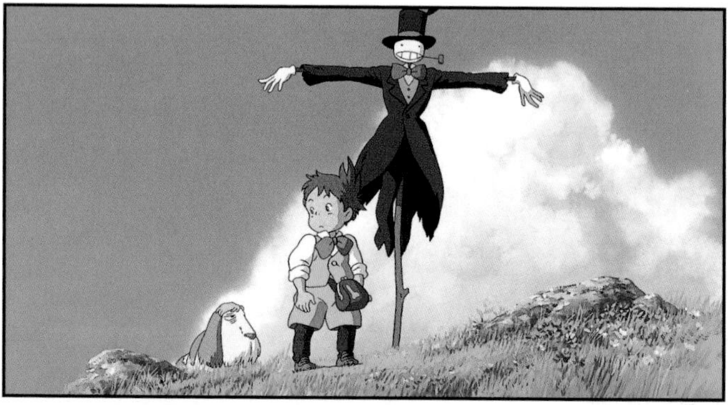

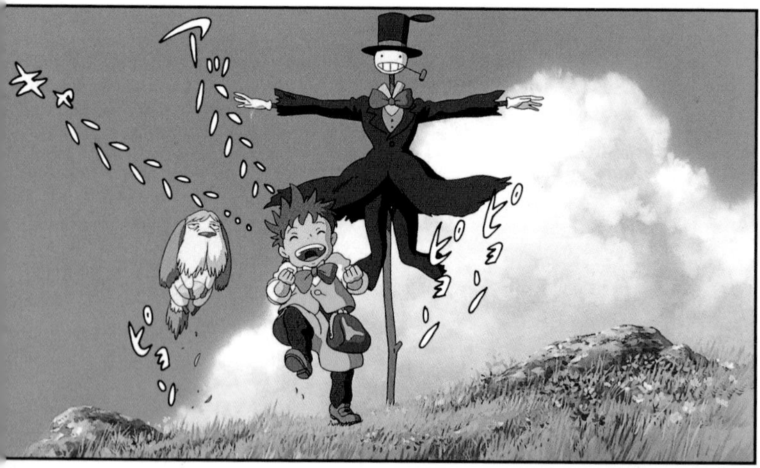

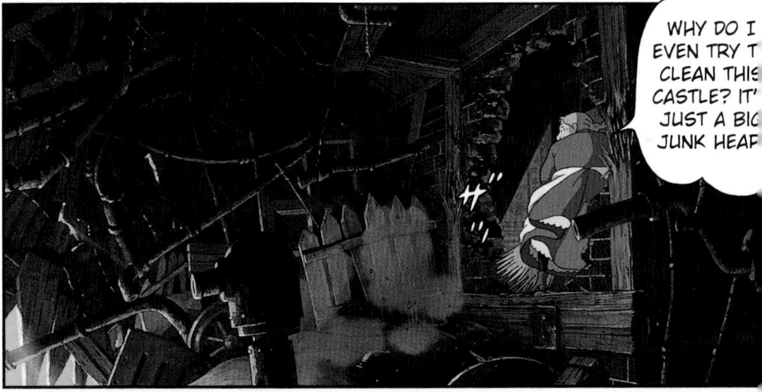
WHY DO I EVEN TRY T CLEAN THIS CASTLE? IT' JUST A BIG JUNK HEAP
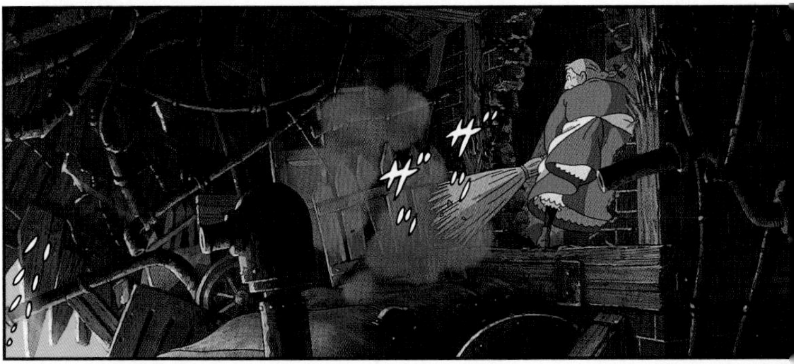
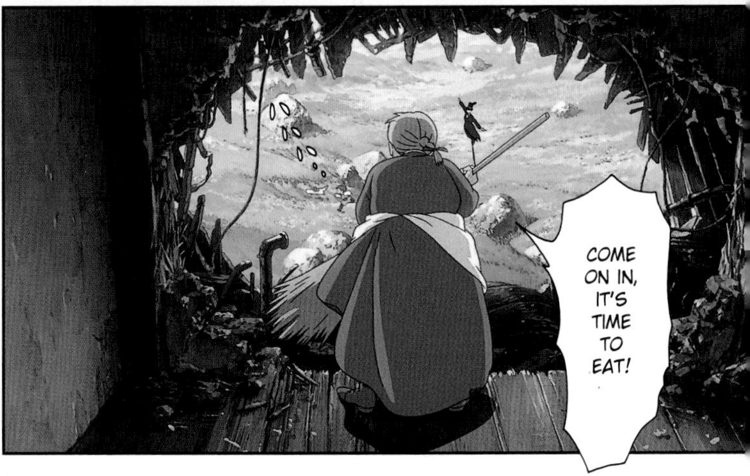
COME ON IN, IT'S TIME TO EAT!

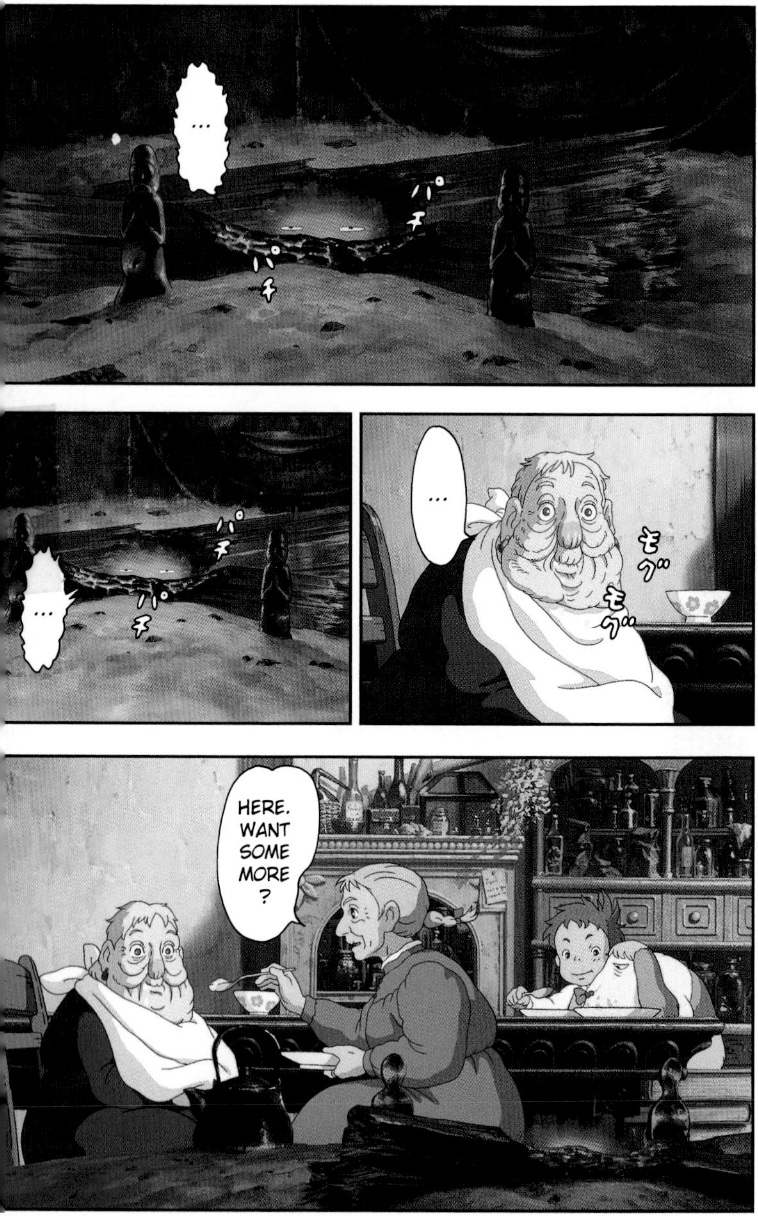
...
パチ
パチ
...
モグ
モグ
...
パチ
パチ
HERE. WANT SOME MORE?

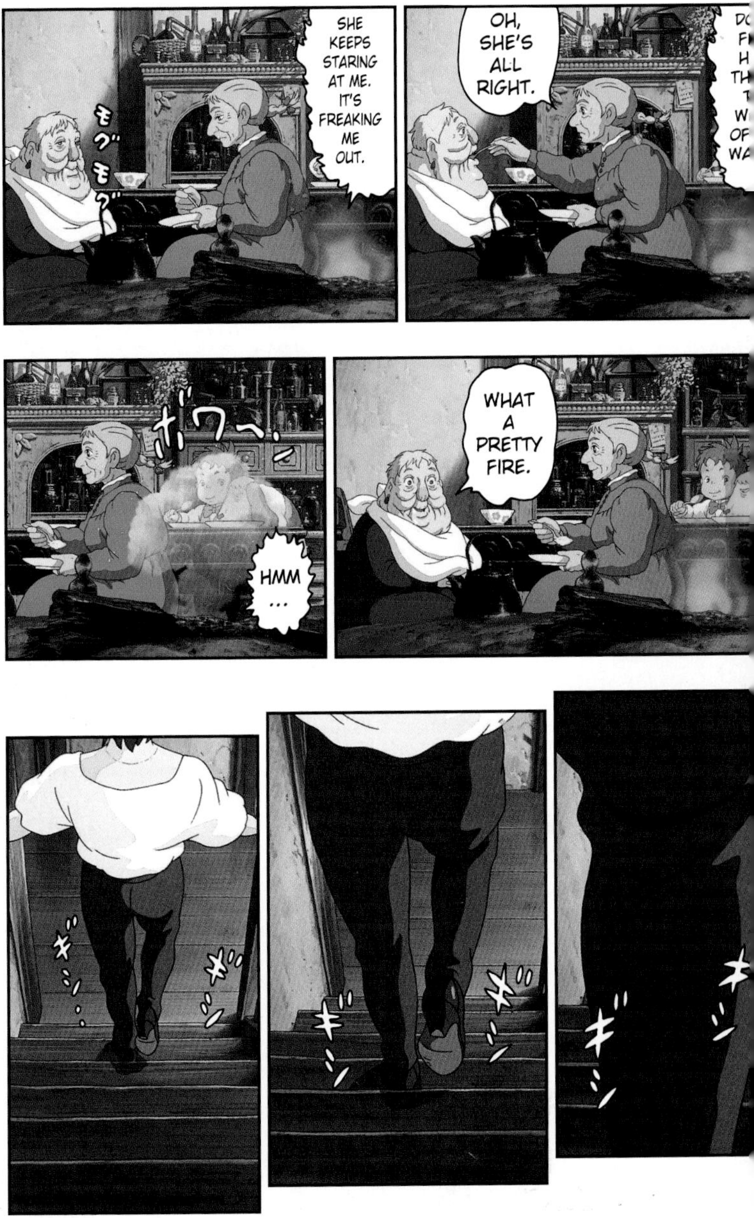
OH, SHE'S ALL RIGHT.
SHE KEEPS STARING AT ME. IT'S FREAKING ME OUT.
モグモグ
WHAT A PRETTY FIRE.
ボワ〜
HMM ...

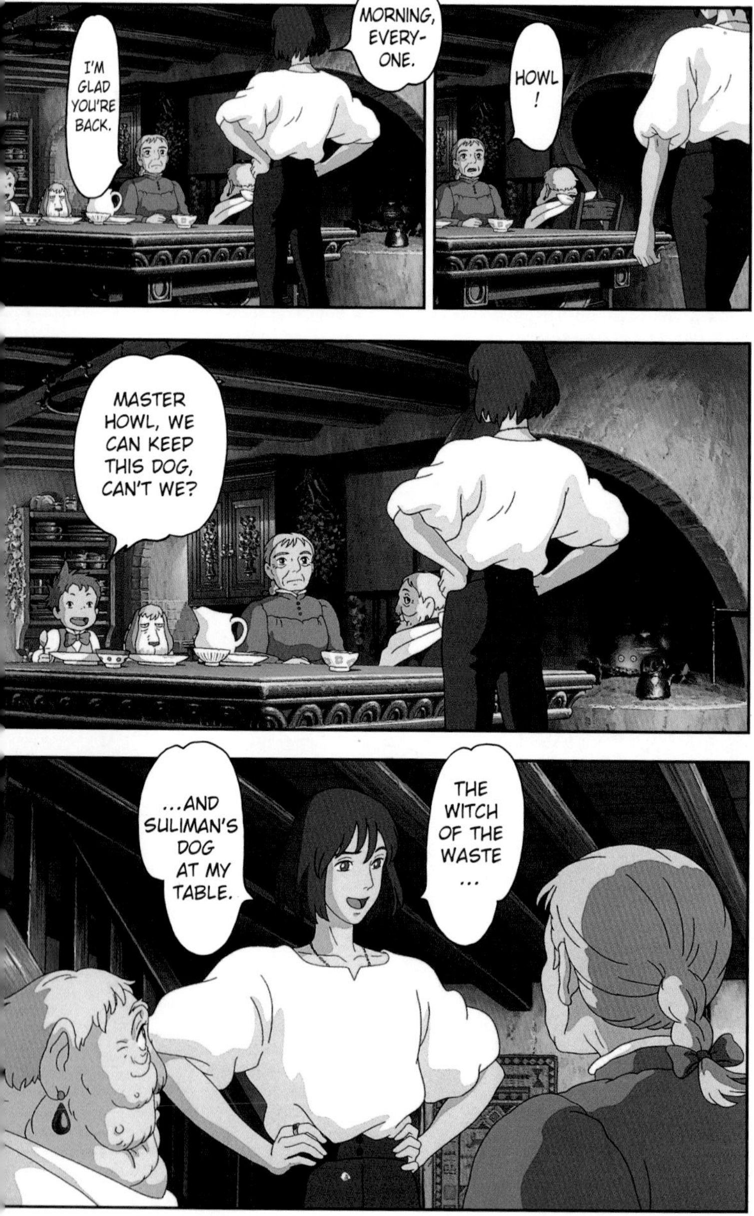
HOWL!
MORNING, EVERY-ONE.
I'M GLAD YOU'RE BACK.
MASTER HOWL, WE CAN KEEP THIS DOG, CAN'T WE?
THE WITCH OF THE WASTE...
...AND SULIMAN'S DOG AT MY TABLE.

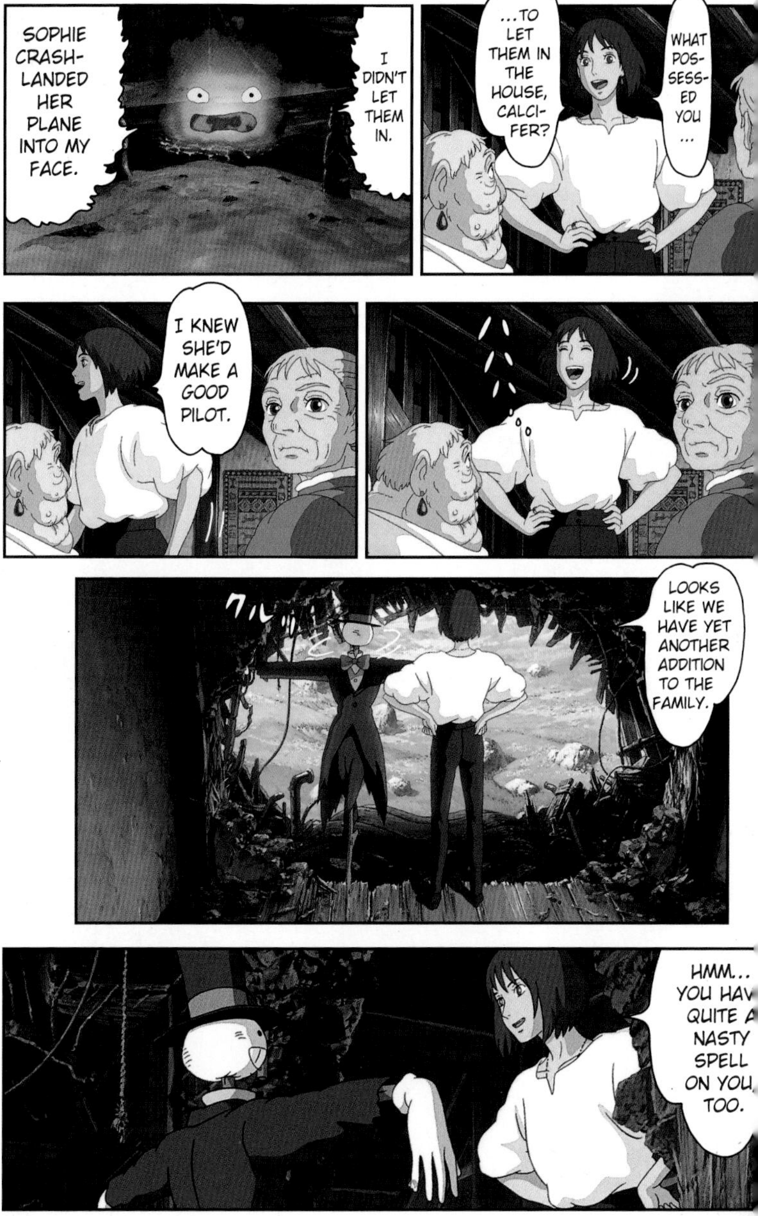
WHAT POSSESSED YOU...
...TO LET THEM IN THE HOUSE, CALCIFER?
I DIDN'T LET THEM IN.
SOPHIE CRASH-LANDED HER PLANE INTO MY FACE.
I KNEW SHE'D MAKE A GOOD PILOT.
LOOKS LIKE WE HAVE YET ANOTHER ADDITION TO THE FAMILY.
HMM... YOU HAV QUITE A NASTY SPELL ON YOU TOO.

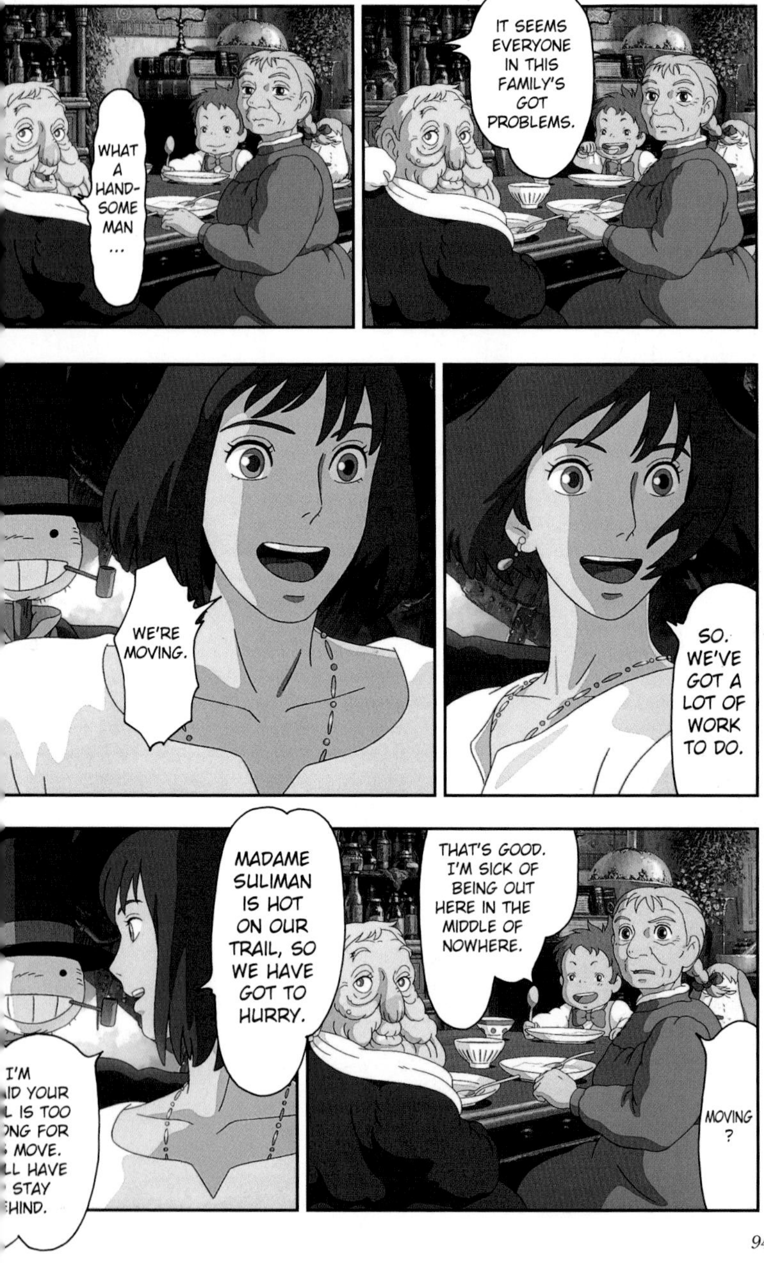
WHAT A HAND-SOME MAN ...
IT SEEMS EVERYONE IN THIS FAMILY'S GOT PROBLEMS.
WE'RE MOVING.
SO. WE'VE GOT A LOT OF WORK TO DO.
MADAME SULIMAN IS HOT ON OUR TRAIL, SO WE HAVE GOT TO HURRY.
THAT'S GOOD. I'M SICK OF BEING OUT HERE IN THE MIDDLE OF NOWHERE.
MOVING?
I'M
ID YOUR
L IS TOO
NG FOR
MOVE.
LL HAVE
STAY
HIND.

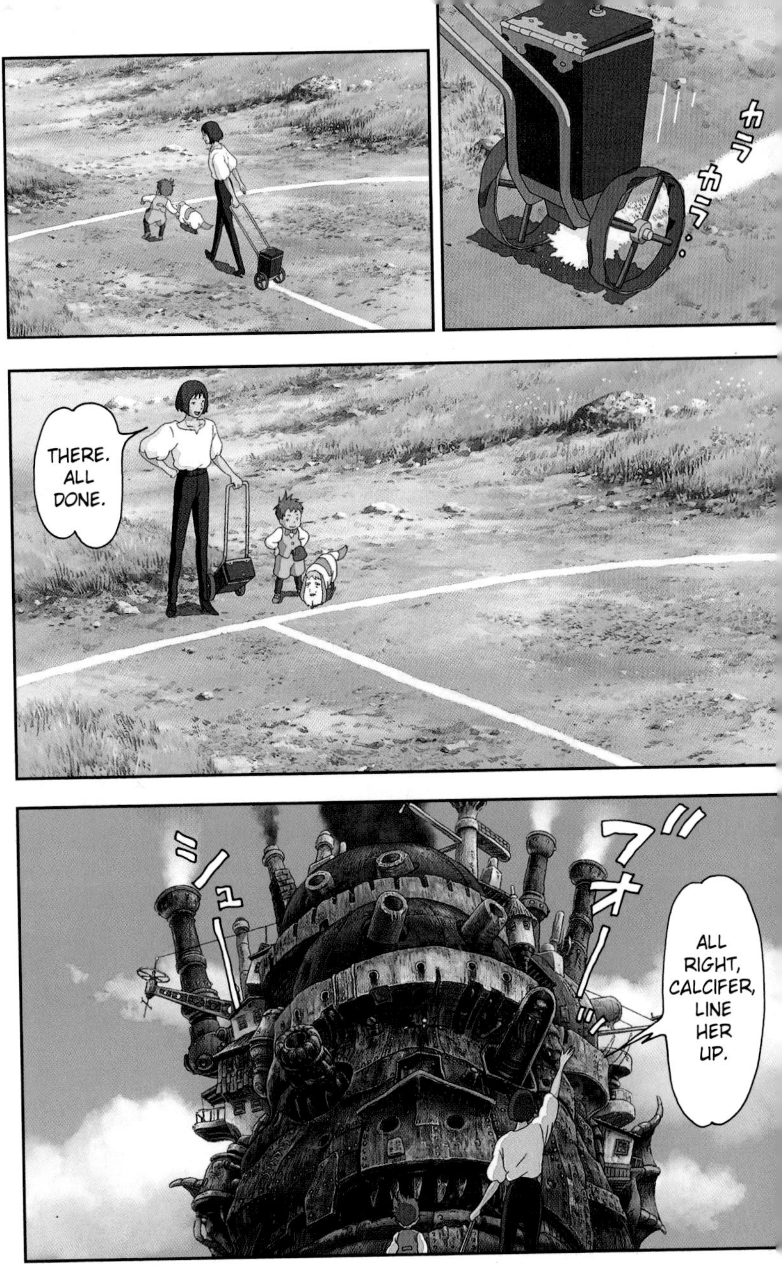
カラカラ…
THERE. ALL DONE.
ブオーッ
ALL RIGHT, CALCIFER, LINE HER UP.
シュー

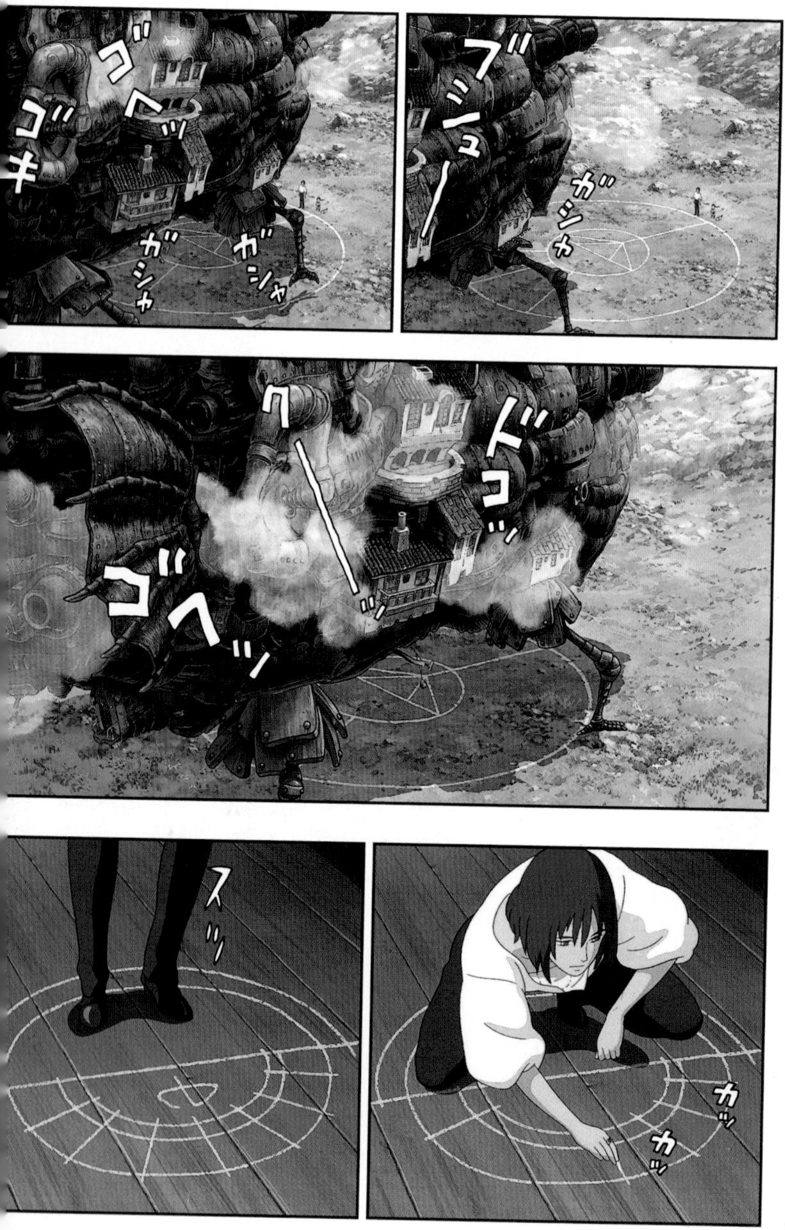
ブシュー
ガシャ
ゴベッ
ゴキ
ガシャ
ガシャ
ドコッ
クーッ
ゴベッ
カッ
カッ
スッ

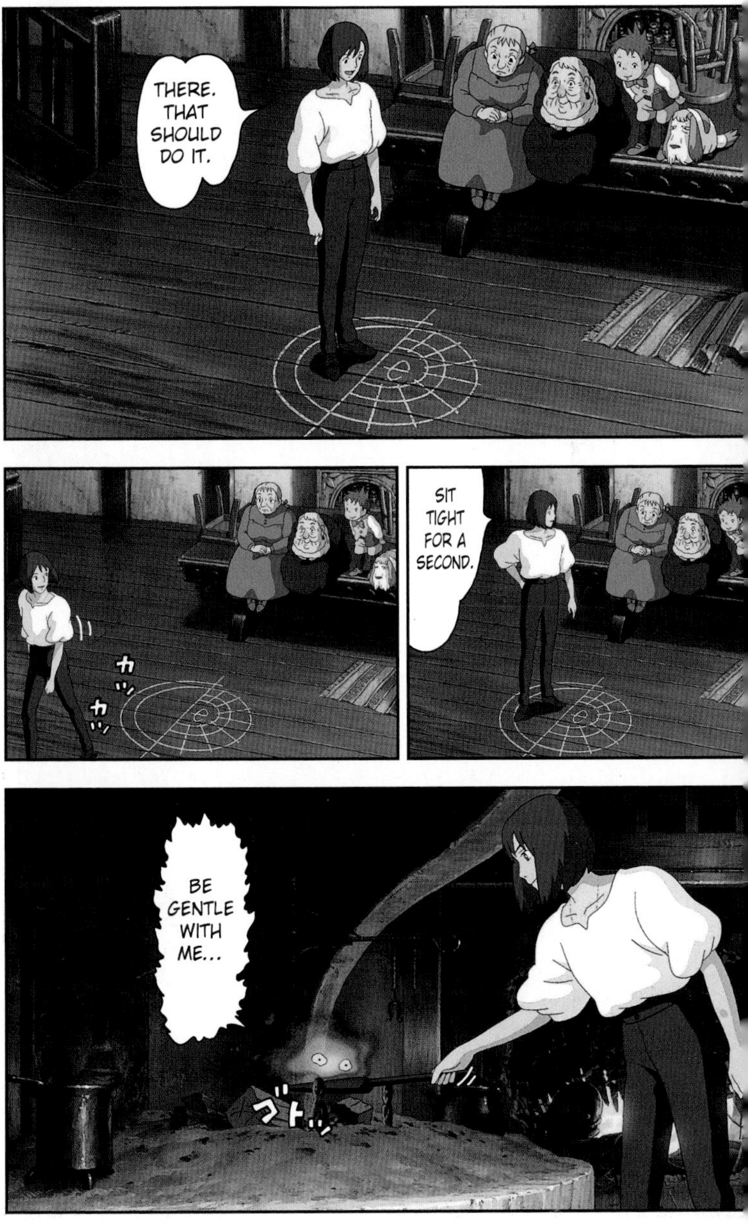
THERE. THAT SHOULD DO IT.
SIT TIGHT FOR A SECOND.
カッ
カッ
BE GENTLE WITH ME...
ゴトッ

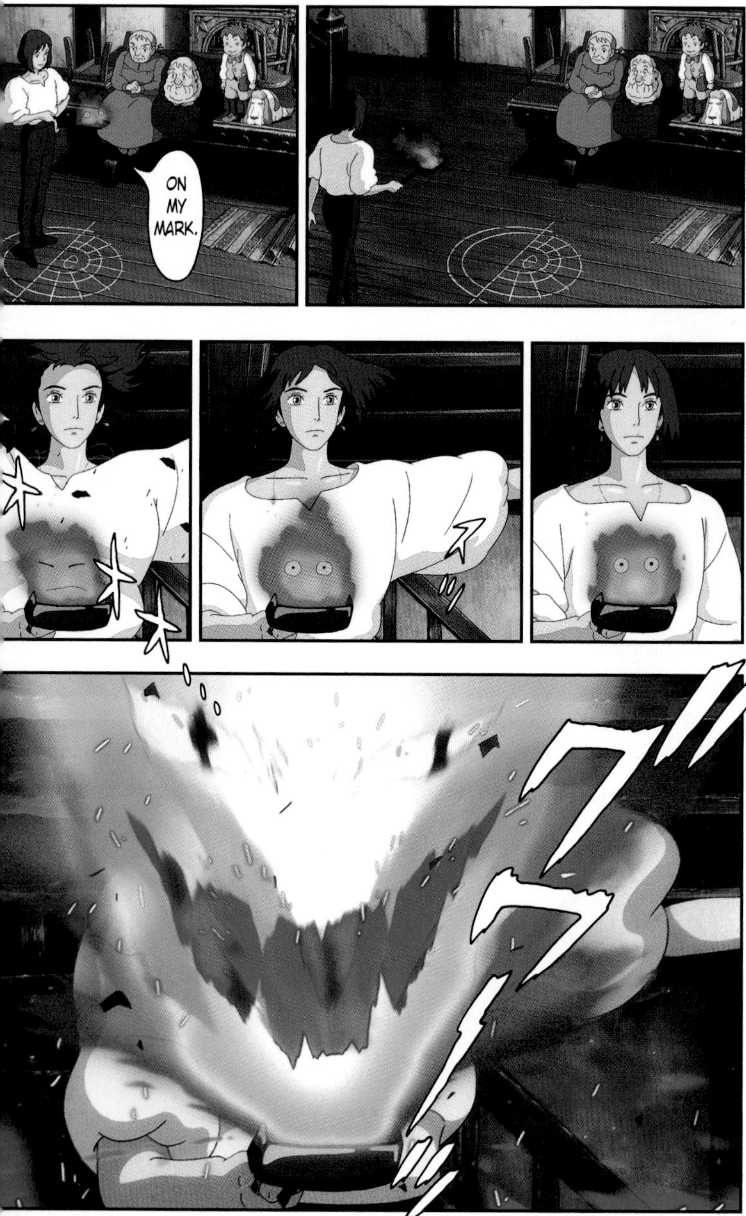
ON MY MARK.

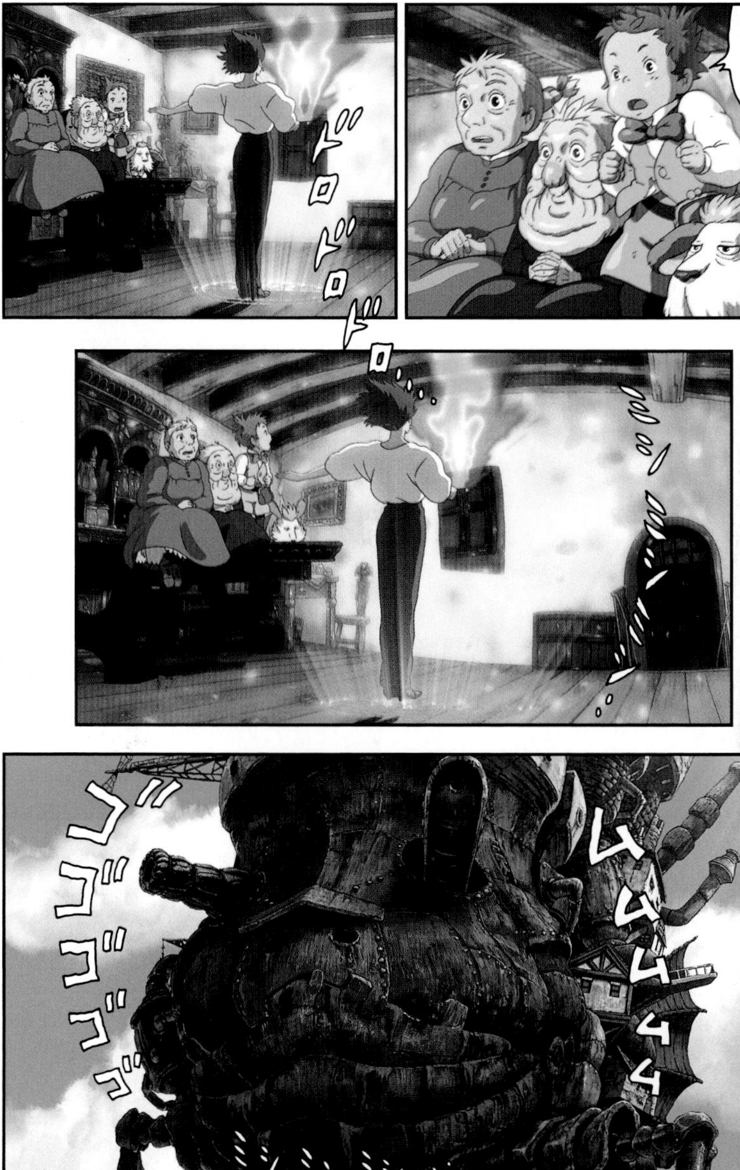
ドロドロドロ…
ゴゴゴゴゴ
ムムムムム

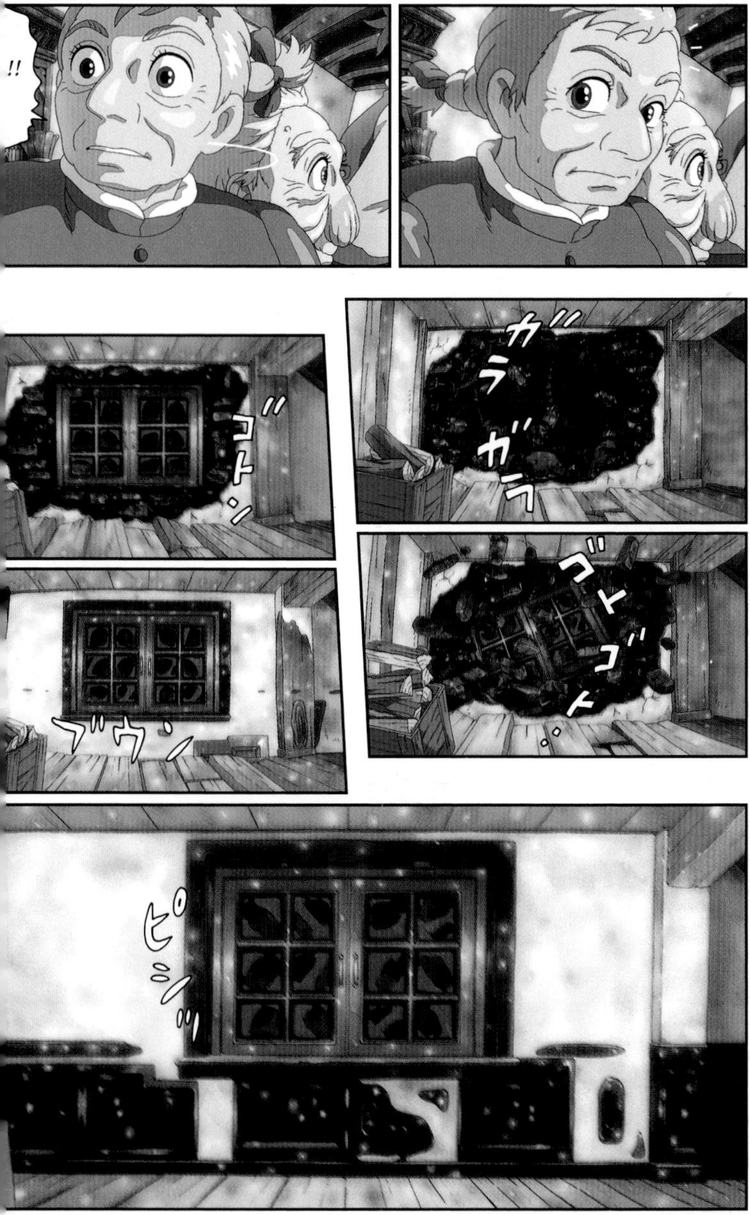
!!
ガラガラ
ゴトゴト
ゴトン
ブウン
ピシッ

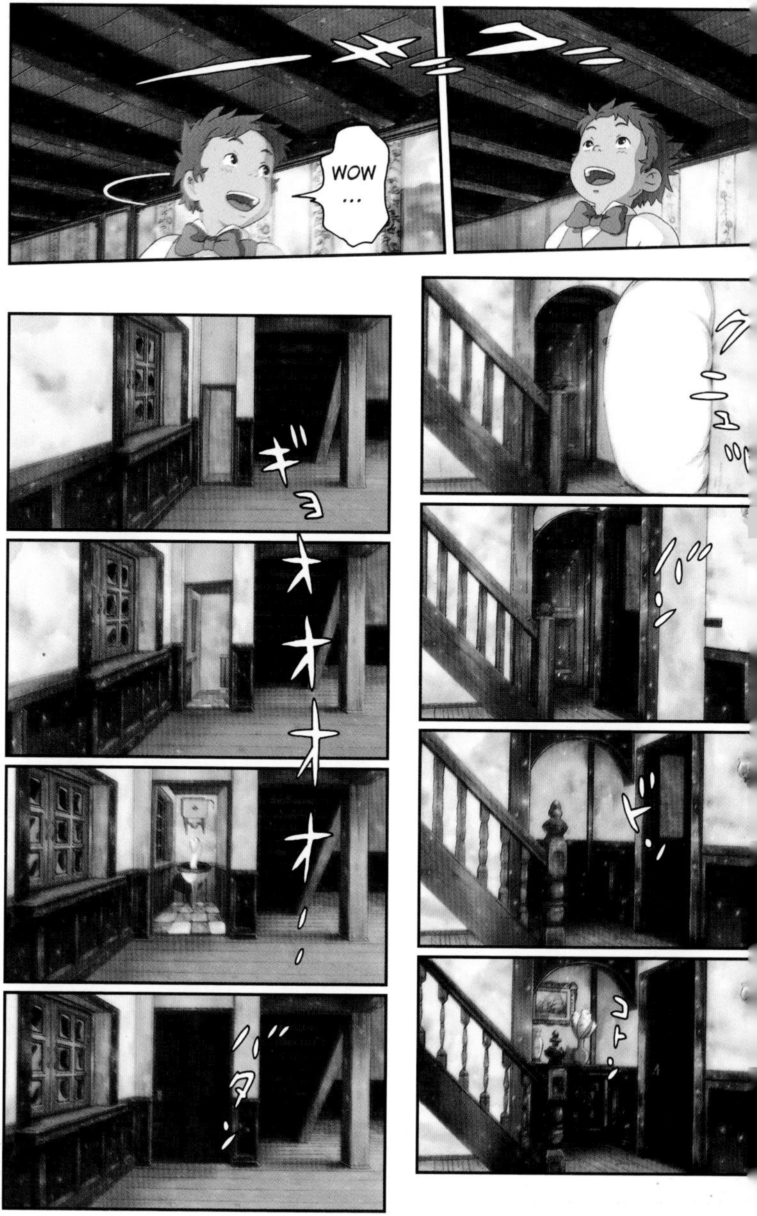
WOW
...
ギョオオオオ
バタン

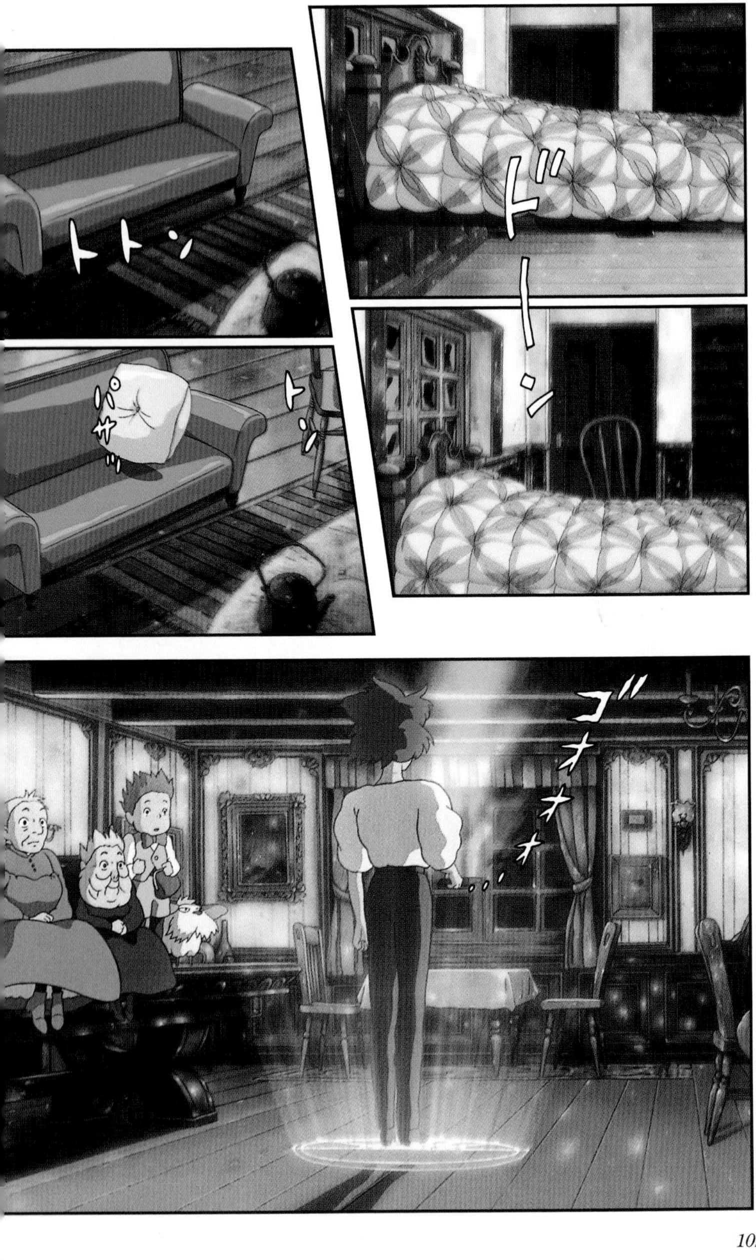
ドドーン
トトン
トン
パサ…
ゴォォォ…

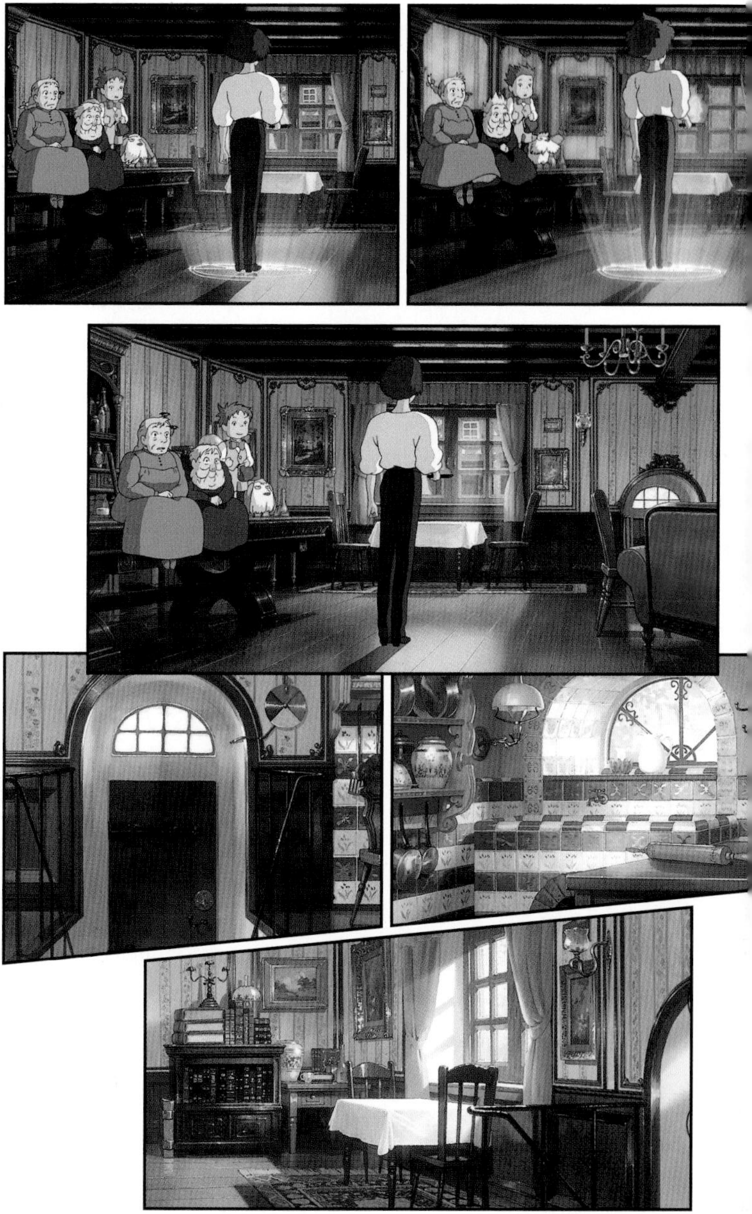

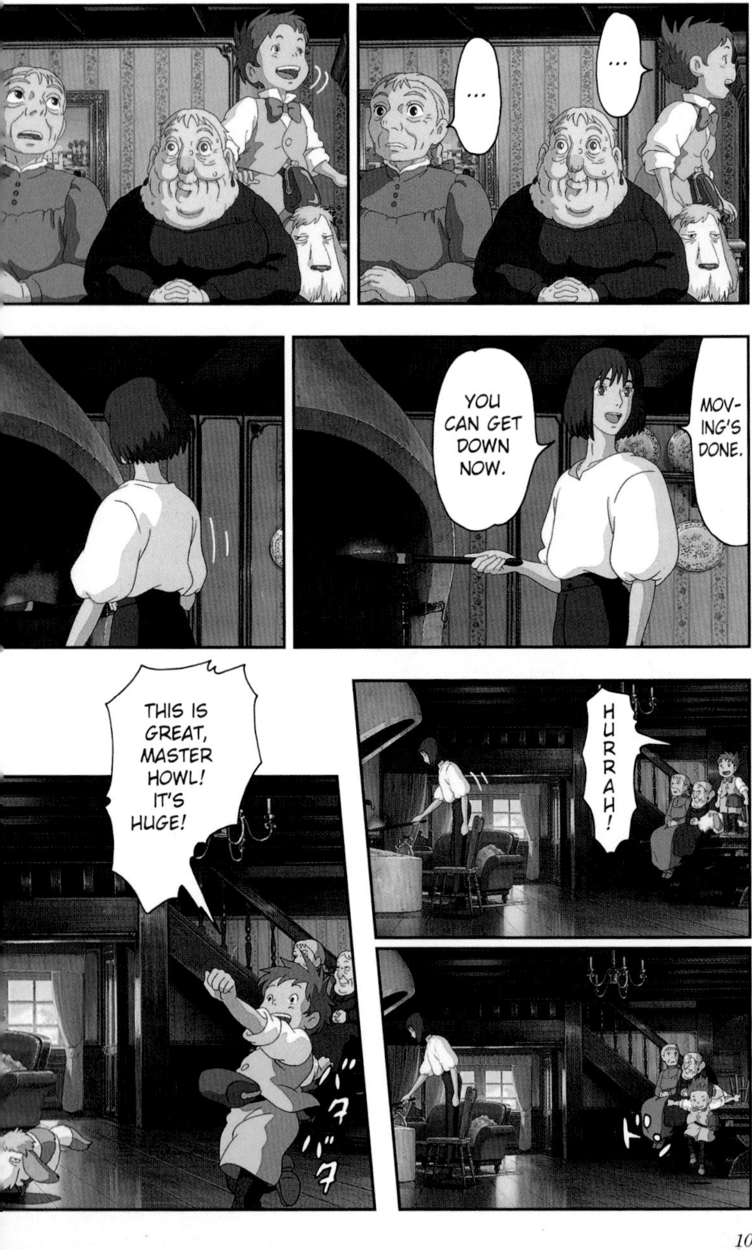
...
...
MOV-ING'S DONE.
YOU CAN GET DOWN NOW.
HURRAH!
ド
THIS IS GREAT, MASTER HOWL! IT'S HUGE!
バタバタ

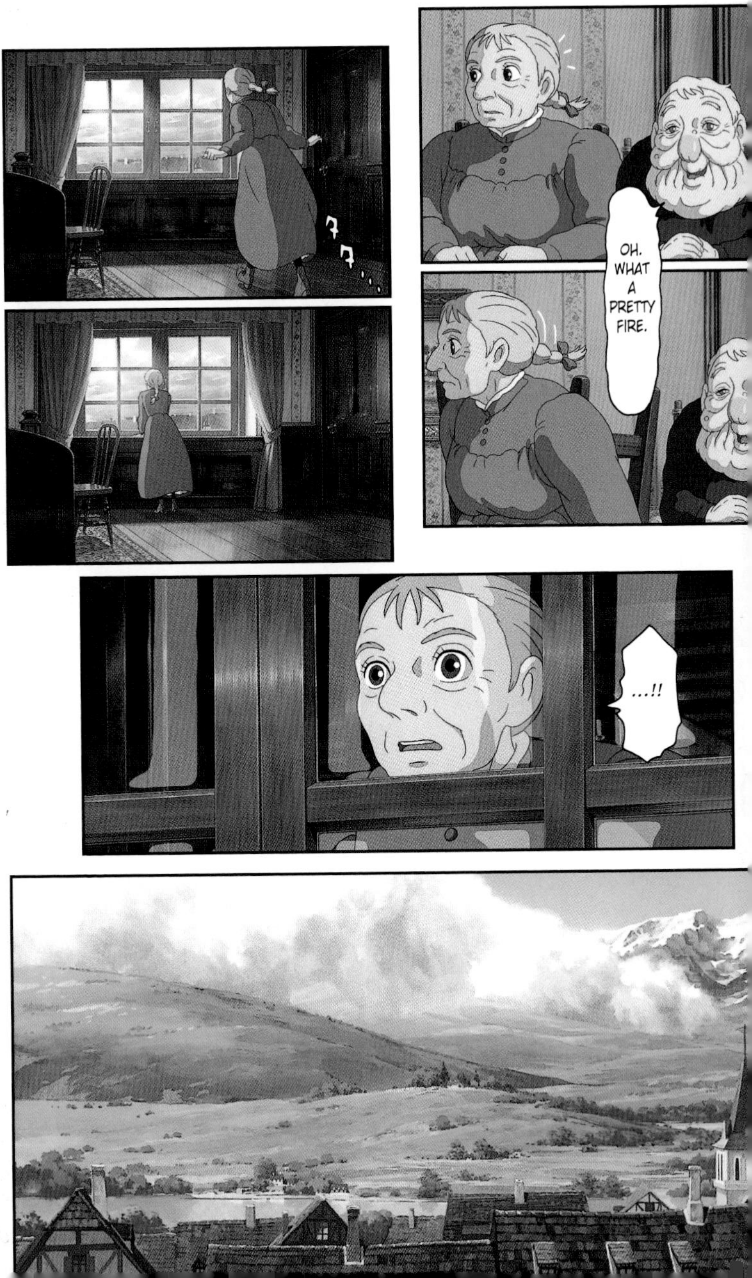
OH. WHAT A PRETTY FIRE.
...!!

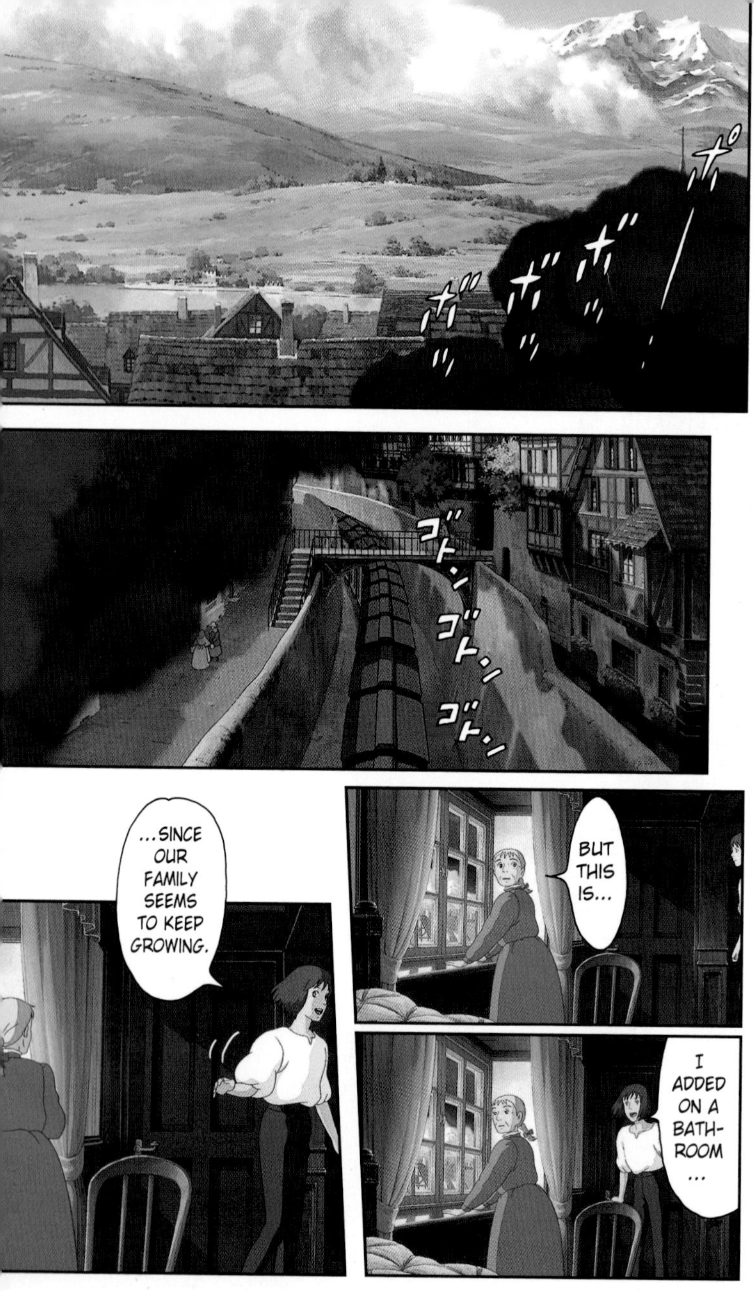
ゴトン
ゴトン
ゴトン
BUT THIS IS...
I ADDED ON A BATH-ROOM...
...SINCE OUR FAMILY SEEMS TO KEEP GROWING.

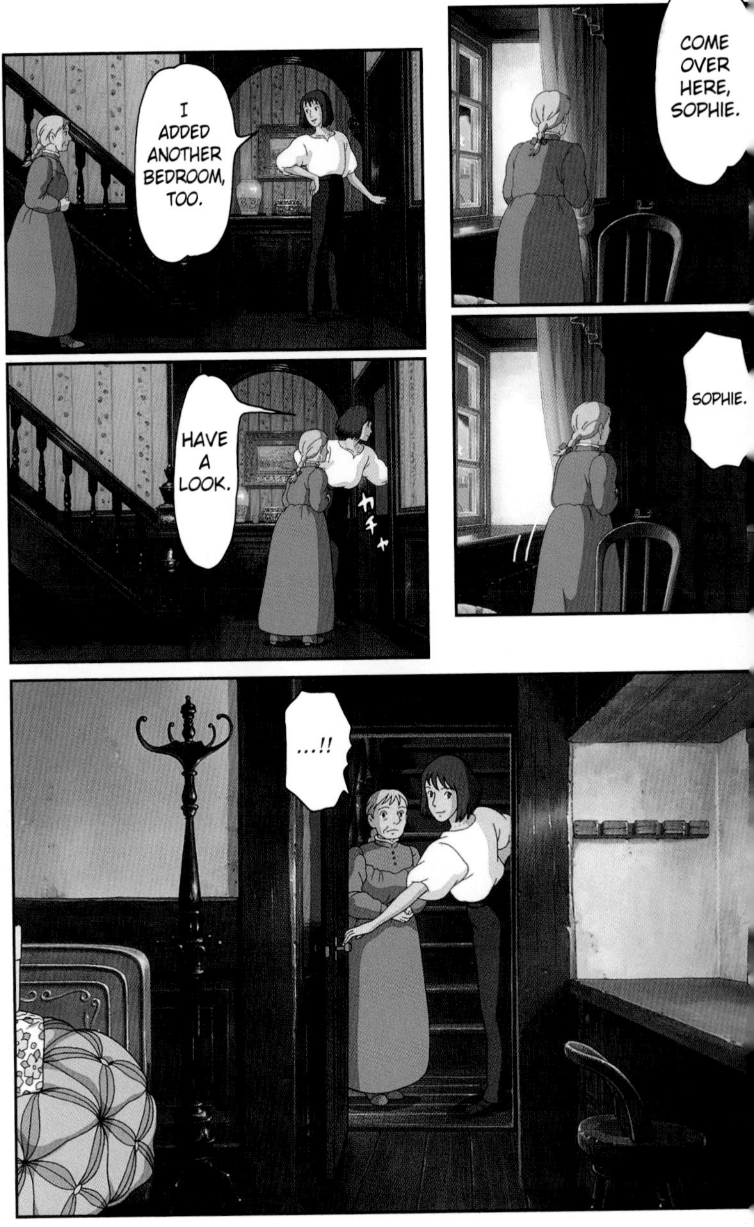
COME OVER HERE, SOPHIE.
SOPHIE.
I ADDED ANOTHER BEDROOM, TOO.
HAVE A LOOK.
カチャ
...!!

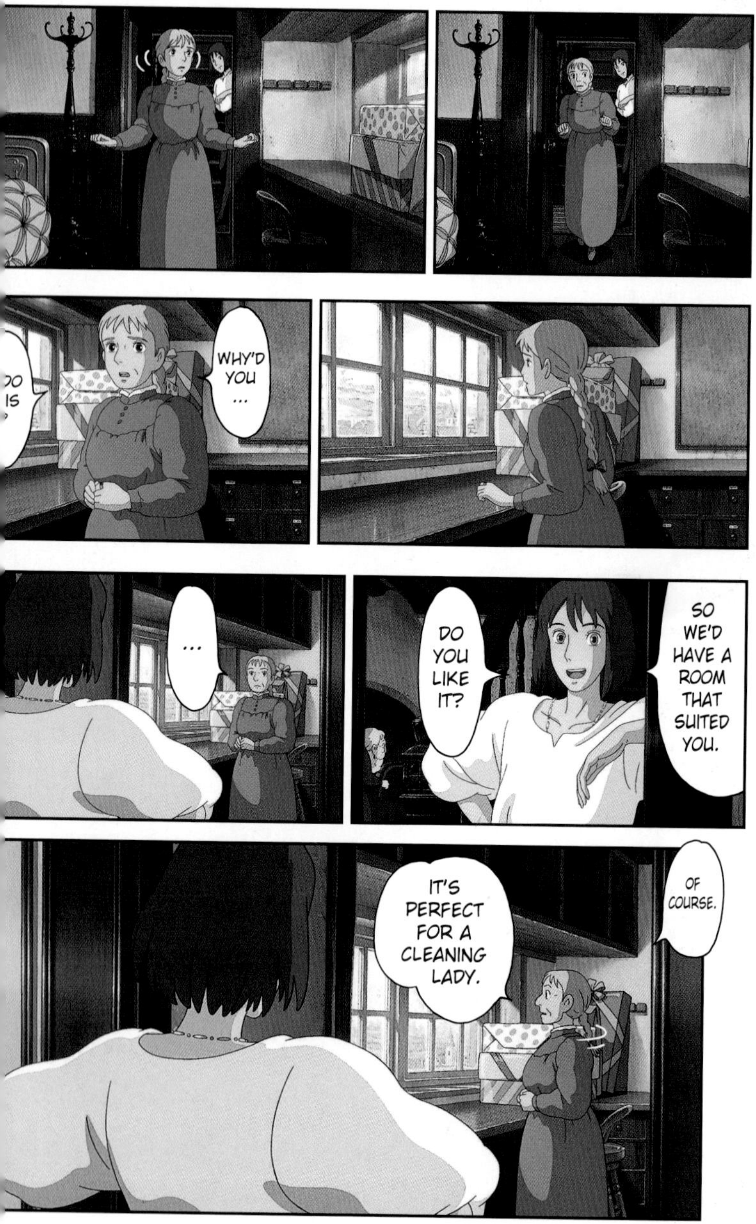
WHY'D YOU ...
SO WE'D HAVE A ROOM THAT SUITED YOU.
DO YOU LIKE IT?
...
OF COURSE.
IT'S PERFECT FOR A CLEANING LADY.

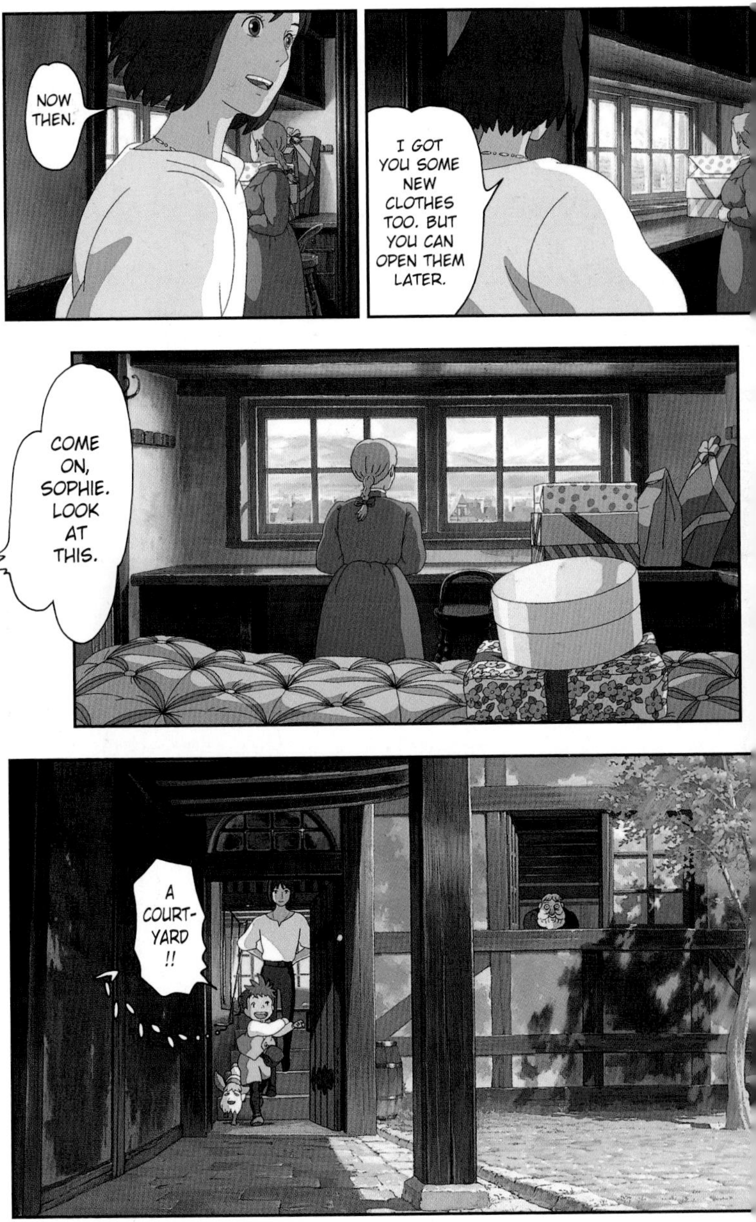
NOW THEN.
I GOT YOU SOME NEW CLOTHES TOO. BUT YOU CAN OPEN THEM LATER.
COME ON, SOPHIE. LOOK AT THIS.
A COURT-YARD !!

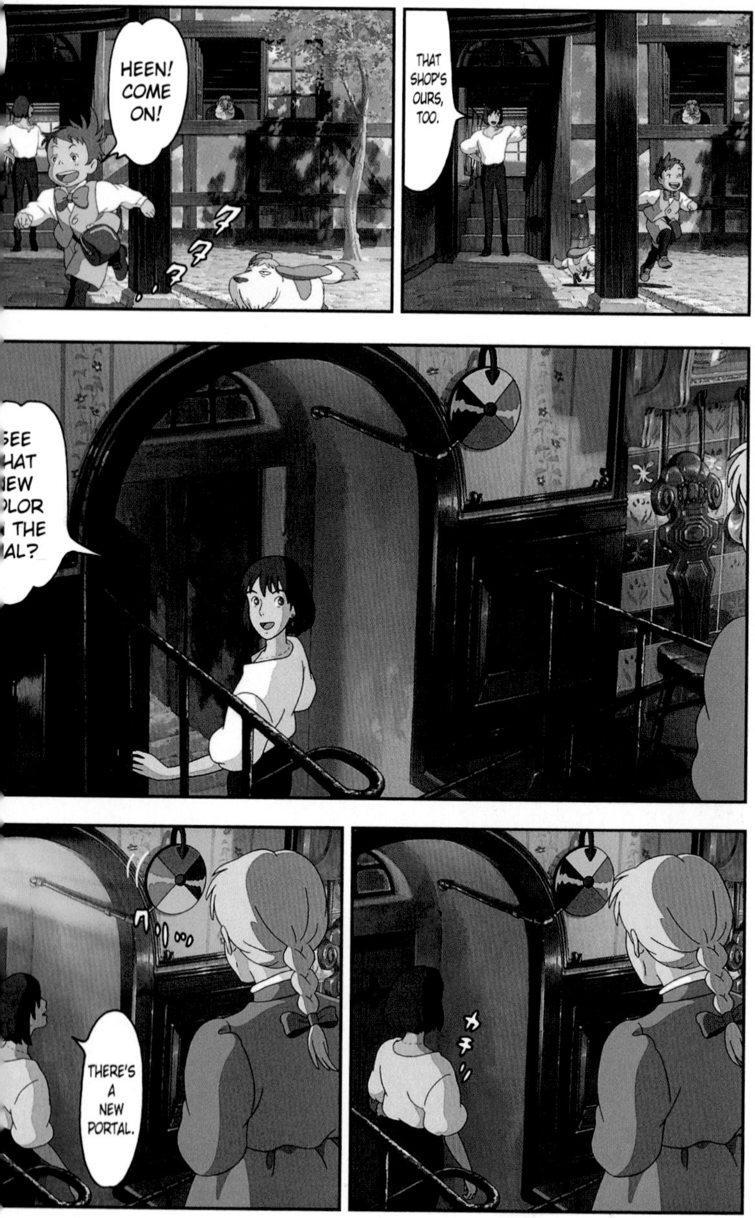
THAT SHOP'S OURS, TOO.
HEEN! COME ON!
SEE HAT IEW OLOR THE AL?
THERE'S A NEW PORTAL.

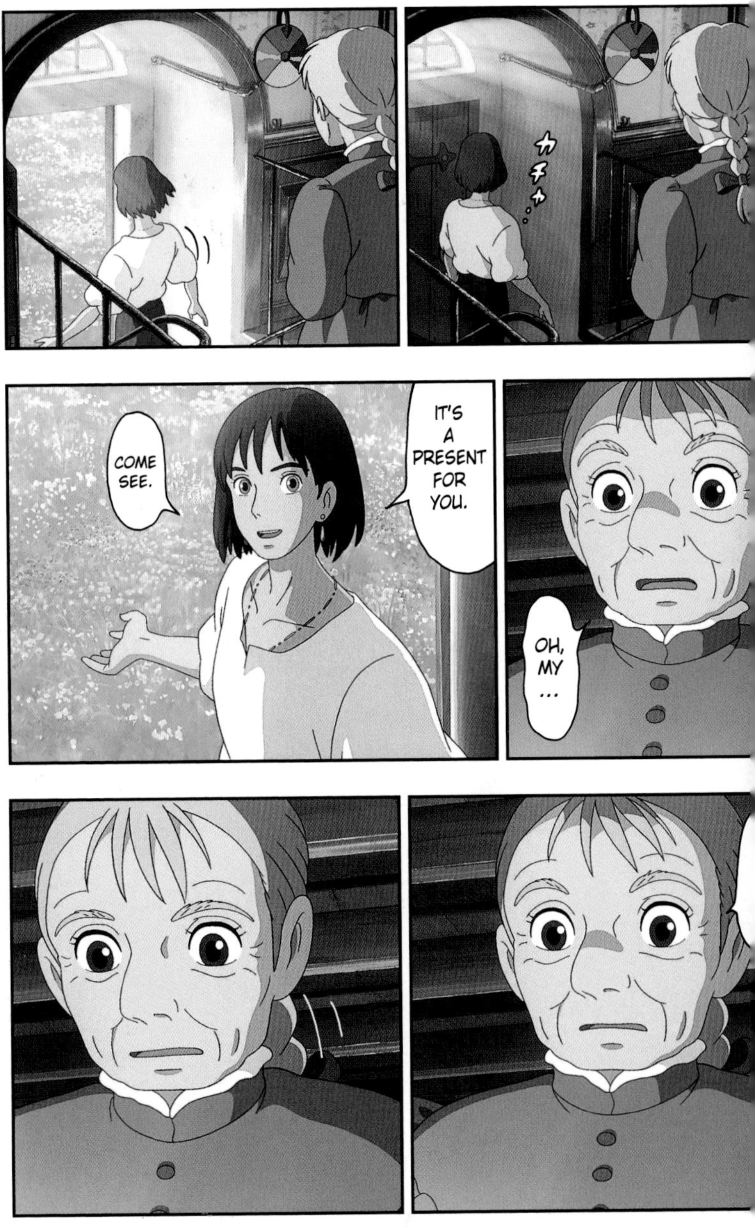
カチャ...
COME SEE.
IT'S A PRESENT FOR YOU.
OH, MY ...

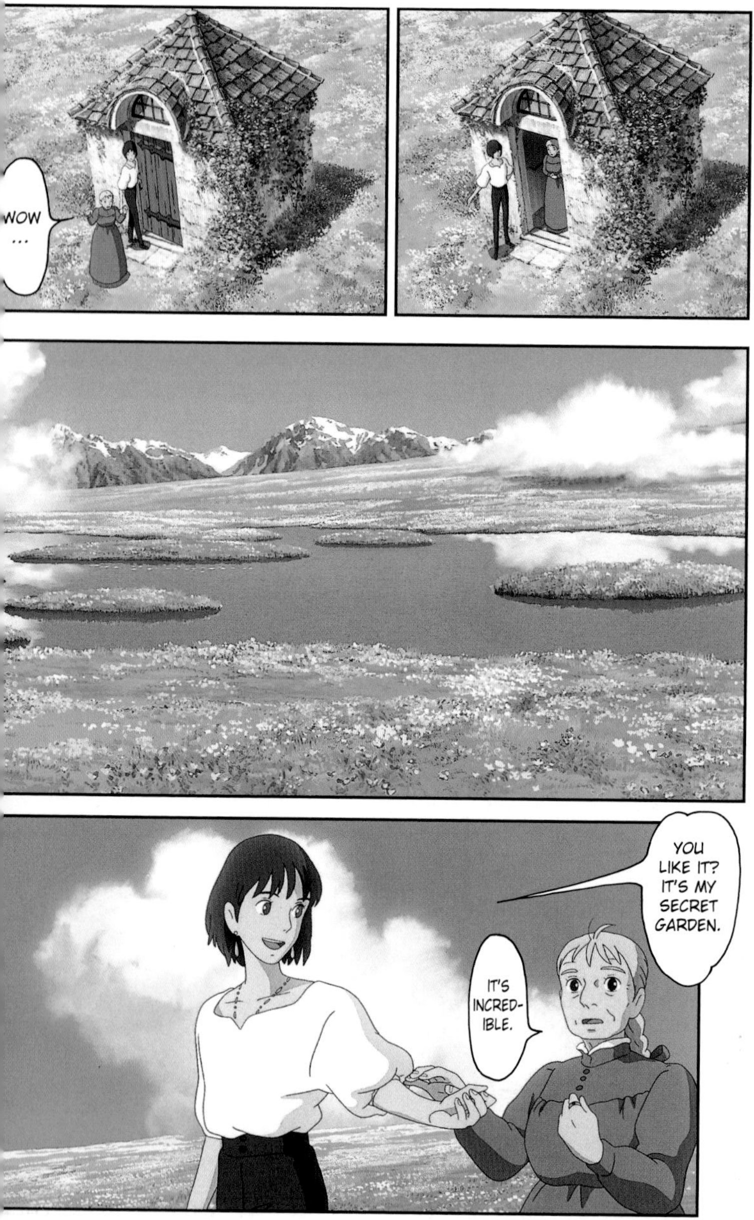
WOW ...
YOU LIKE IT? IT'S MY SECRET GARDEN.
IT'S INCRED-IBLE.

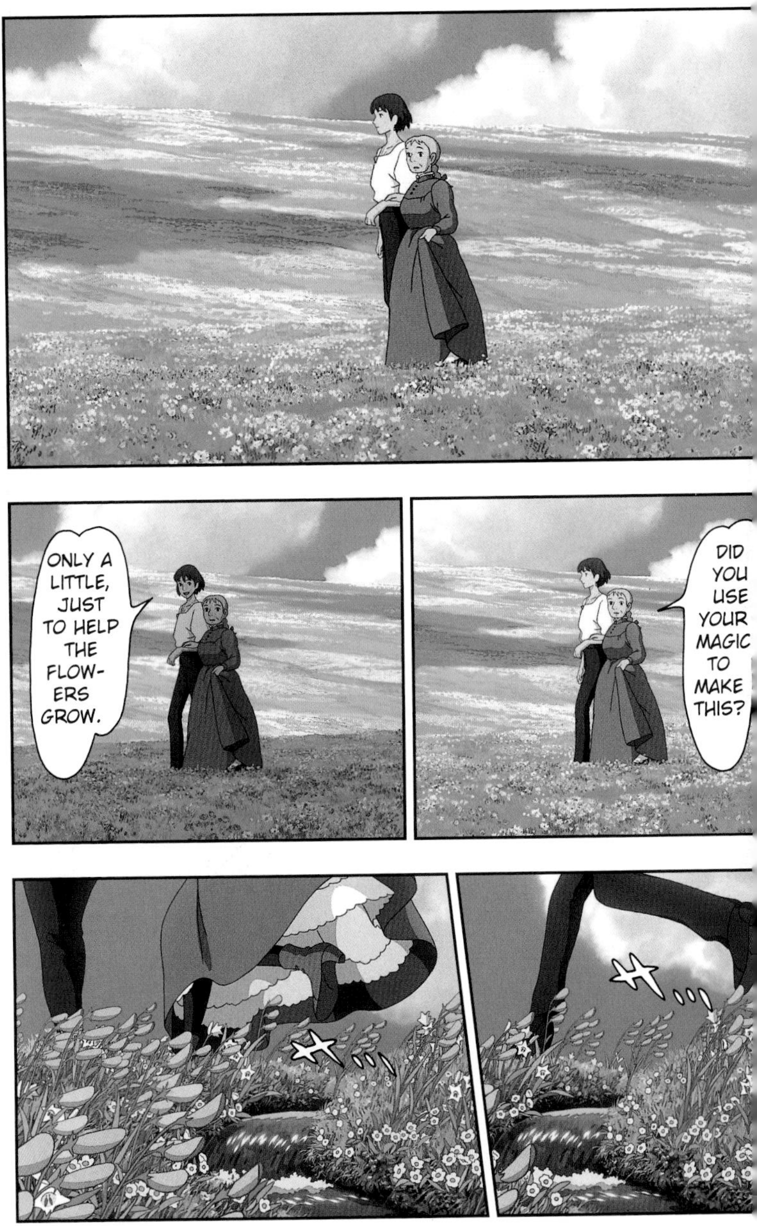
DID YOU USE YOUR MAGIC TO MAKE THIS?
ONLY A LITTLE, JUST TO HELP THE FLOW-ERS GROW.

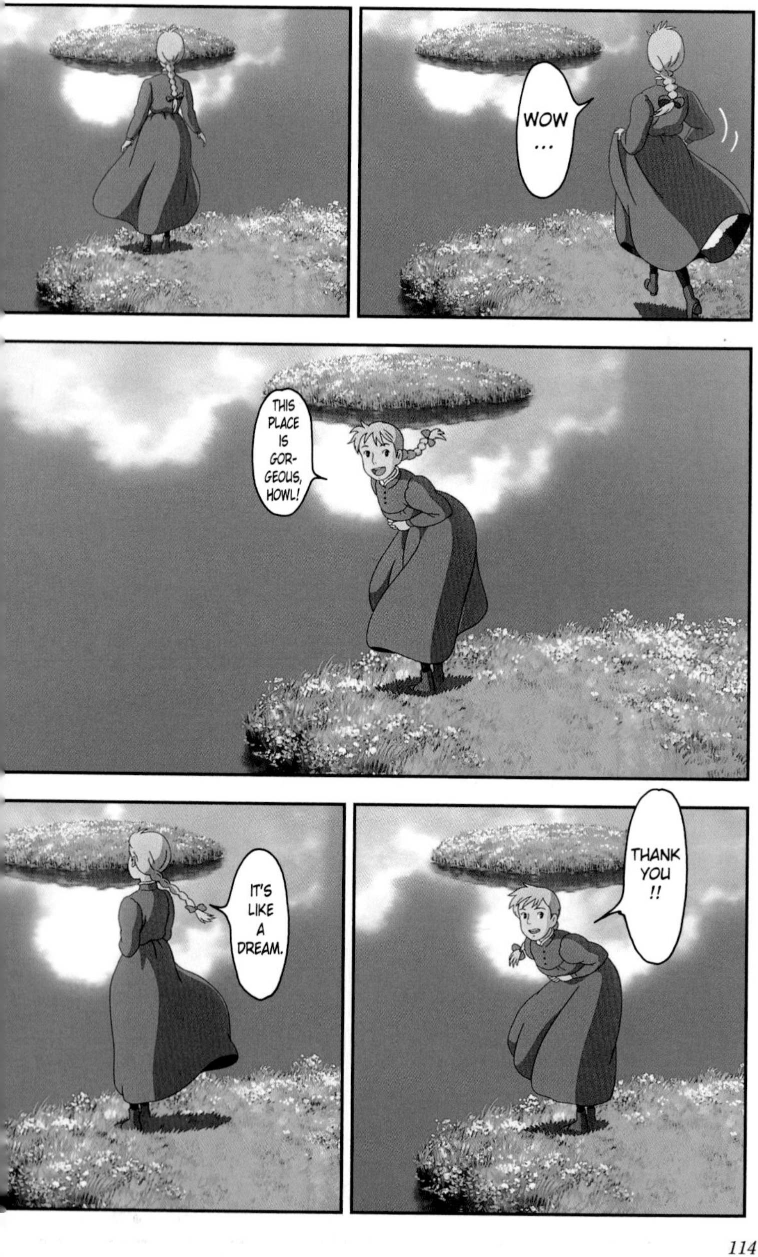
WOW ...
THIS PLACE IS GORGEOUS, HOWL!
IT'S LIKE A DREAM.
THANK YOU !!

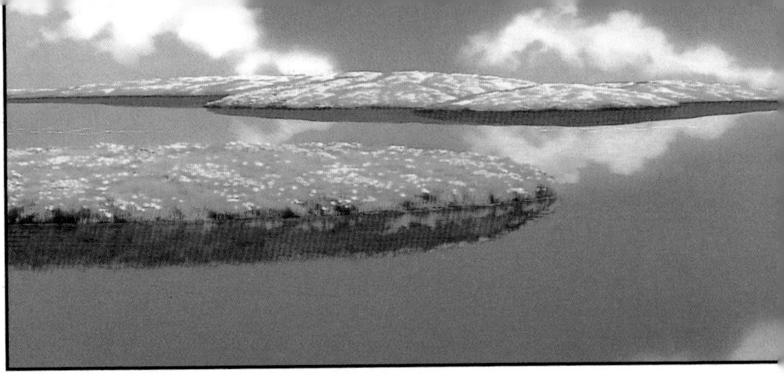

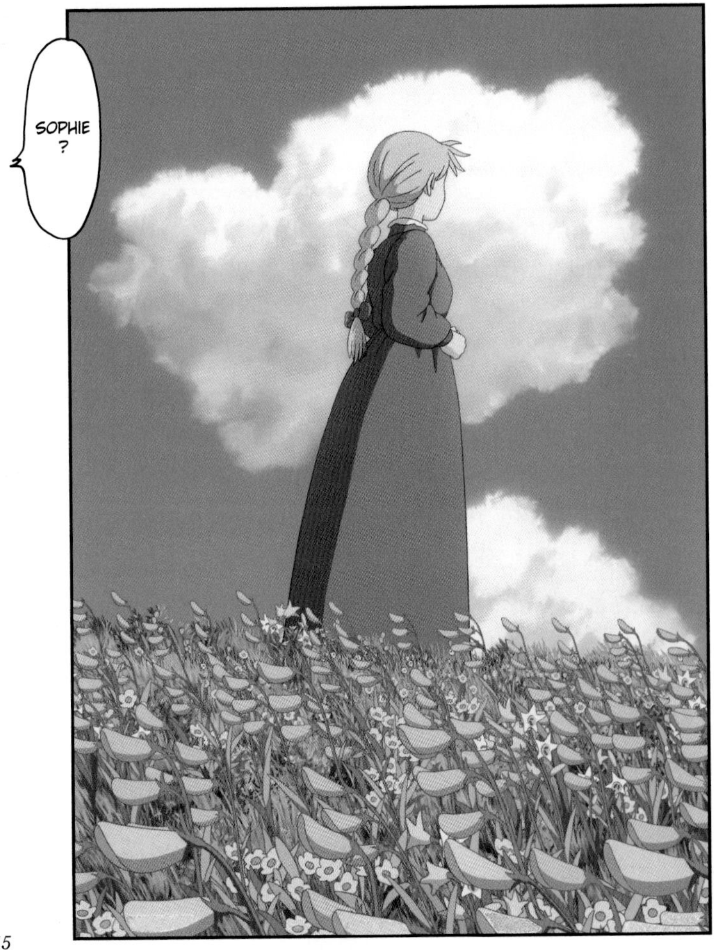
SOPHIE
?

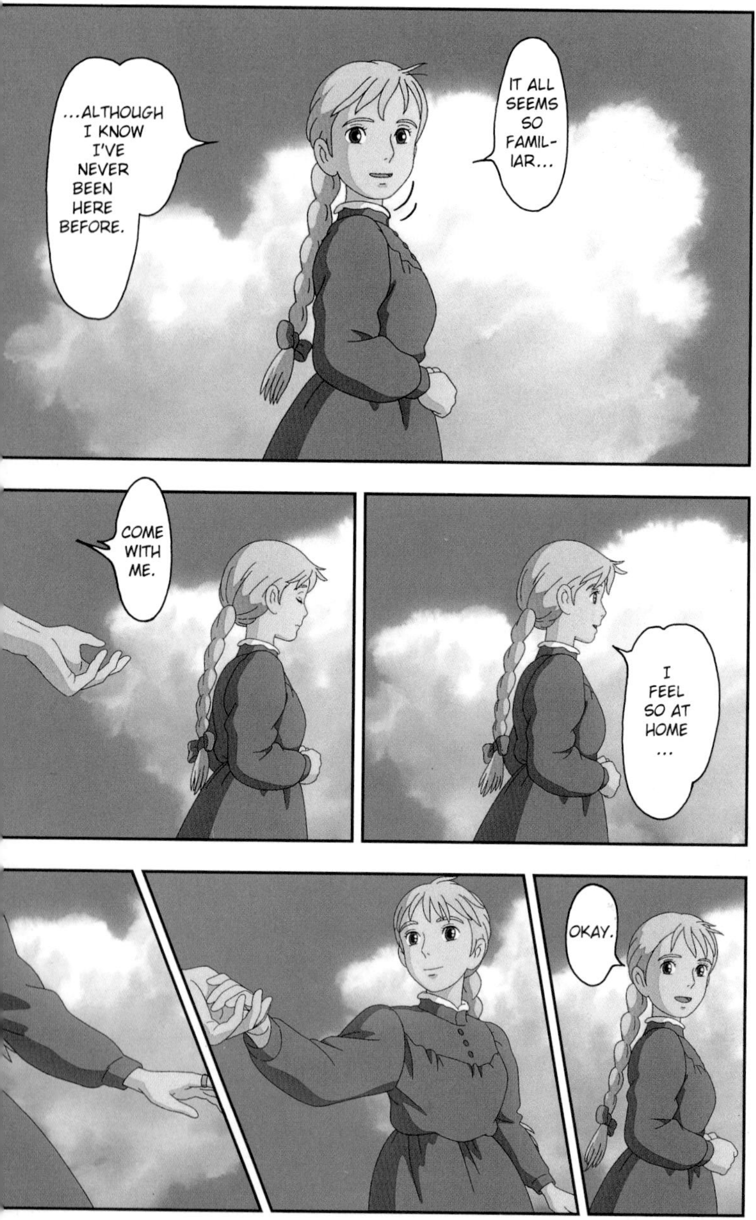
IT ALL SEEMS SO FAMIL-IAR...
...ALTHOUGH I KNOW I'VE NEVER BEEN HERE BEFORE.
I FEEL SO AT HOME ...
COME WITH ME.
OKAY.

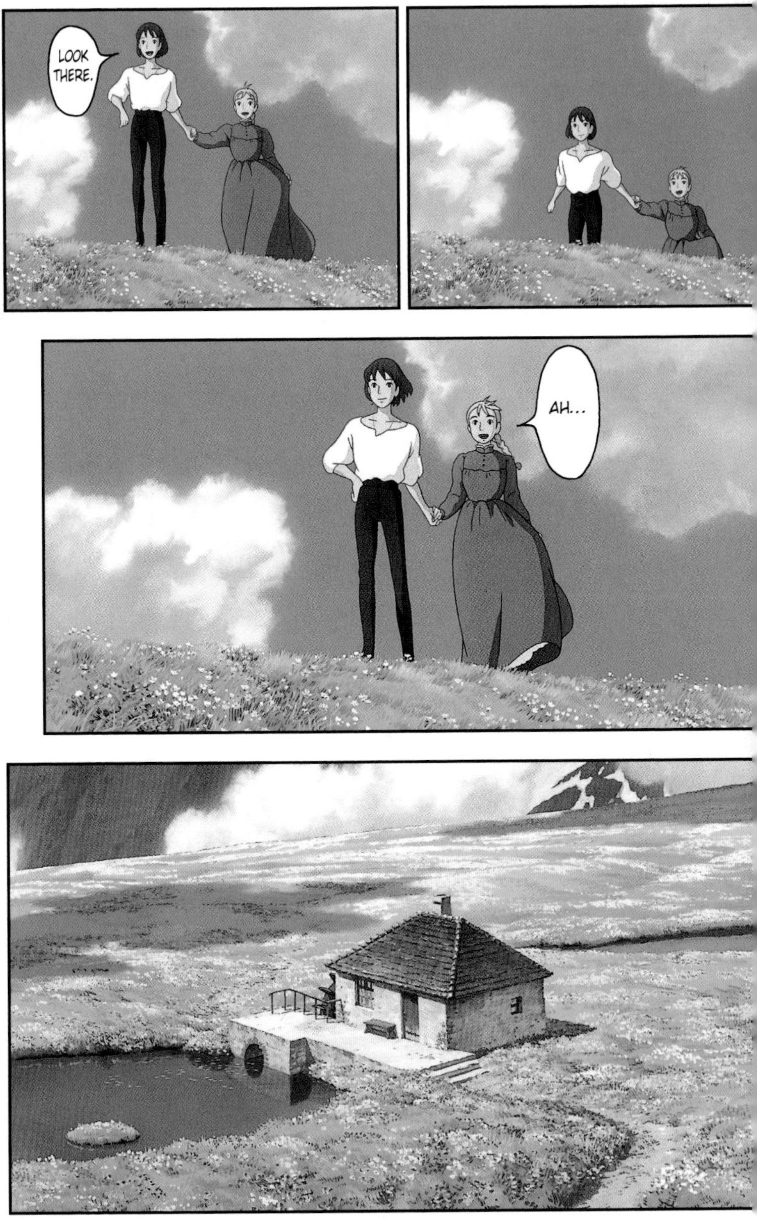
LOOK THERE.
AH...

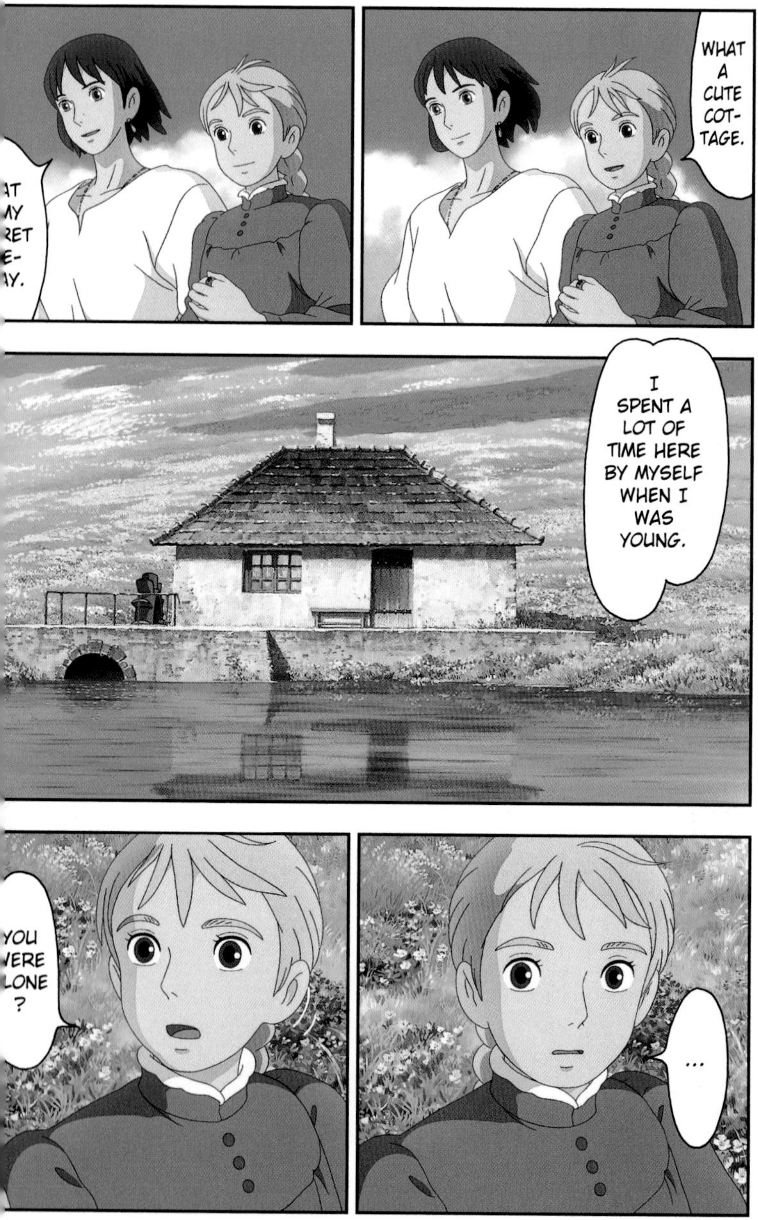
WHAT A CUTE COTTAGE.
I SPENT A LOT OF TIME HERE BY MYSELF WHEN I WAS YOUNG.
...

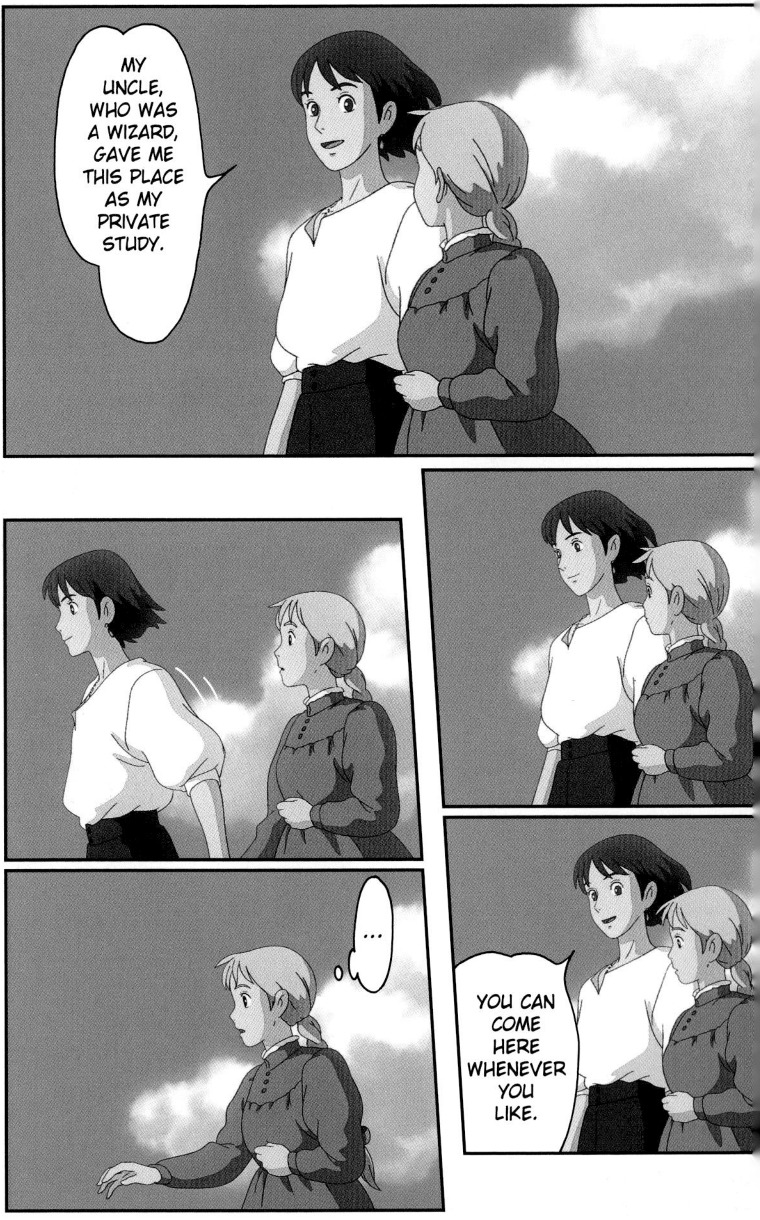
MY UNCLE, WHO WAS A WIZARD, GAVE ME THIS PLACE AS MY PRIVATE STUDY.
YOU CAN COME HERE WHENEVER YOU LIKE.
...

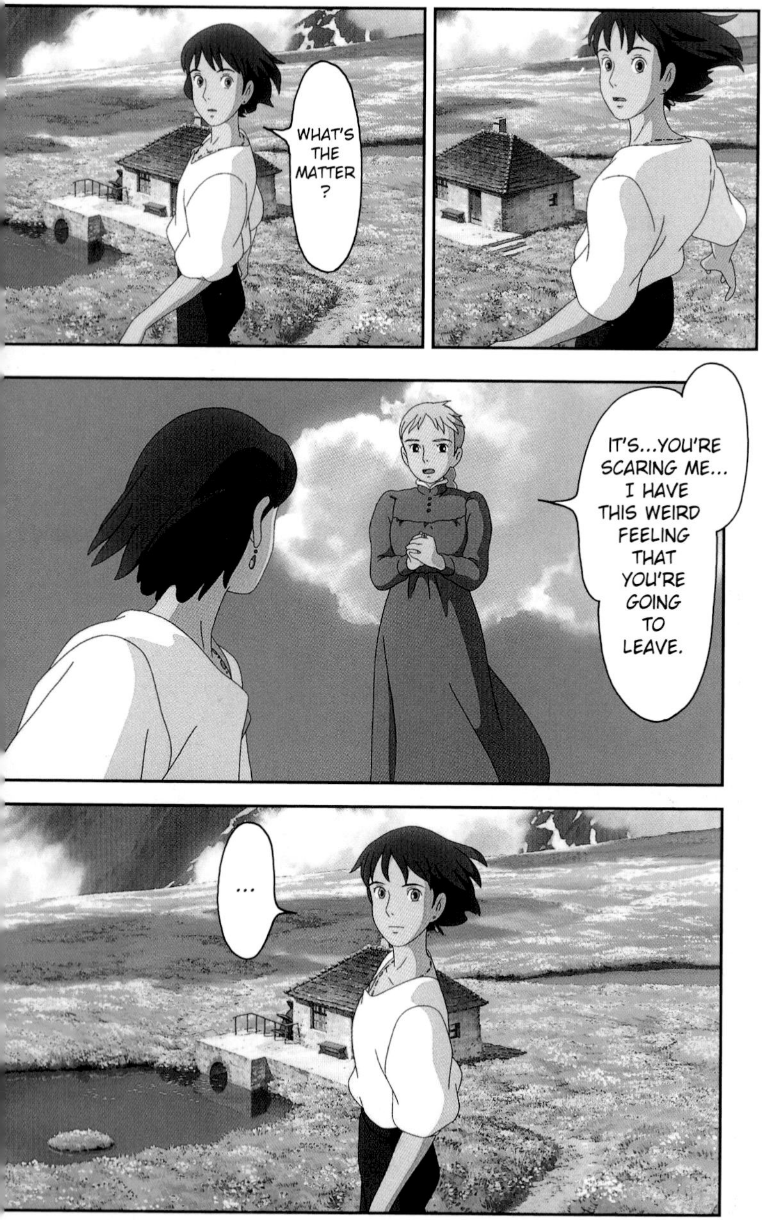
WHAT'S THE MATTER?
IT'S...YOU'RE SCARING ME... I HAVE THIS WEIRD FEELING THAT YOU'RE GOING TO LEAVE.
...

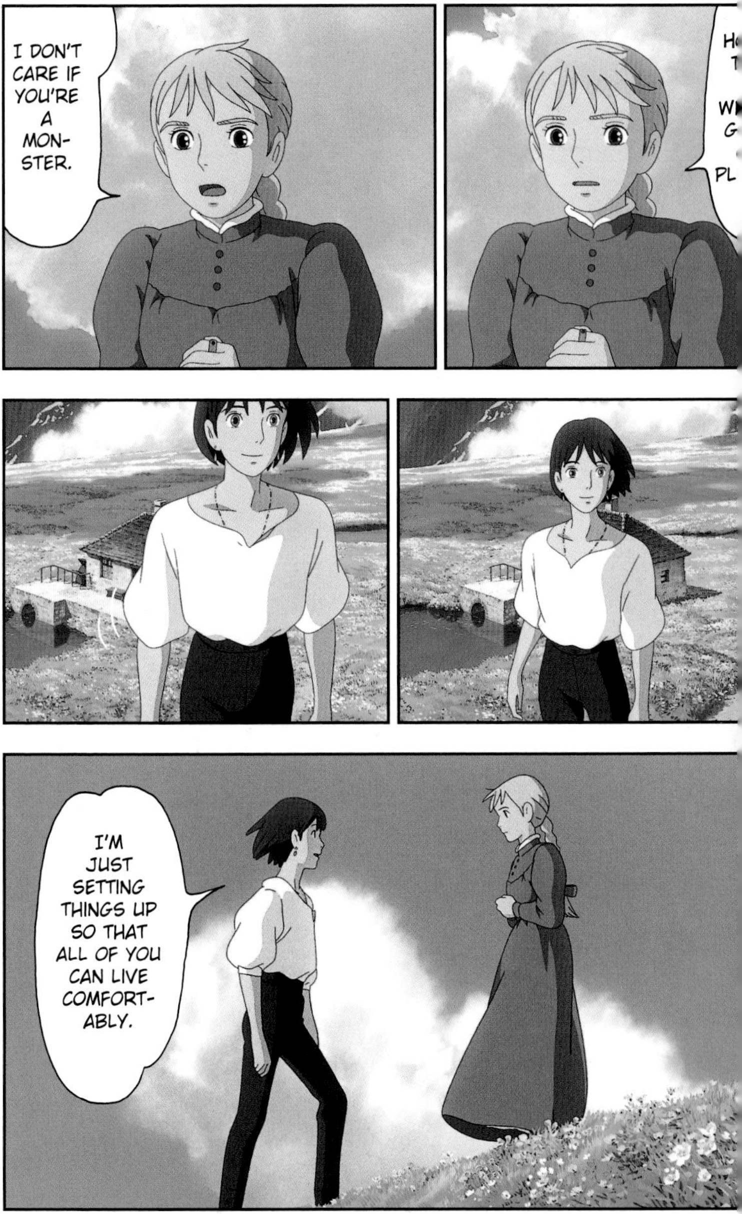
I DON'T CARE IF YOU'RE A MONSTER.
I'M JUST SETTING THINGS UP SO THAT ALL OF YOU CAN LIVE COMFORTABLY.

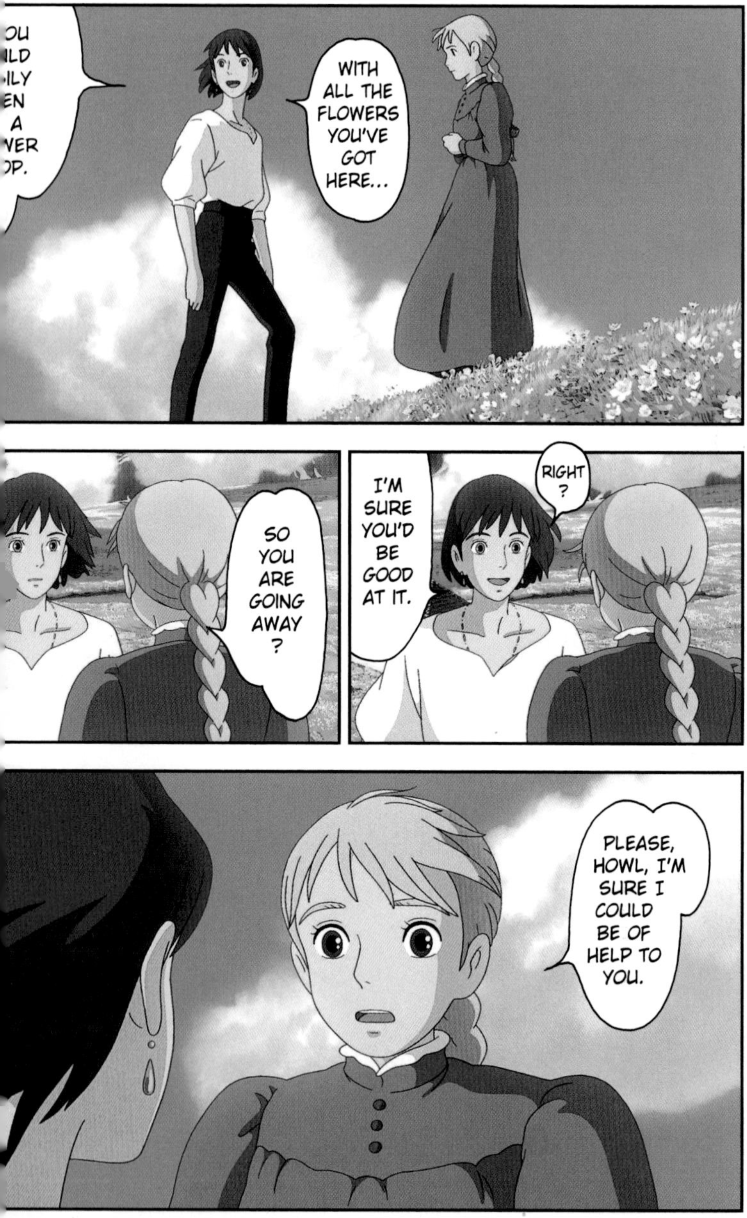
WITH ALL THE FLOWERS YOU'VE GOT HERE...
I'M SURE YOU'D BE GOOD AT IT.
RIGHT?
SO YOU ARE GOING AWAY?
PLEASE, HOWL, I'M SURE I COULD BE OF HELP TO YOU.

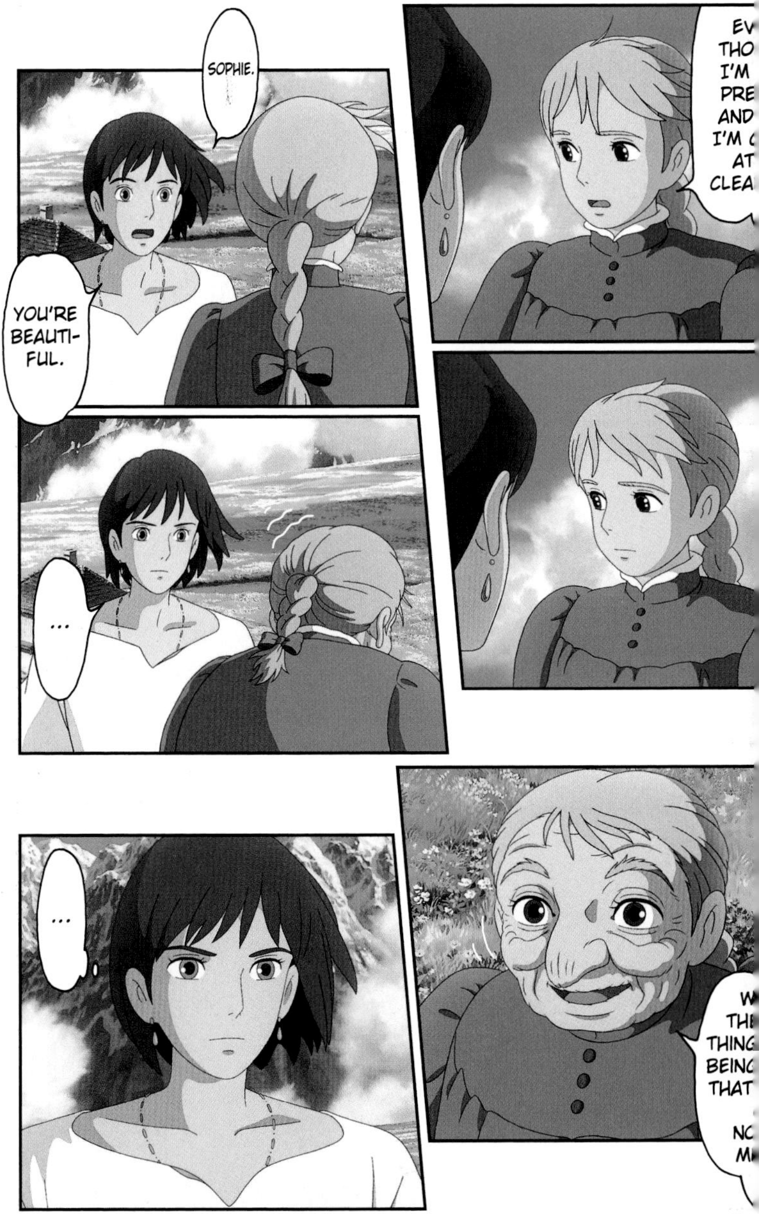
SOPHIE.
YOU'RE BEAUTI-FUL.
...
...

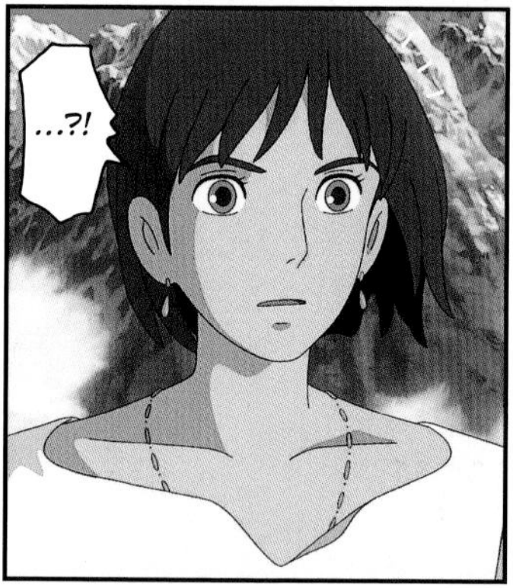
...?!
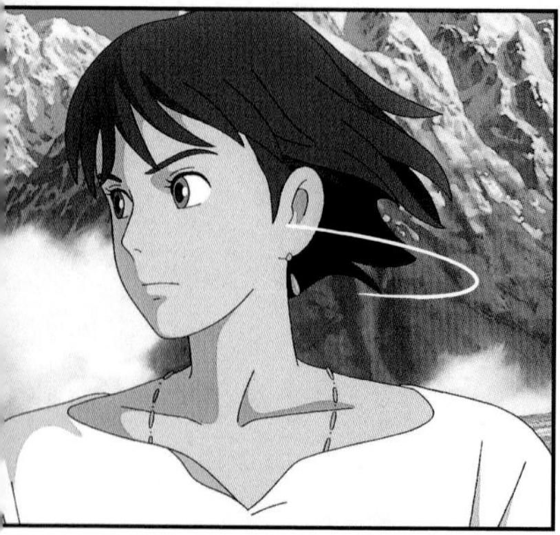
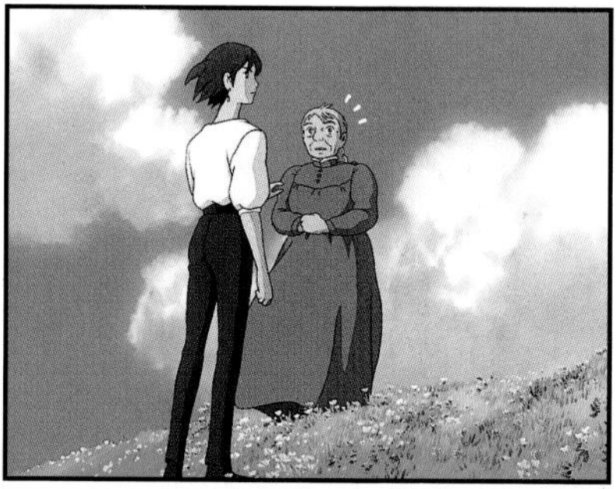
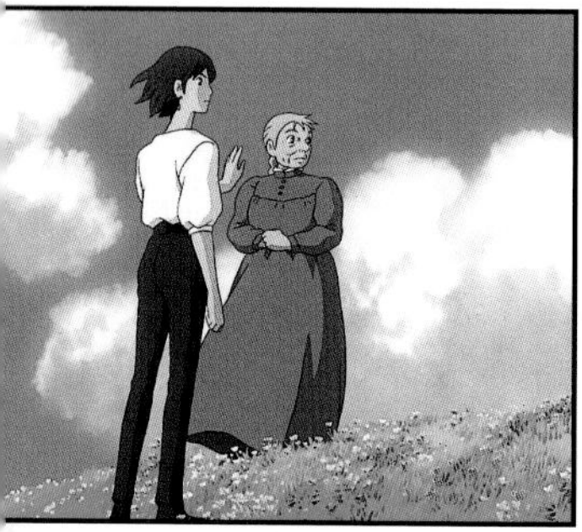
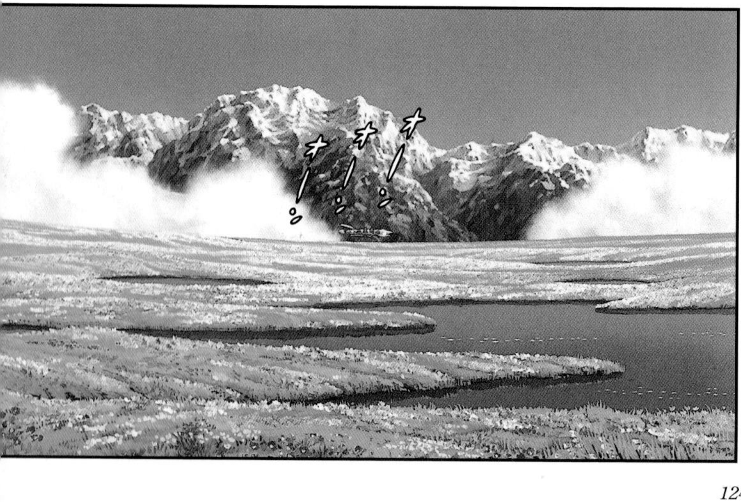
オー
オー
オー

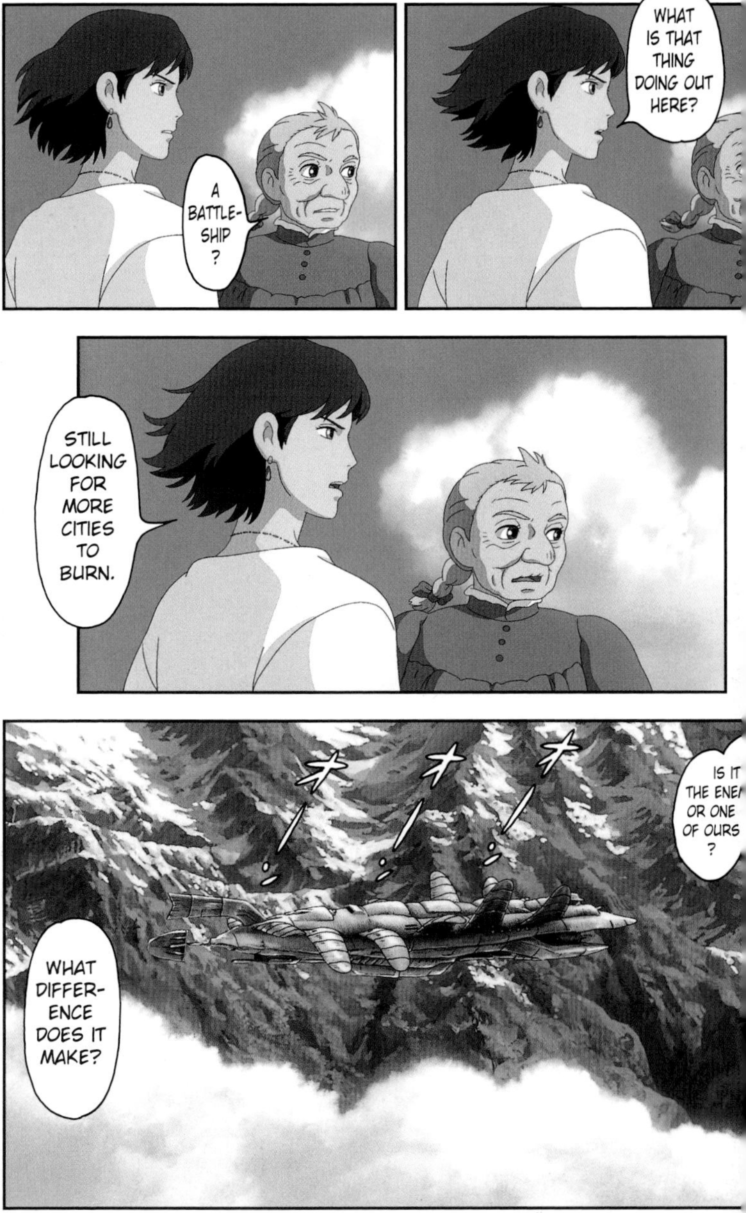
WHAT IS THAT THING DOING OUT HERE?
A BATTLE-SHIP ?
STILL LOOKING FOR MORE CITIES TO BURN.
IS IT THE ENE OR ONE OF OURS ?
WHAT DIFFER-ENCE DOES IT MAKE?

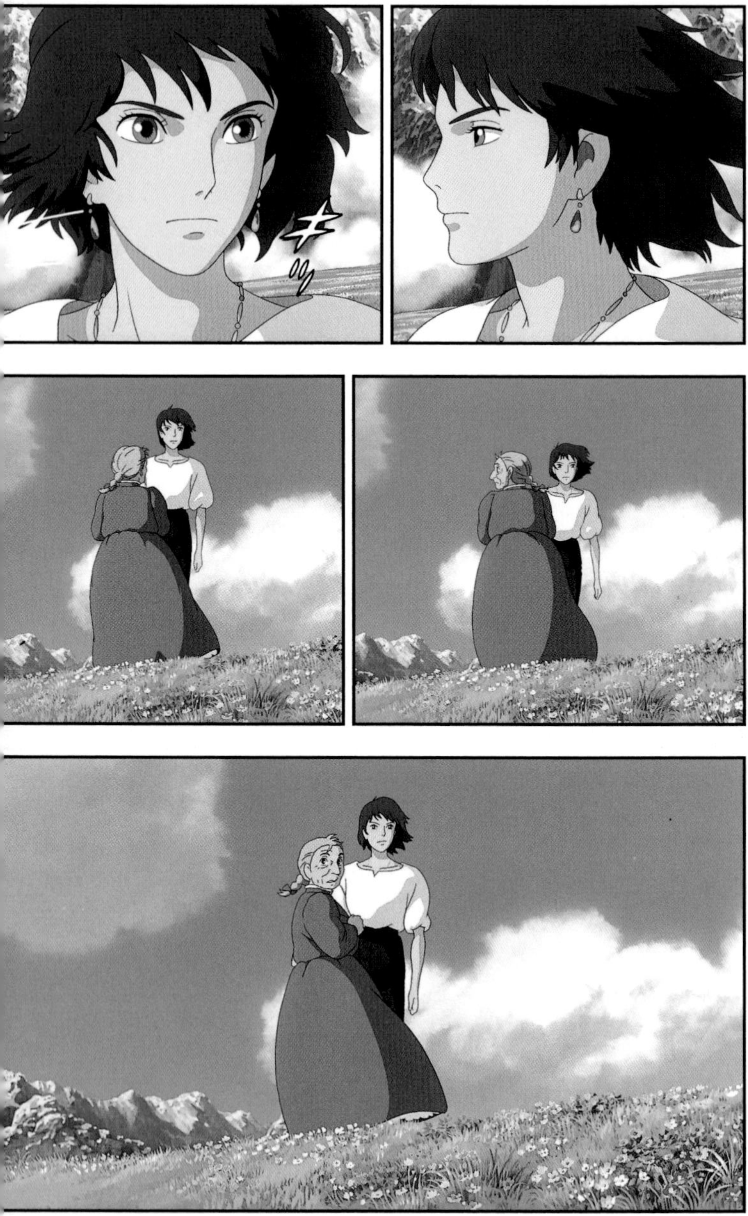

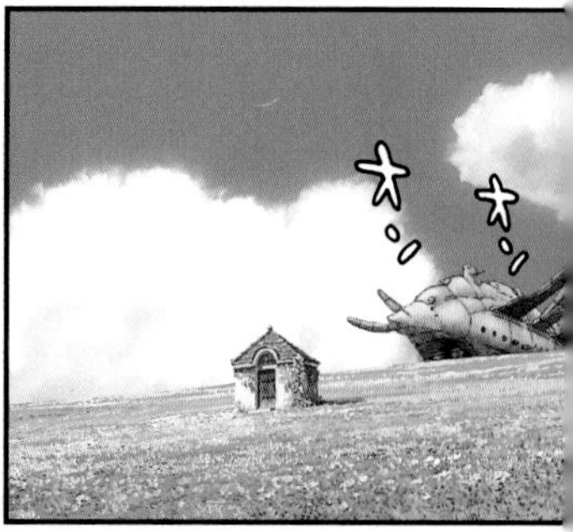

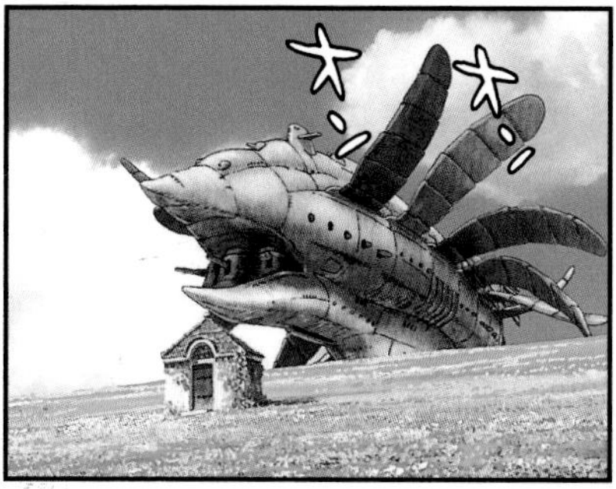

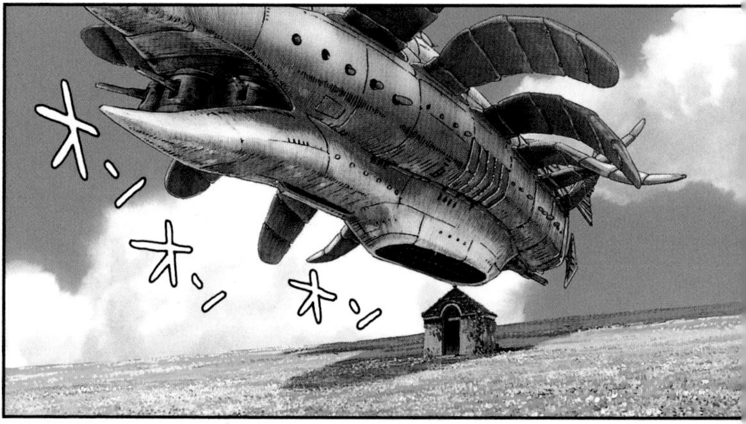

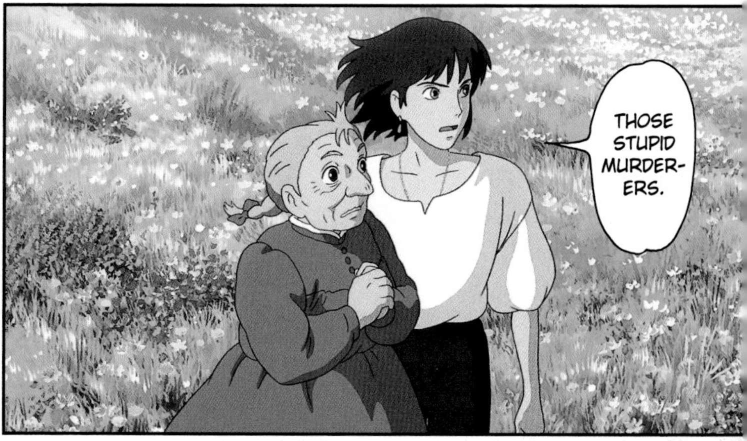
THOSE STUPID MURDERER-ERS.

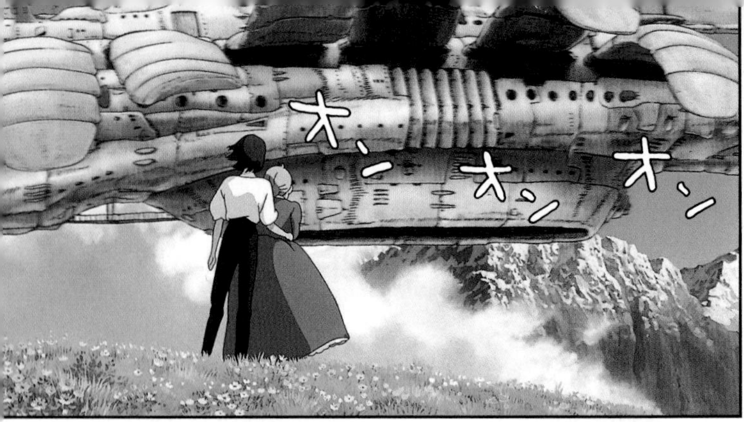
オ〜ン
オ〜ン
オ〜ン
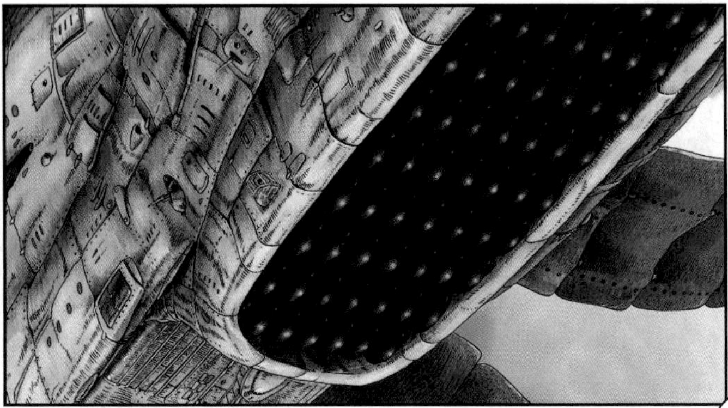
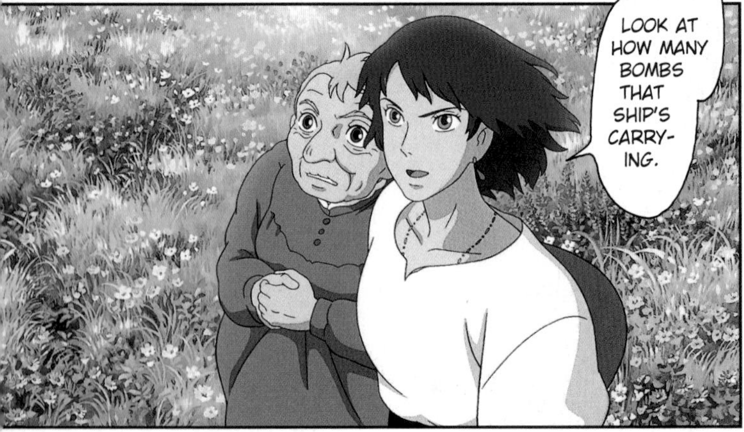
LOOK AT HOW MANY BOMBS THAT SHIP'S CARRY-ING.

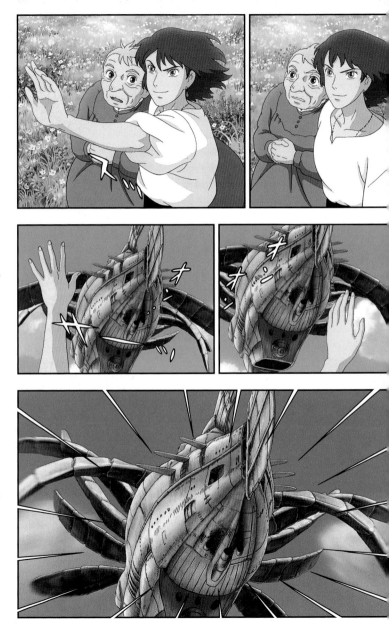

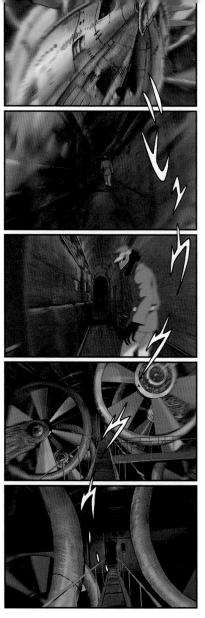

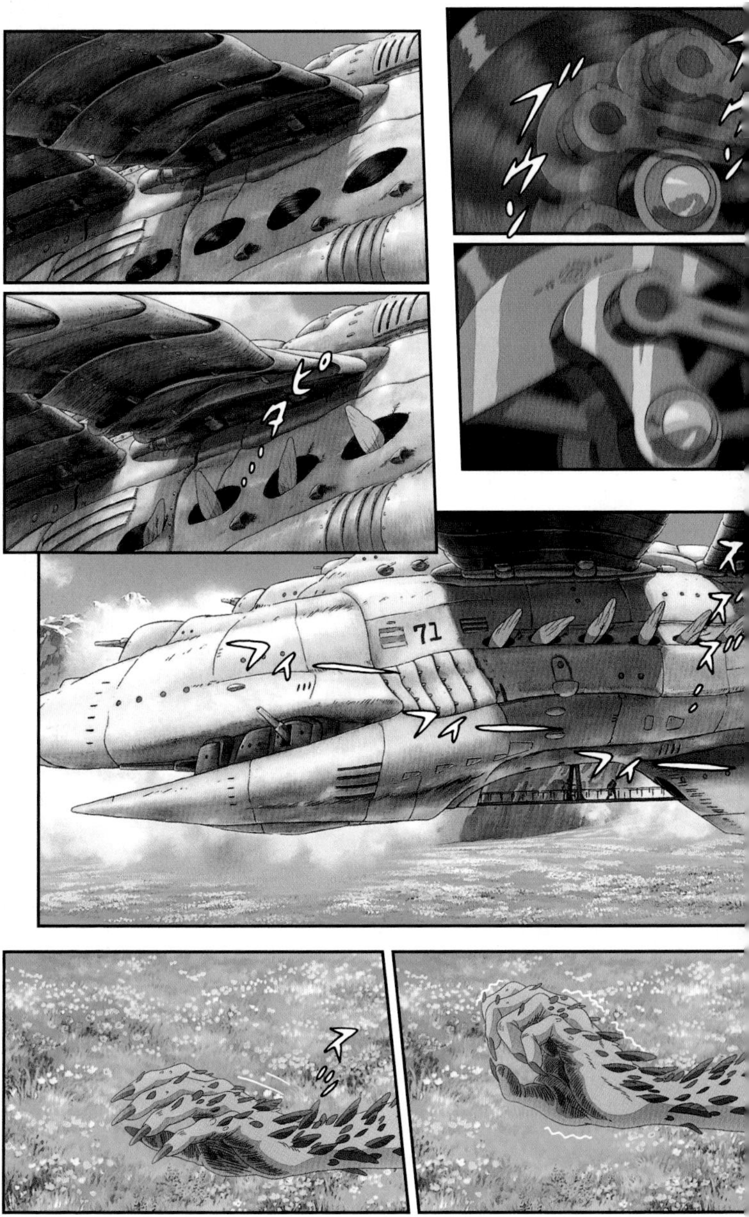
ブゥン
ピタ…
フィー
フィー
フィー
ス…

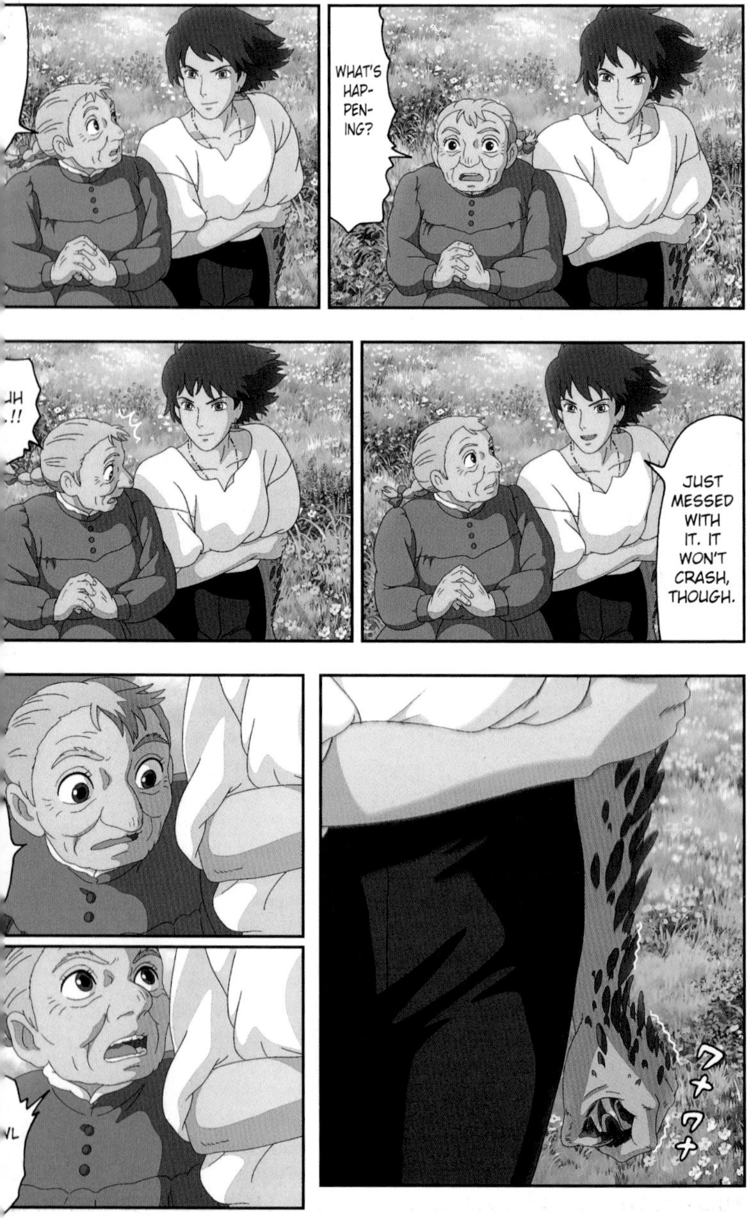
WHAT'S HAP-PEN-ING?
JUST MESSED WITH IT. IT WON'T CRASH, THOUGH.
ワナワナ

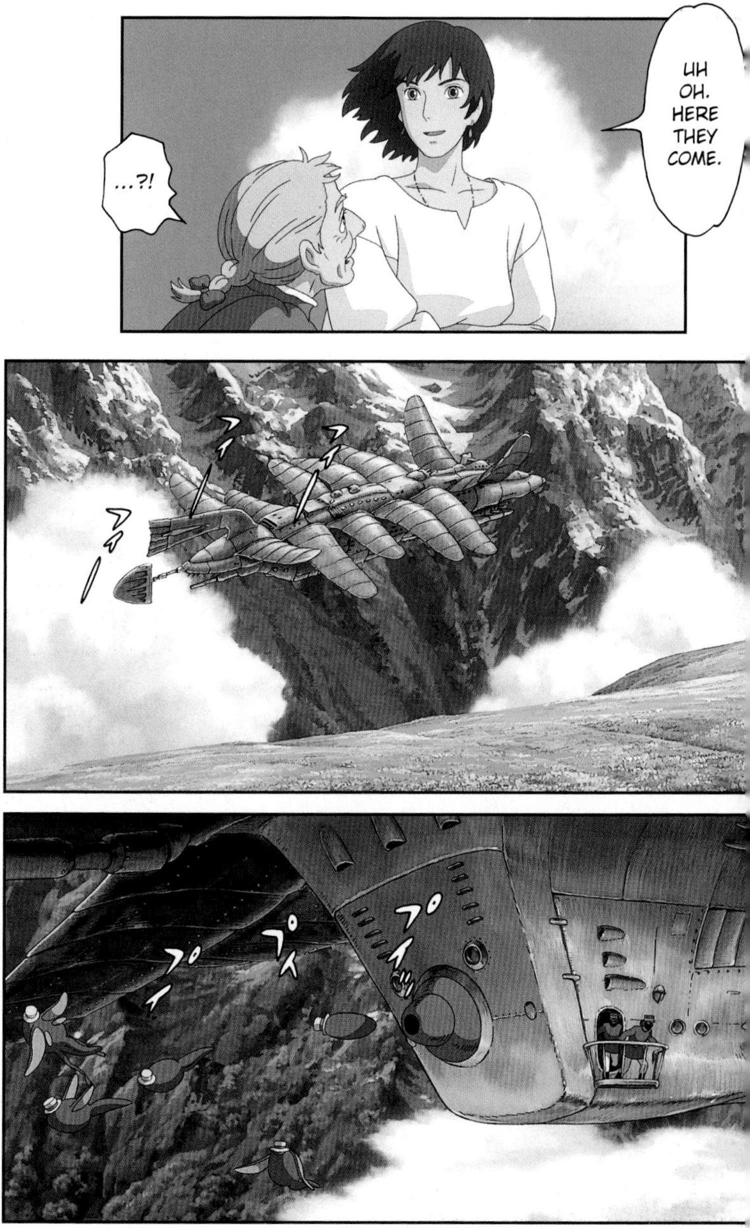
UH OH. HERE THEY COME.
...?!

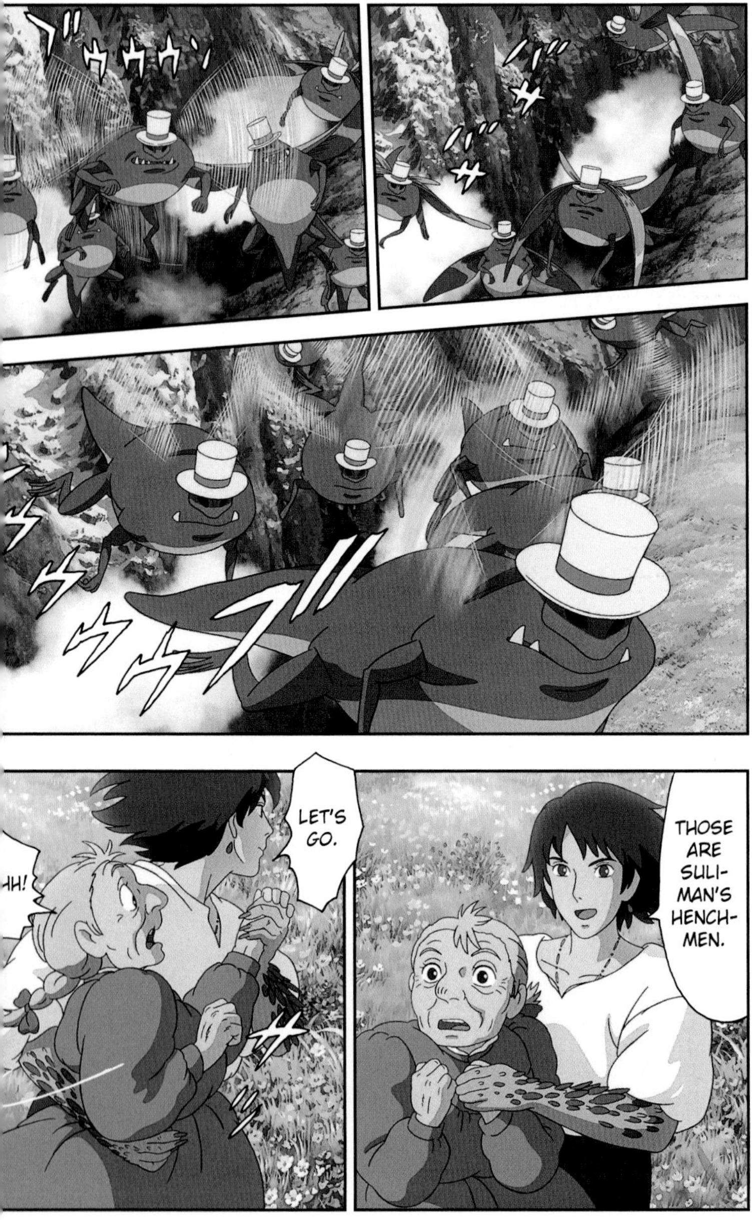
THOSE ARE SULI-MAN'S HENCH-MEN.
LET'S GO.

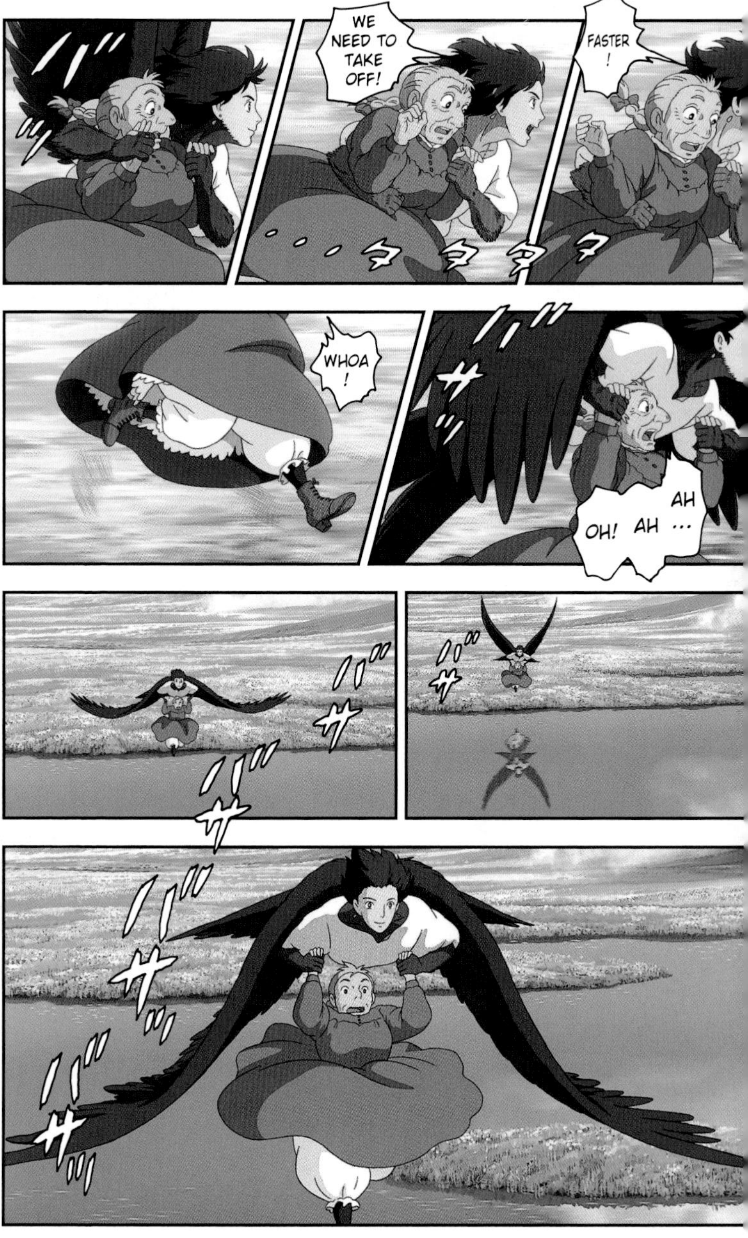
WE NEED TO TAKE OFF!
FASTER!
WHOA!
OH! AH AH...

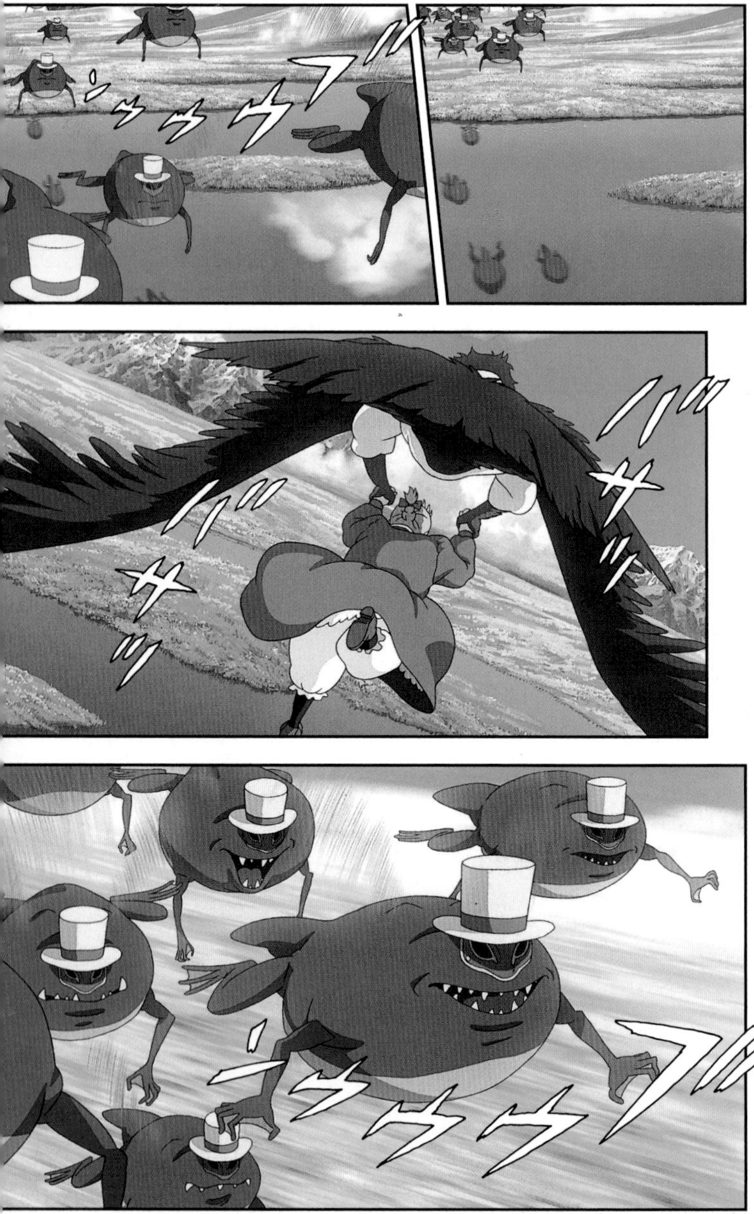
バサッ
バサッ

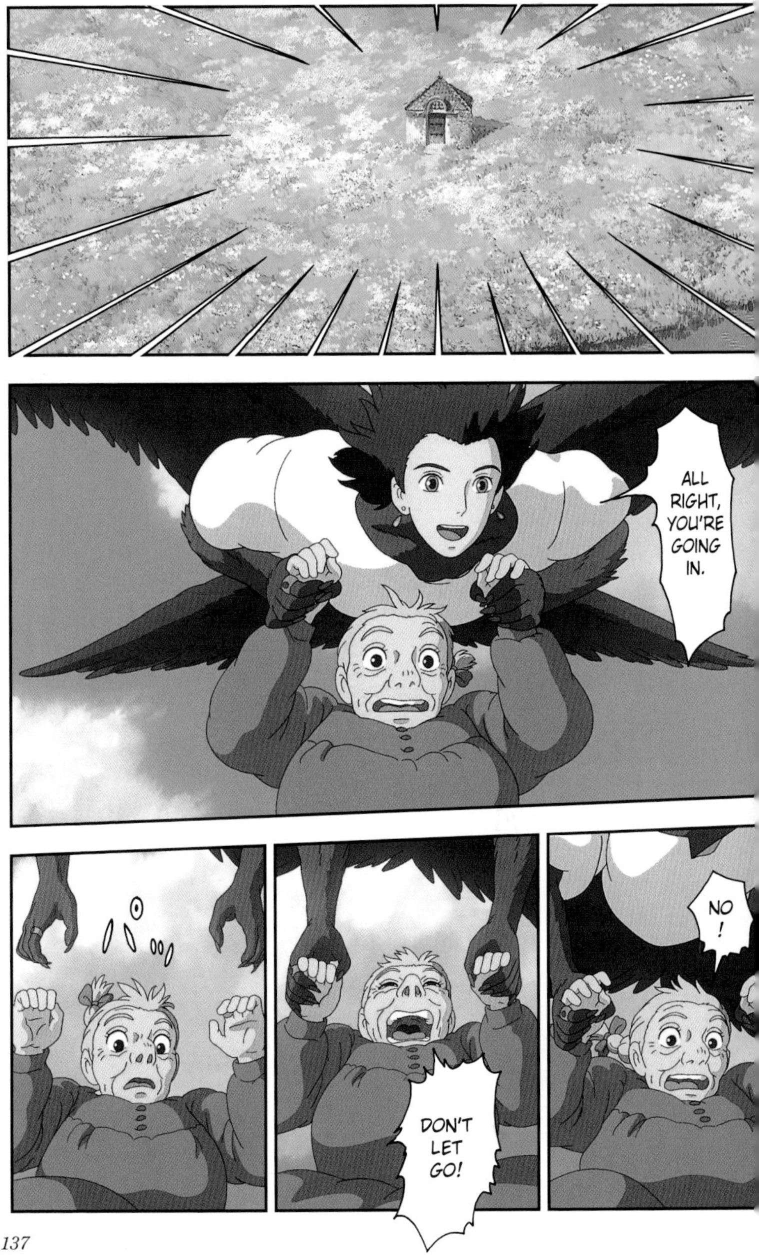
ALL RIGHT, YOU'RE GOING IN.
NO!
DON'T LET GO!

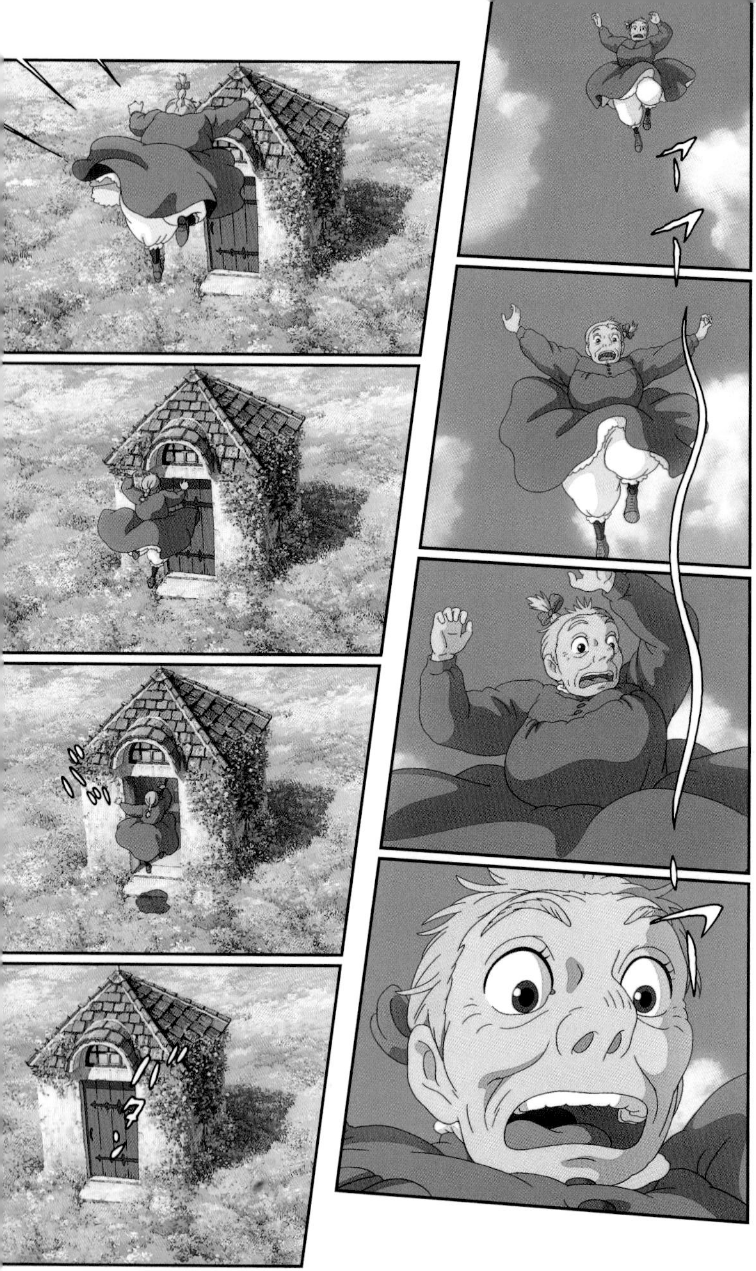

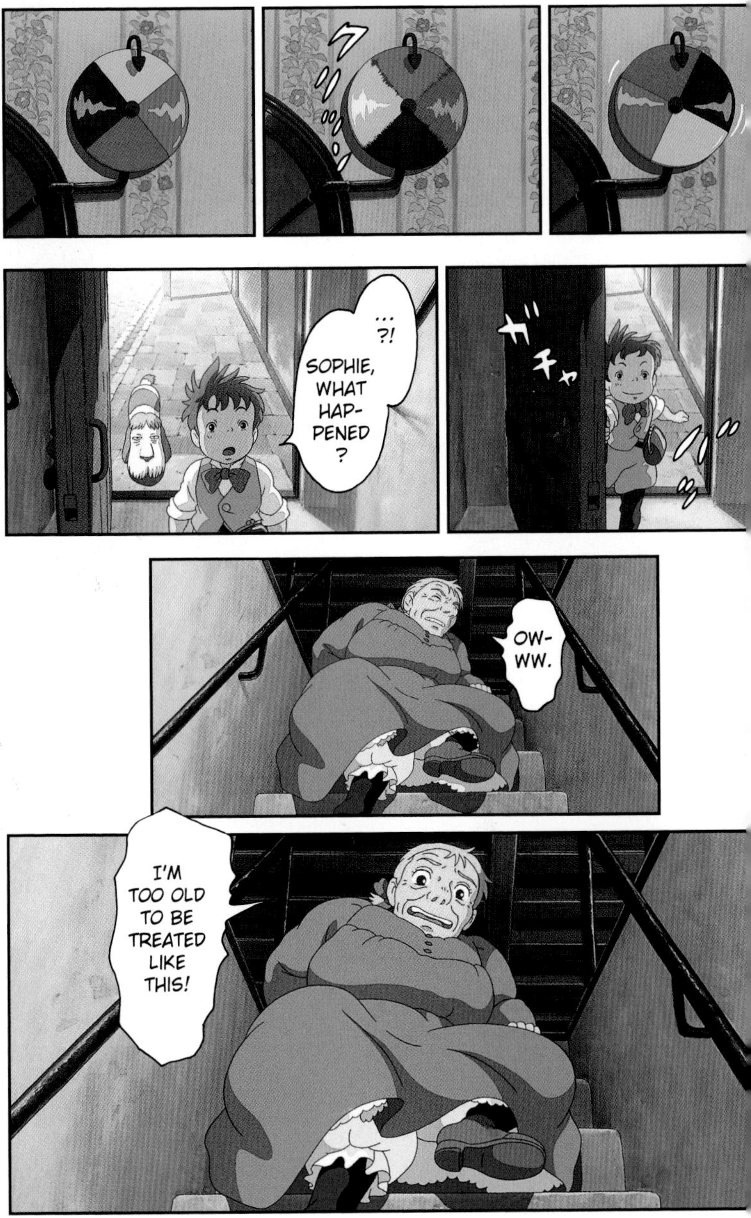
ガチャ
...?! SOPHIE, WHAT HAPPENED?
OW-WW.
I'M TOO OLD TO BE TREATED LIKE THIS!

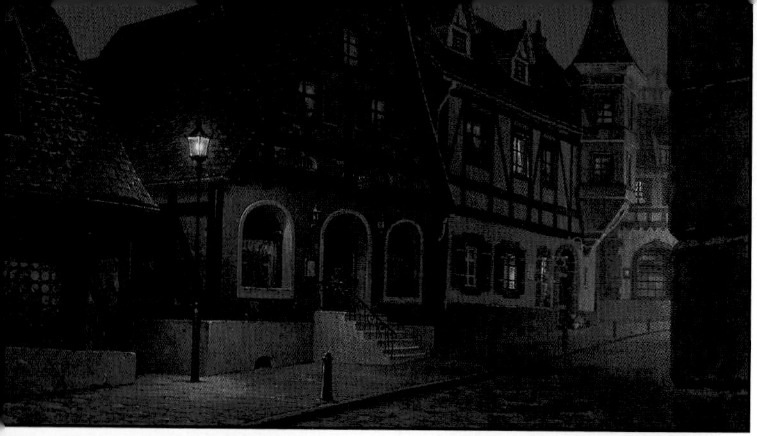

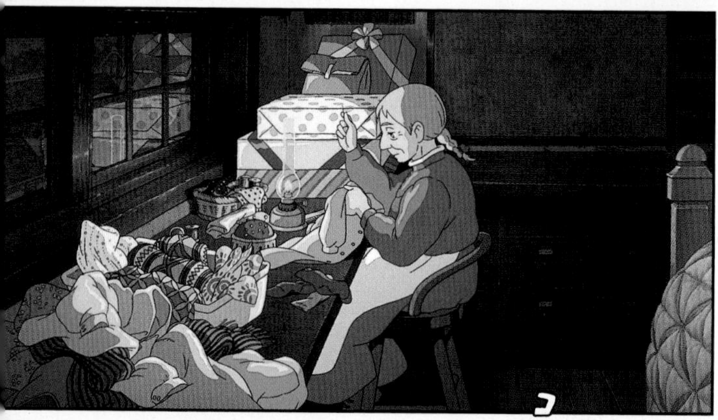

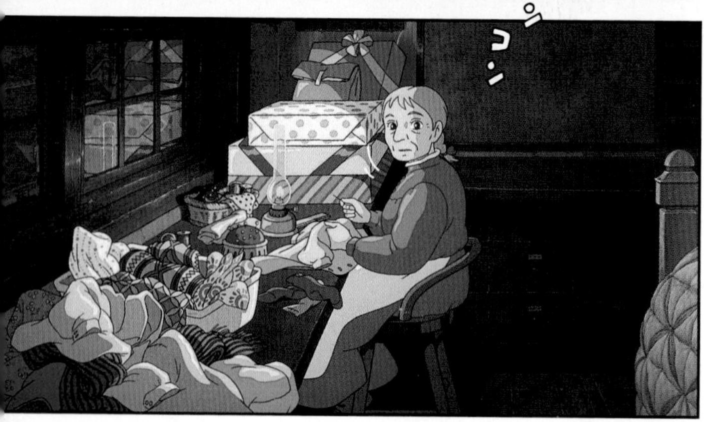
コン コン

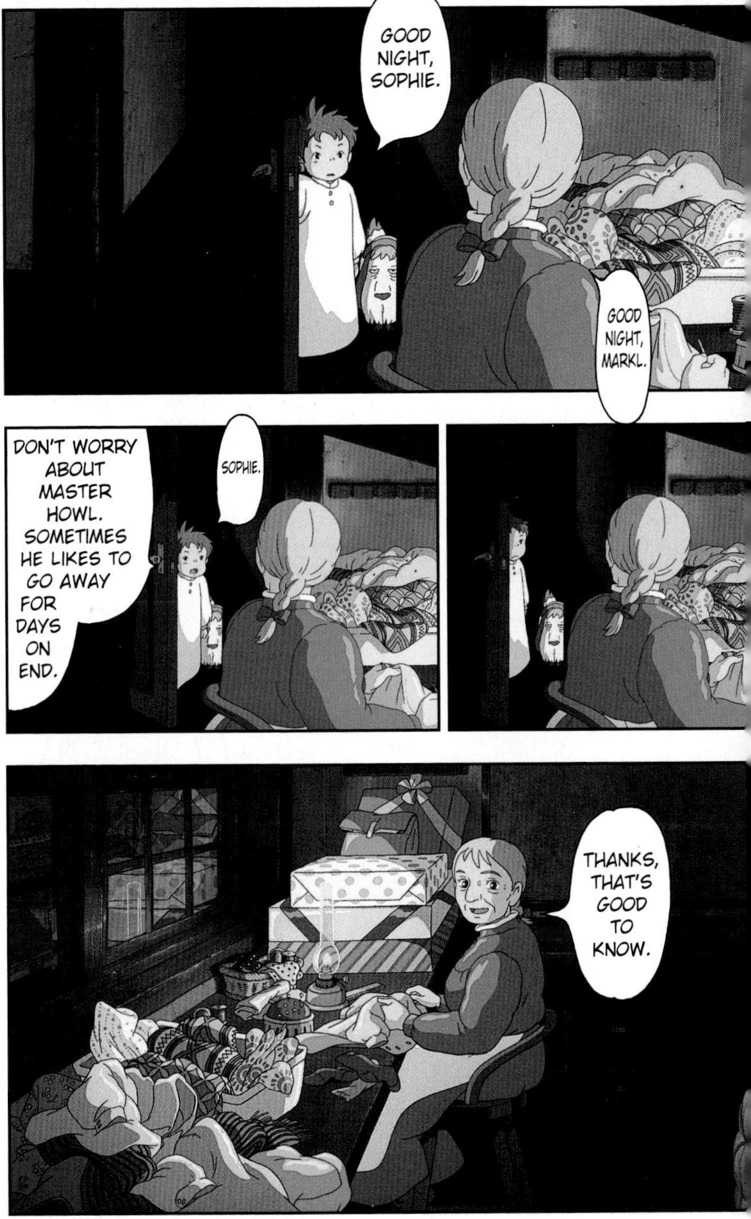
GOOD NIGHT, SOPHIE.
GOOD NIGHT, MARKL.
SOPHIE.
DON'T WORRY ABOUT MASTER HOWL. SOMETIMES HE LIKES TO GO AWAY FOR DAYS ON END.
THANKS, THAT'S GOOD TO KNOW.

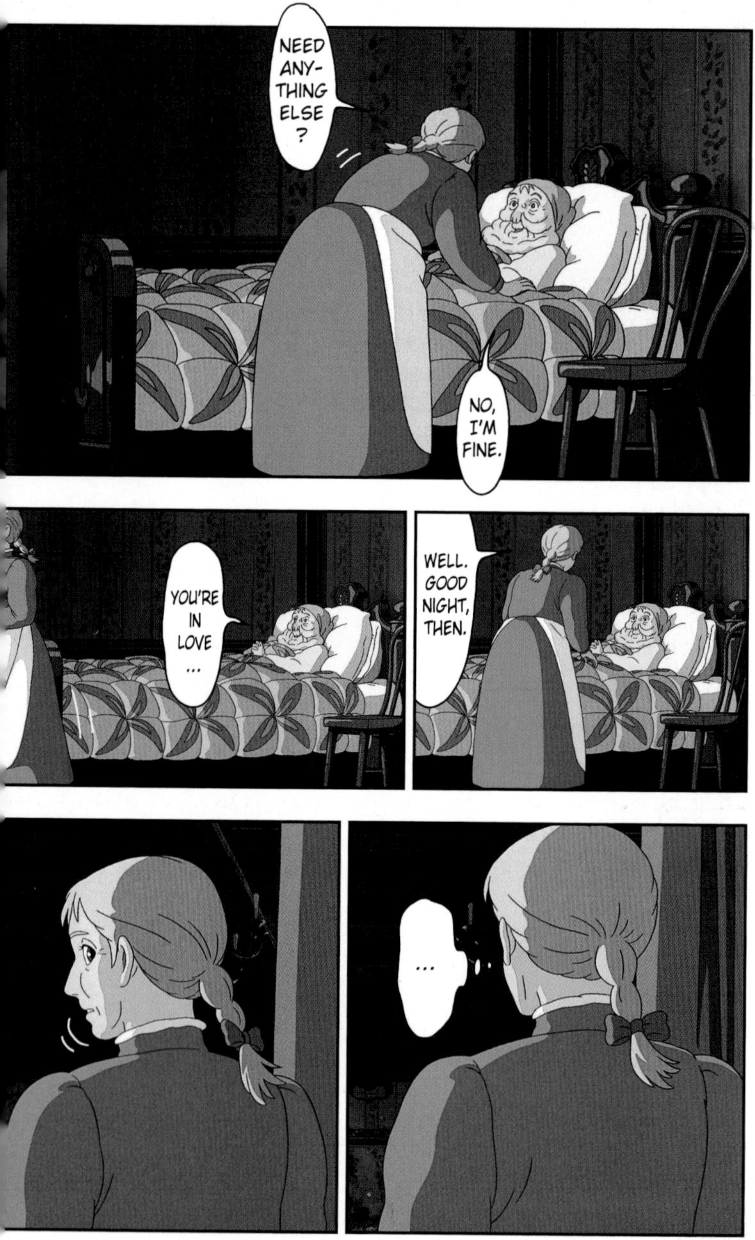
NEED ANY-THING ELSE ?
NO, I'M FINE.
WELL. GOOD NIGHT, THEN.
YOU'RE IN LOVE ...
...

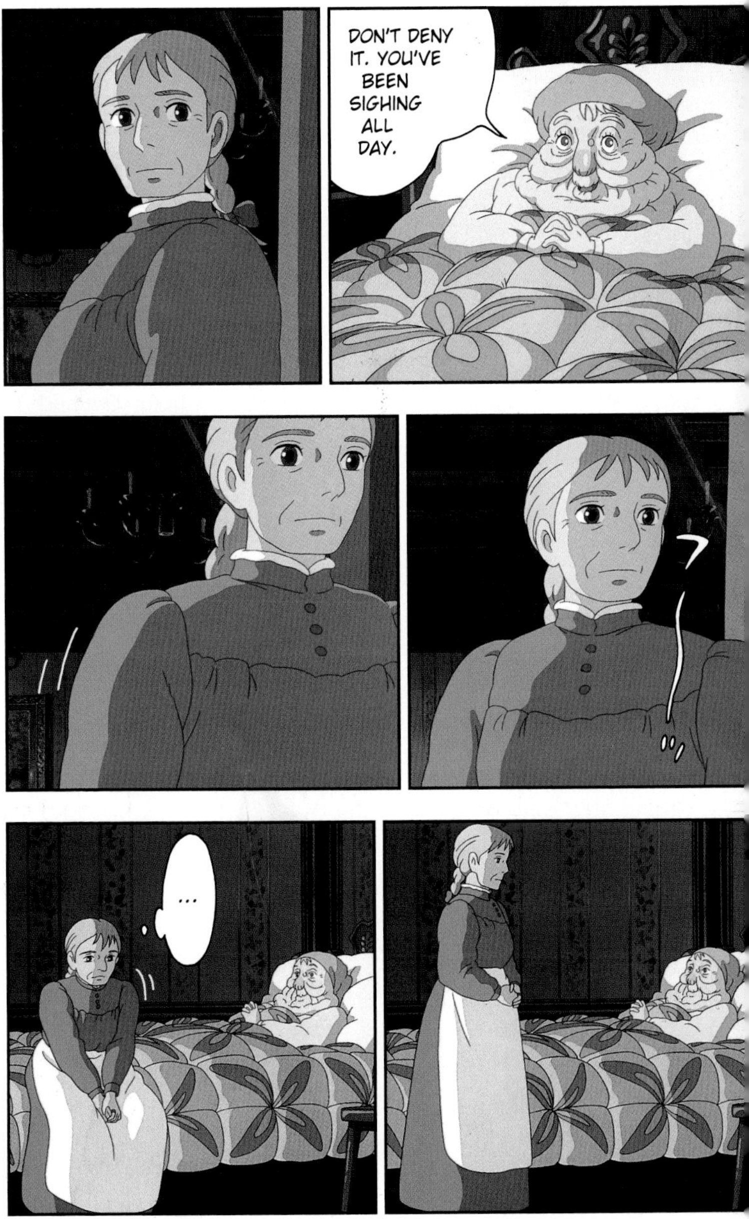
DON'T DENY IT. YOU'VE BEEN SIGHING ALL DAY.
...

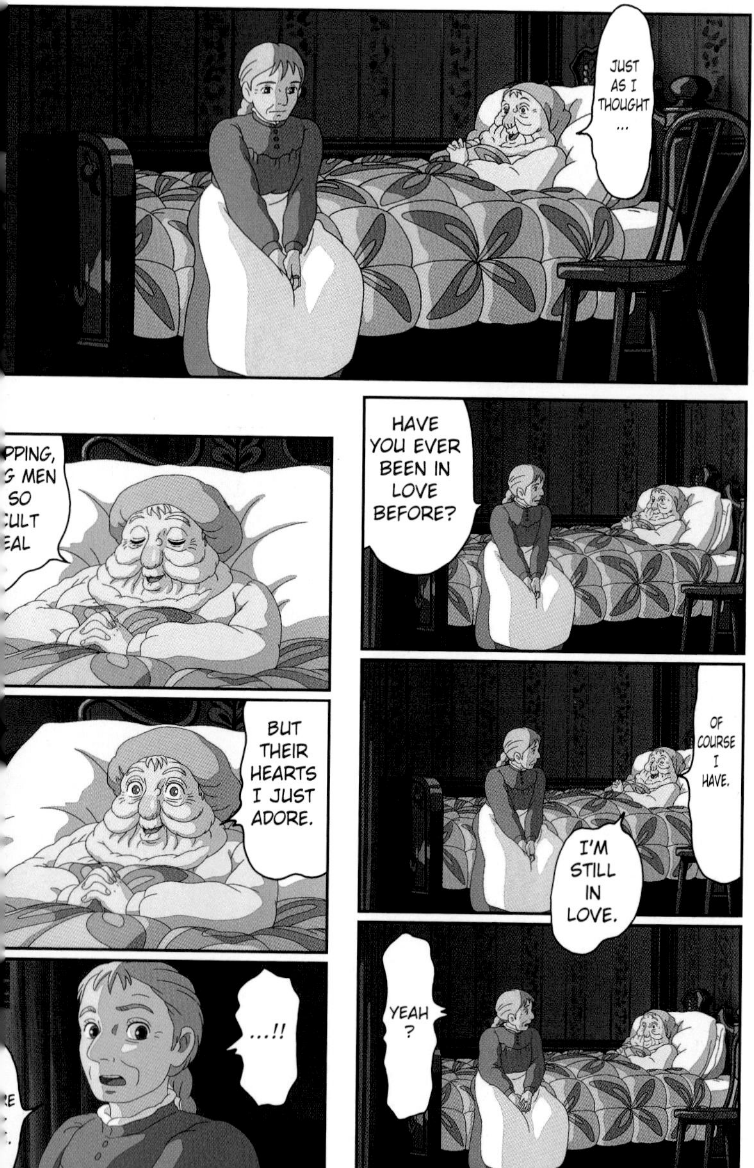

JUST AS I THOUGHT ...
HAVE YOU EVER BEEN IN LOVE BEFORE?
OF COURSE I HAVE.
I'M STILL IN LOVE.
YEAH?
PPING, G MEN SO CULT EAL
BUT THEIR HEARTS I JUST ADORE.
...!!

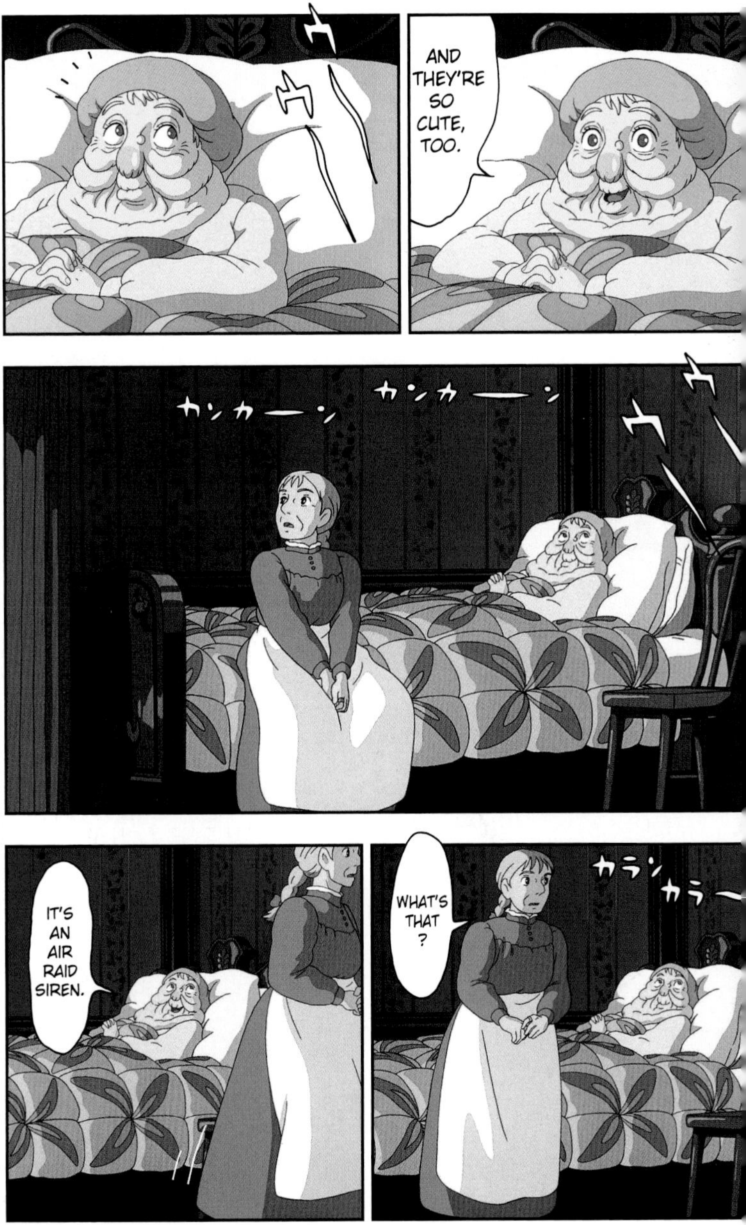
AND THEY'RE SO CUTE, TOO.
カンカーン
カンカーン
WHAT'S THAT?
カランカラー
IT'S AN AIR RAID SIREN.

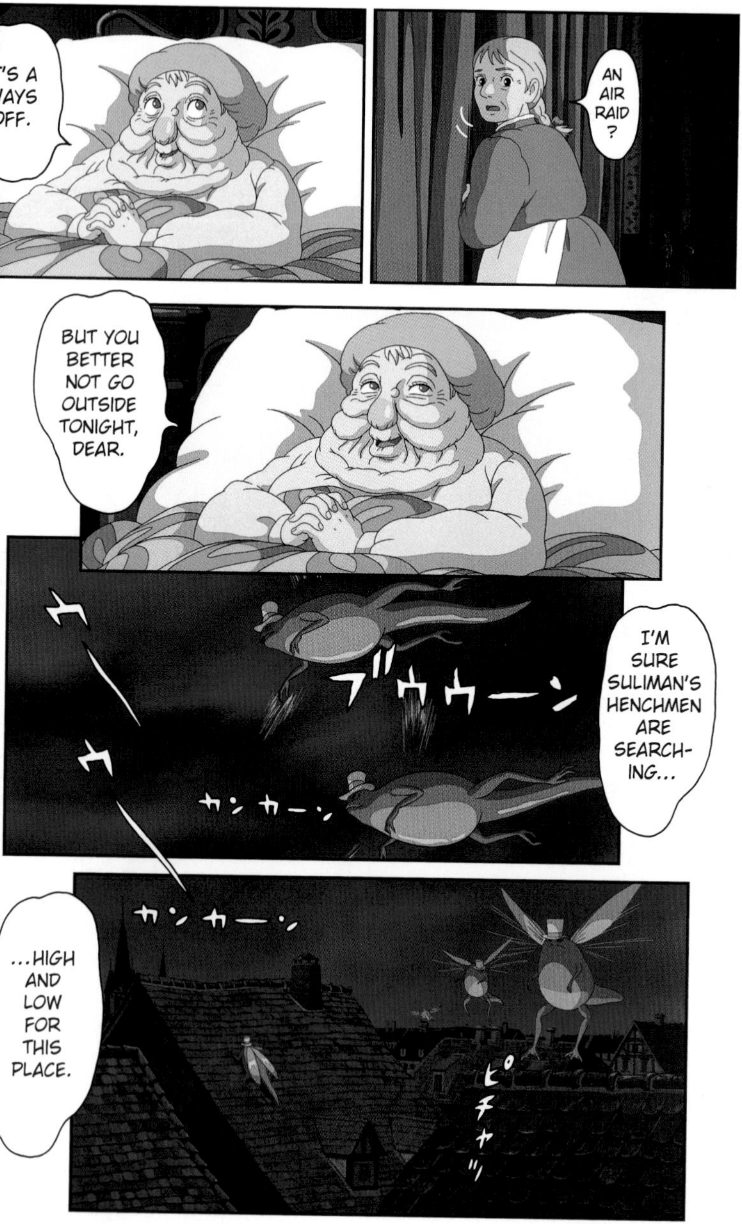
AN AIR RAID?
'S A AYS FF.
BUT YOU BETTER NOT GO OUTSIDE TONIGHT, DEAR.
I'M SURE SULIMAN'S HENCHMEN ARE SEARCH-ING...
ブウウーン
カンカーン
ウーウー
カンカーン
...HIGH AND LOW FOR THIS PLACE.
ピチャッ

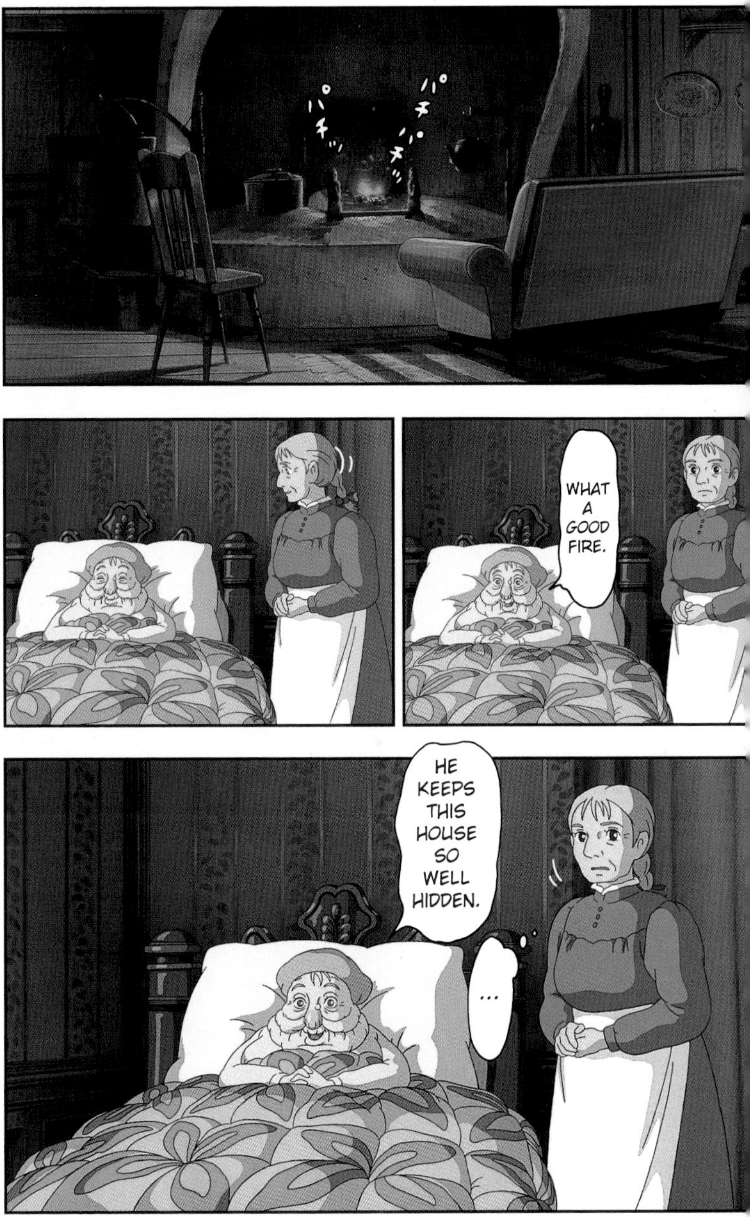
パチパチッ
パチッ
WHAT A GOOD FIRE.
HE KEEPS THIS HOUSE SO WELL HIDDEN.
...

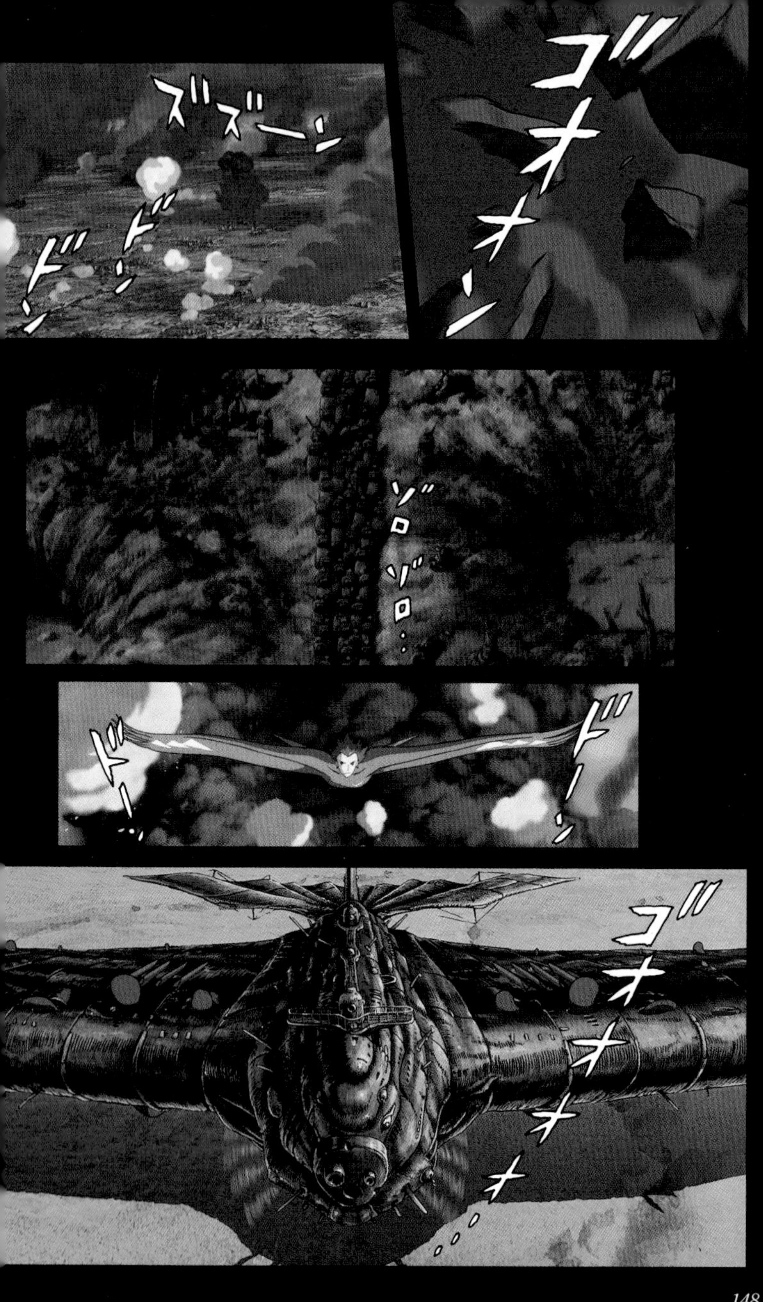
ゴオオーン
ズズーン
ドン
ドン
ゾロゾロ…
ドーン
ドー…
ゴオオオオ…

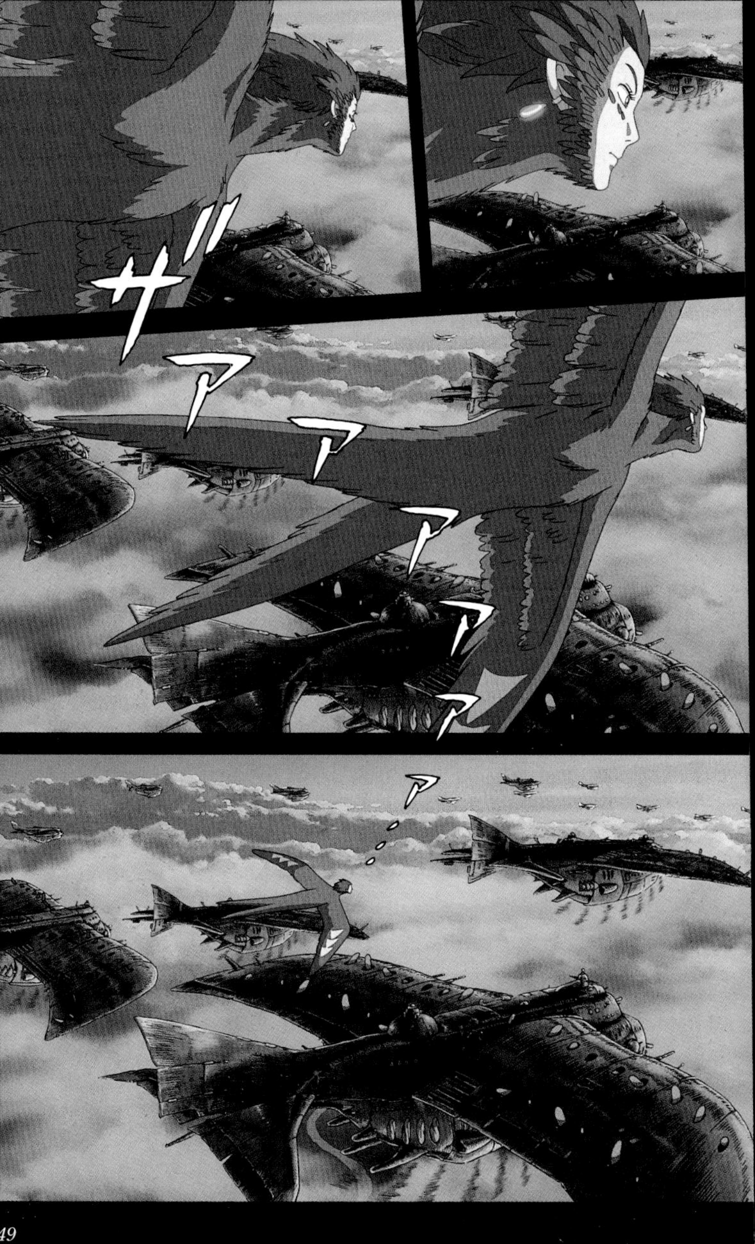
ザァァァァァ
ァ…

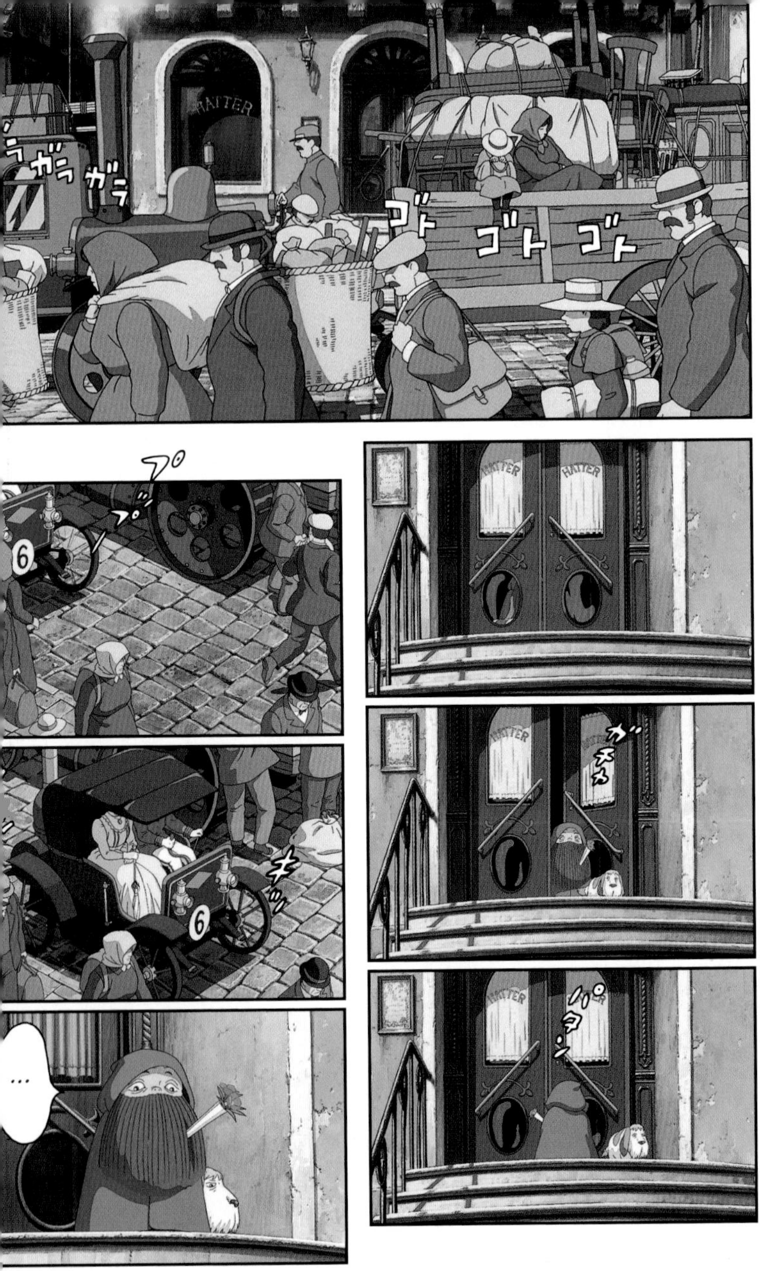
ゴト
ゴト
ゴト
ガラ
ガラ
プ
プ
キッ
…
パタン

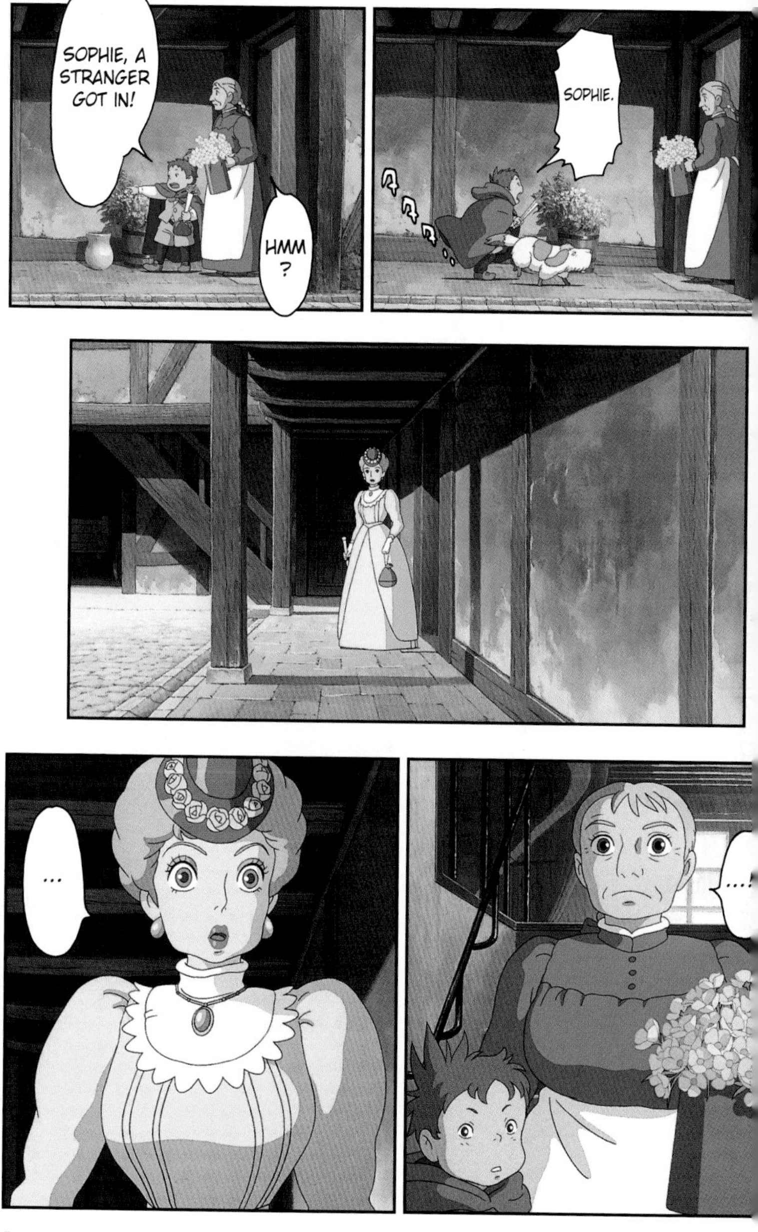
SOPHIE, A STRANGER GOT IN!
HMM?
SOPHIE.
...
...!

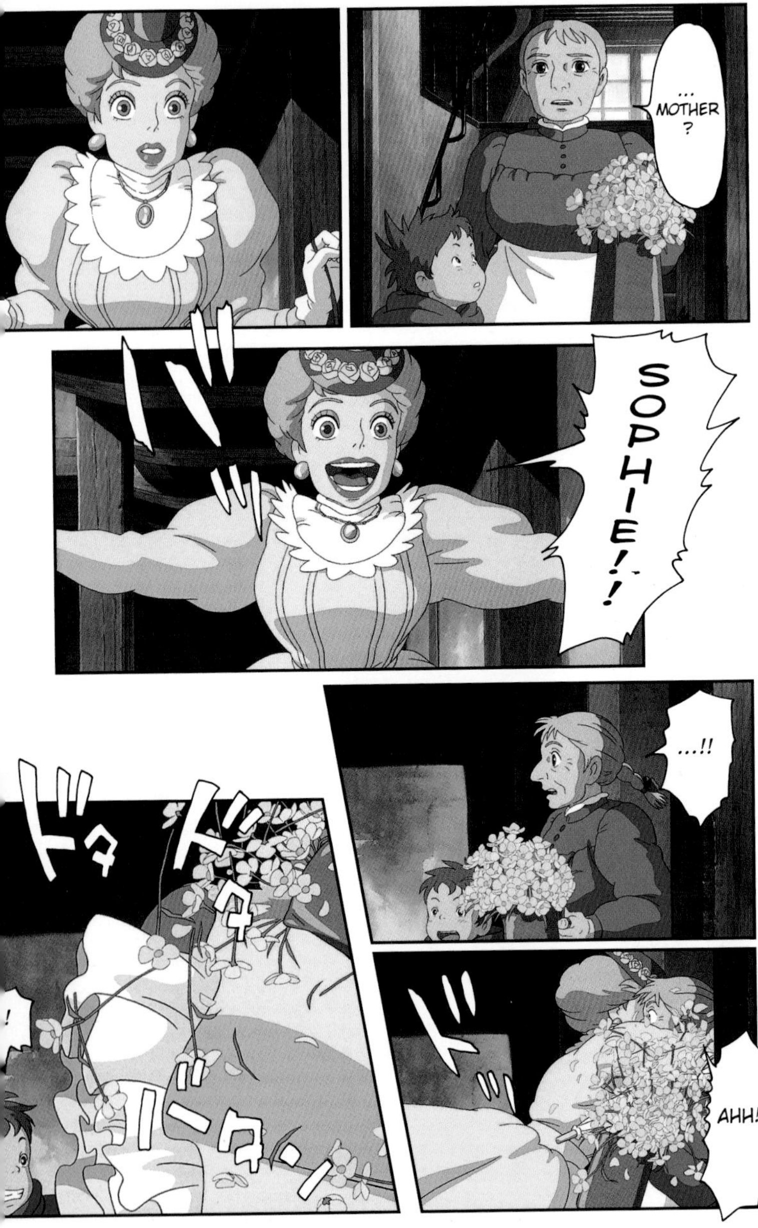
...MOTHER?
SOPHIE!!
...!!
AHH!

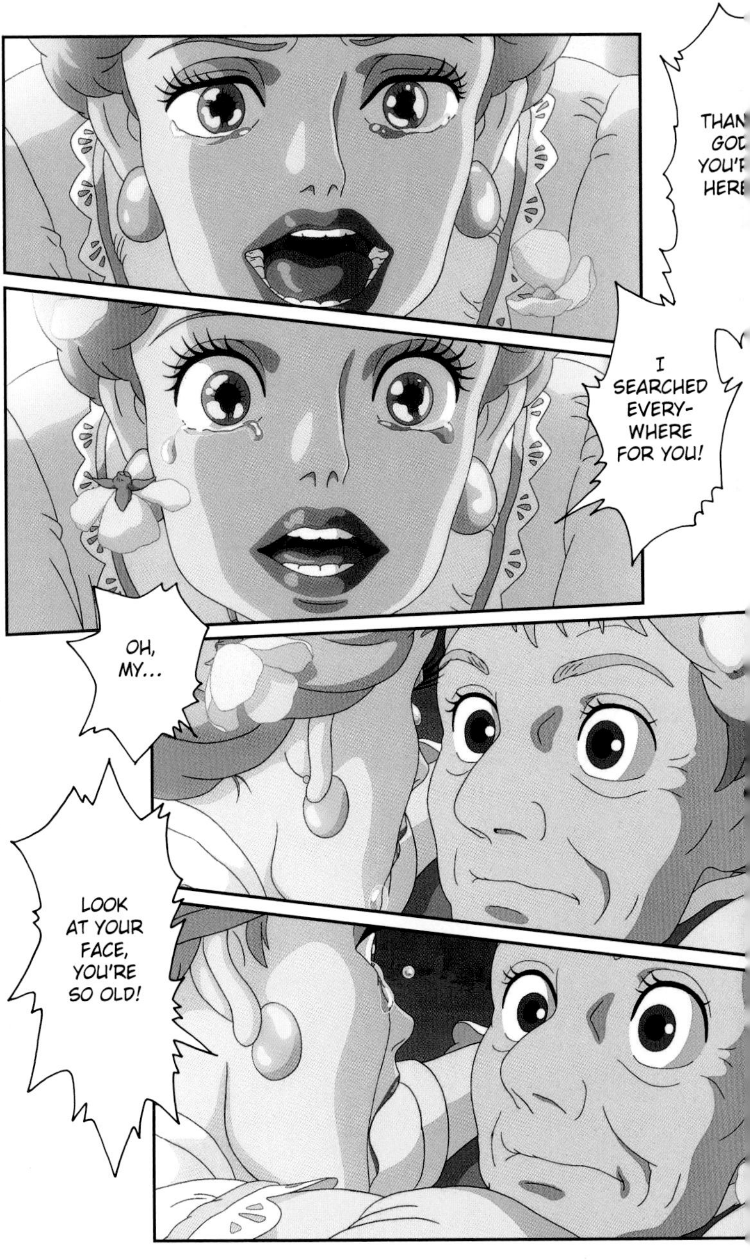
I SEARCHED EVERY-WHERE FOR YOU!
OH, MY...
LOOK AT YOUR FACE, YOU'RE SO OLD!

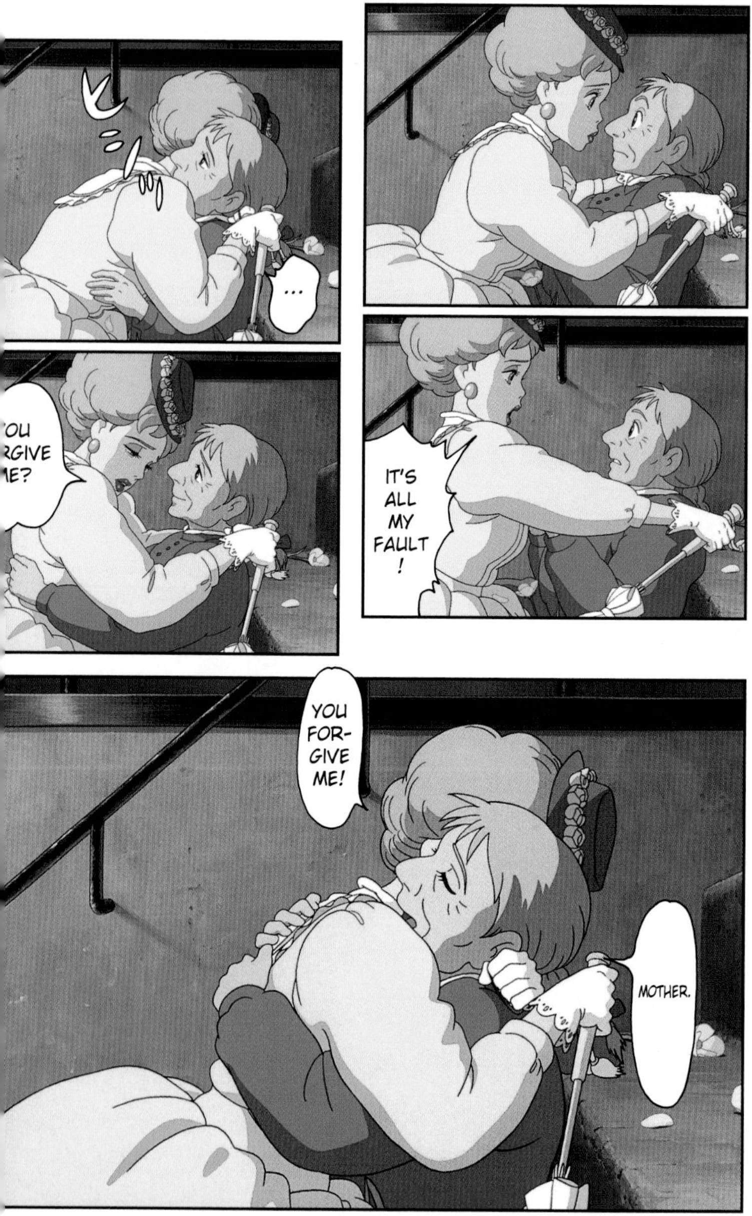
...
IT'S ALL MY FAULT!
YOU FOR-GIVE ME!
MOTHER.

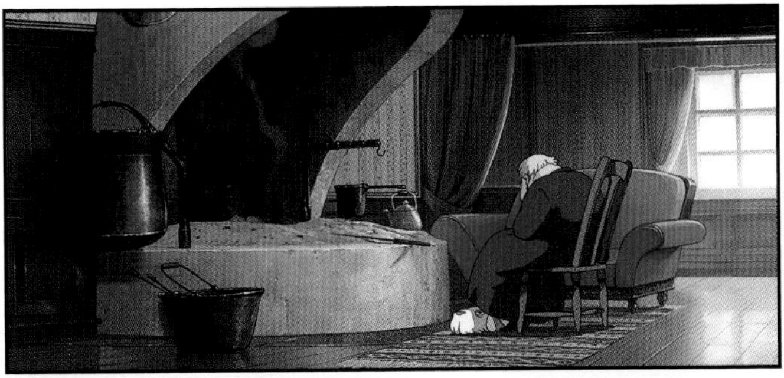

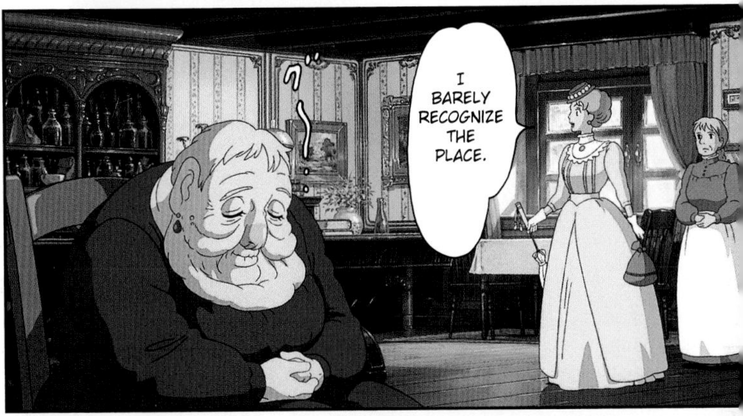
I BARELY RECOGNIZE THE PLACE.

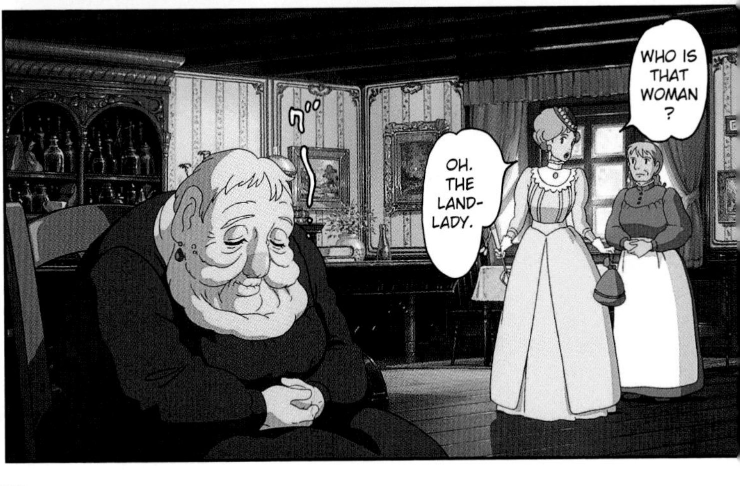
WHO IS THAT WOMAN ?
OH. THE LAND-LADY.

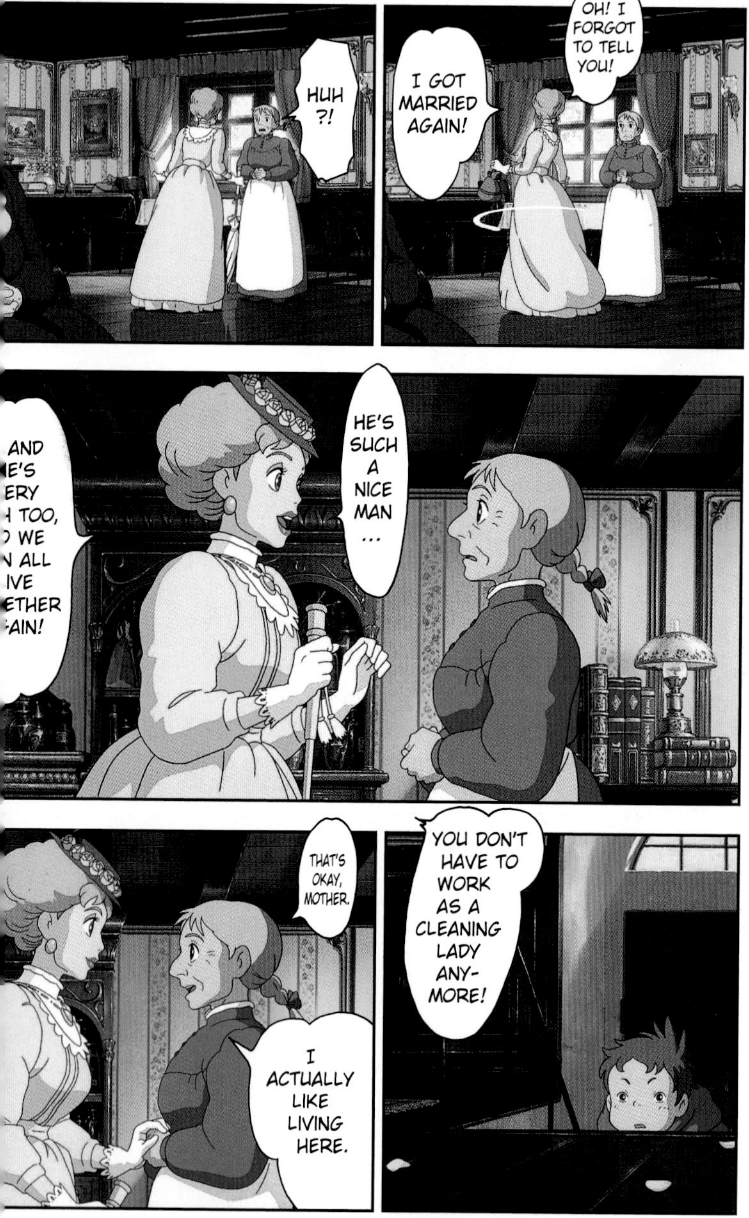
OH! I FORGOT TO TELL YOU!
I GOT MARRIED AGAIN!
HUH ?!
HE'S SUCH A NICE MAN ...
AND E'S ERY TOO, WE ALL IVE ETHER AIN!
YOU DON'T HAVE TO WORK AS A CLEANING LADY ANY-MORE!
THAT'S OKAY, MOTHER.
I ACTUALLY LIKE LIVING HERE.

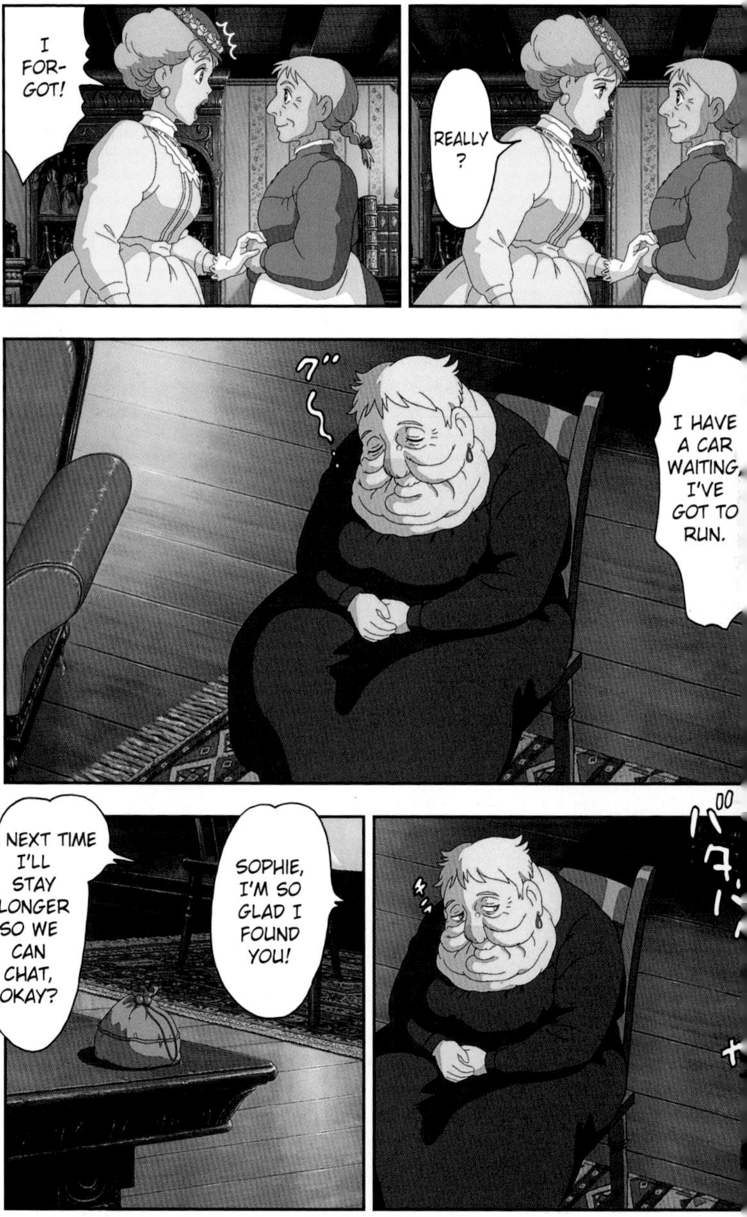
I FOR-GOT!
REALLY?
I HAVE A CAR WAITING, I'VE GOT TO RUN.
SOPHIE, I'M SO GLAD I FOUND YOU!
NEXT TIME I'LL STAY LONGER SO WE CAN CHAT, OKAY?

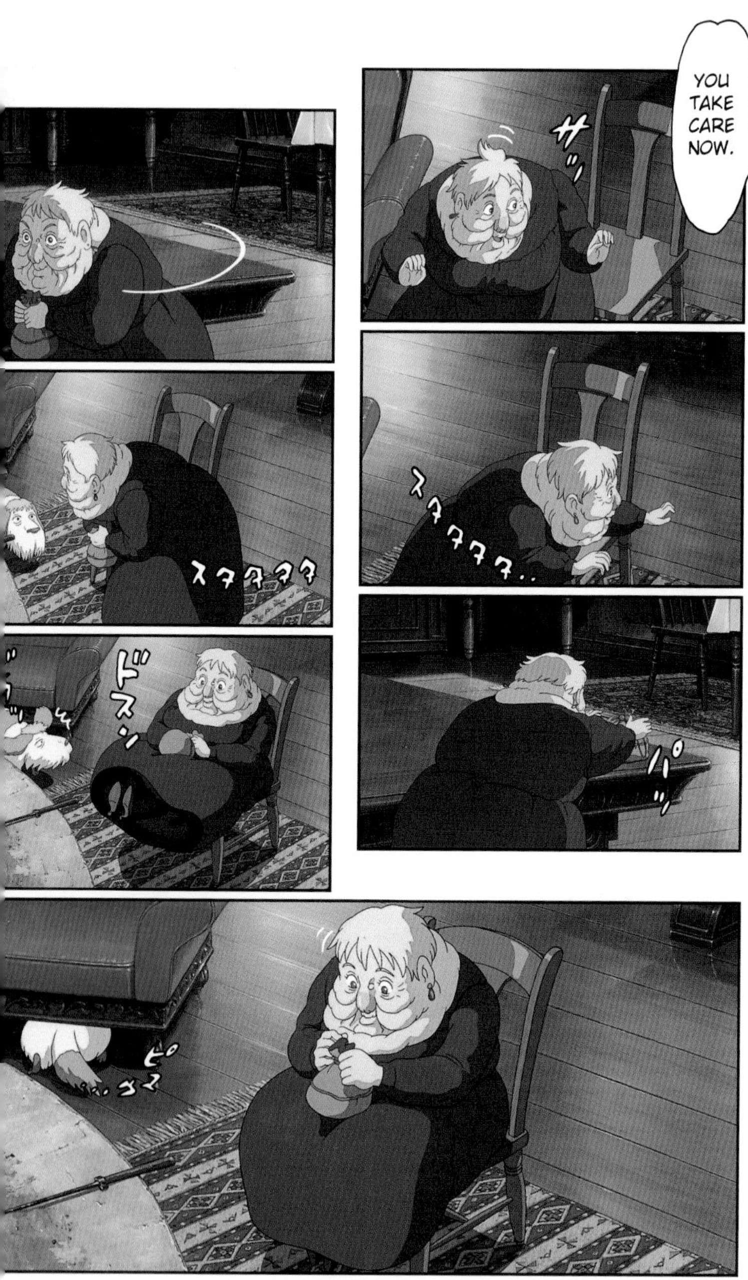
YOU TAKE CARE NOW.
ザッ
スタタタタ..
スタタタタ
パッ
ドスン

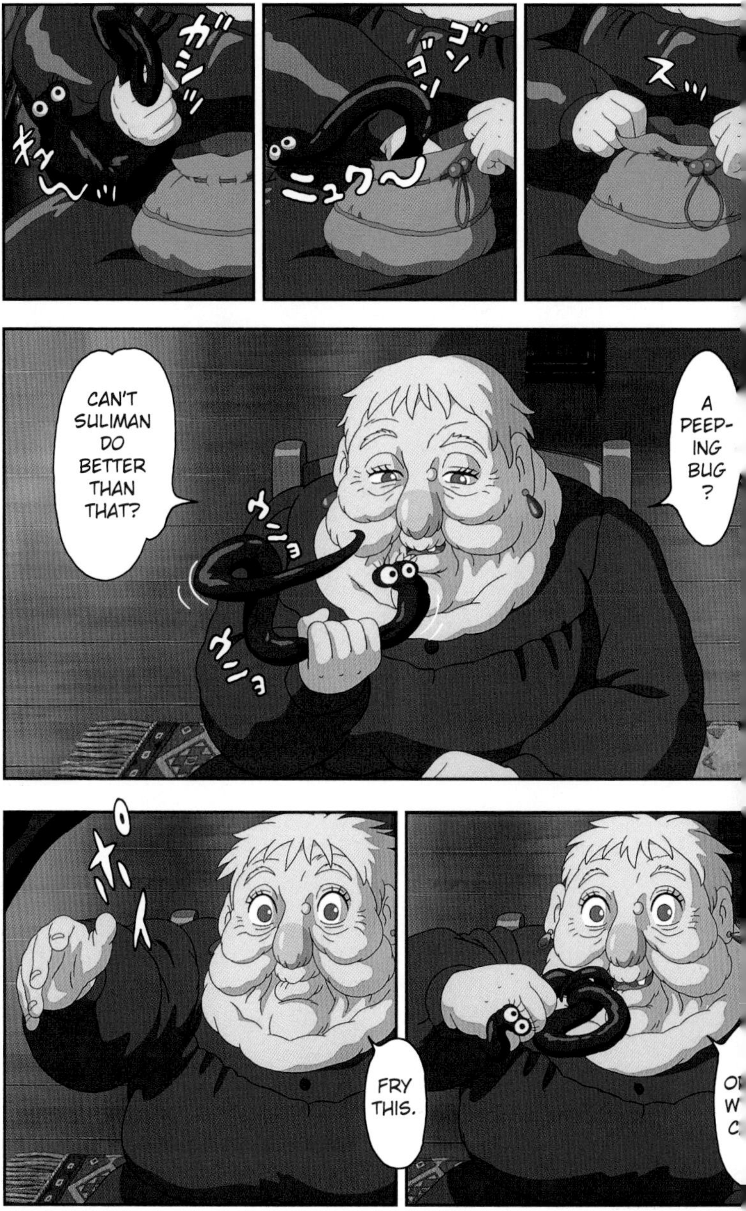

スッ
ゴソゴソ
ニュク〜
ガシッ
キュ〜ッ
A PEEP-ING BUG?
CAN'T SULIMAN DO BETTER THAN THAT?
ウニョ
ウニョ
ポイ
FRY THIS.

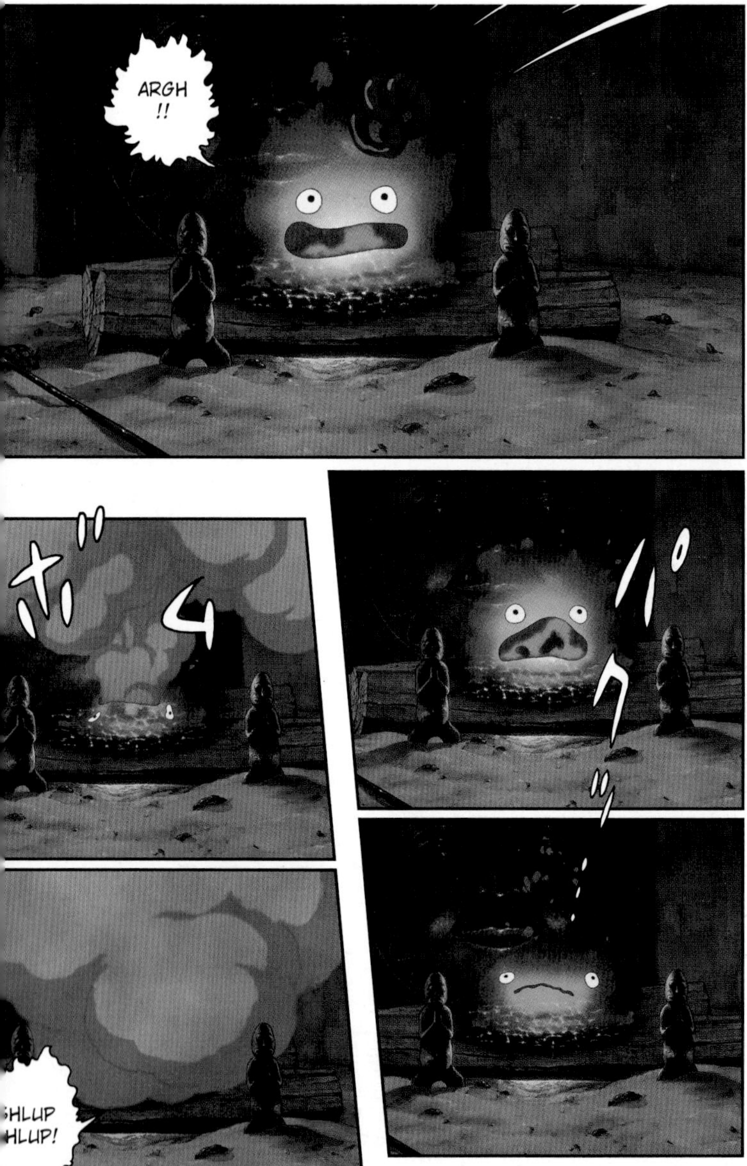
ARGH !!
パク
ボム
HLUP HLUP!

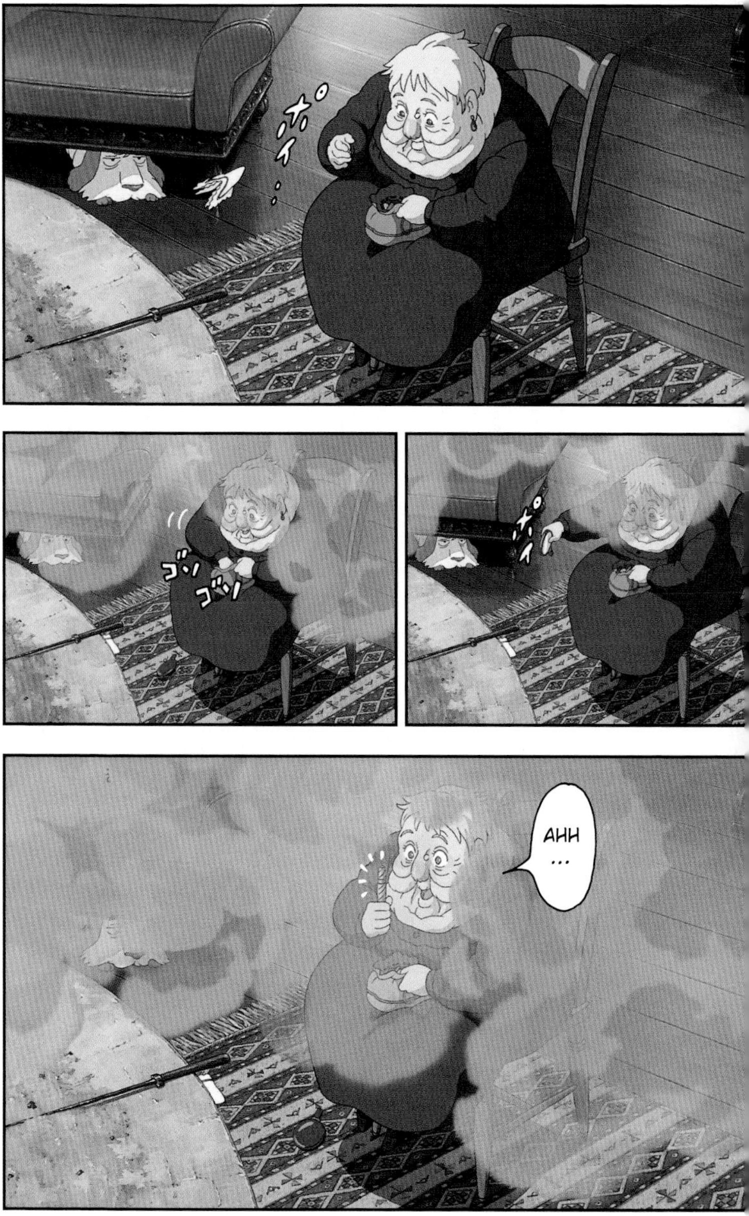
ポイ
ポイ
ゴソ
ゴソ
AHH ...

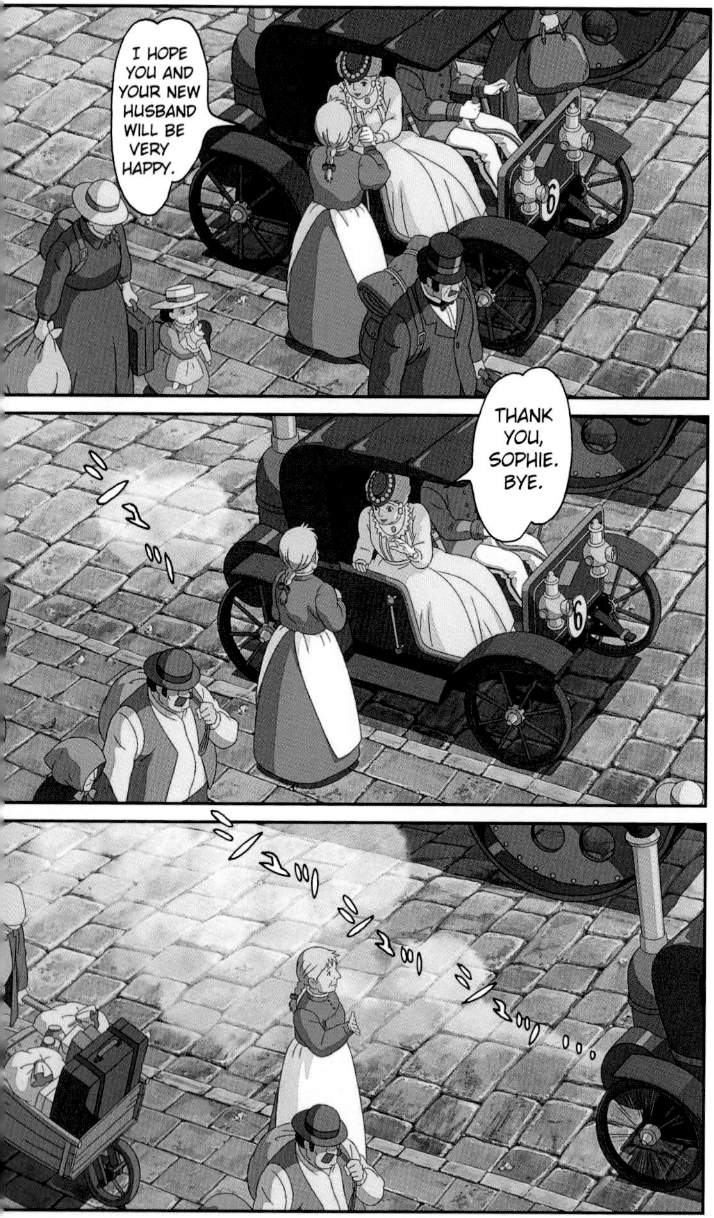
I HOPE YOU AND YOUR NEW HUSBAND WILL BE VERY HAPPY.
THANK YOU, SOPHIE. BYE.

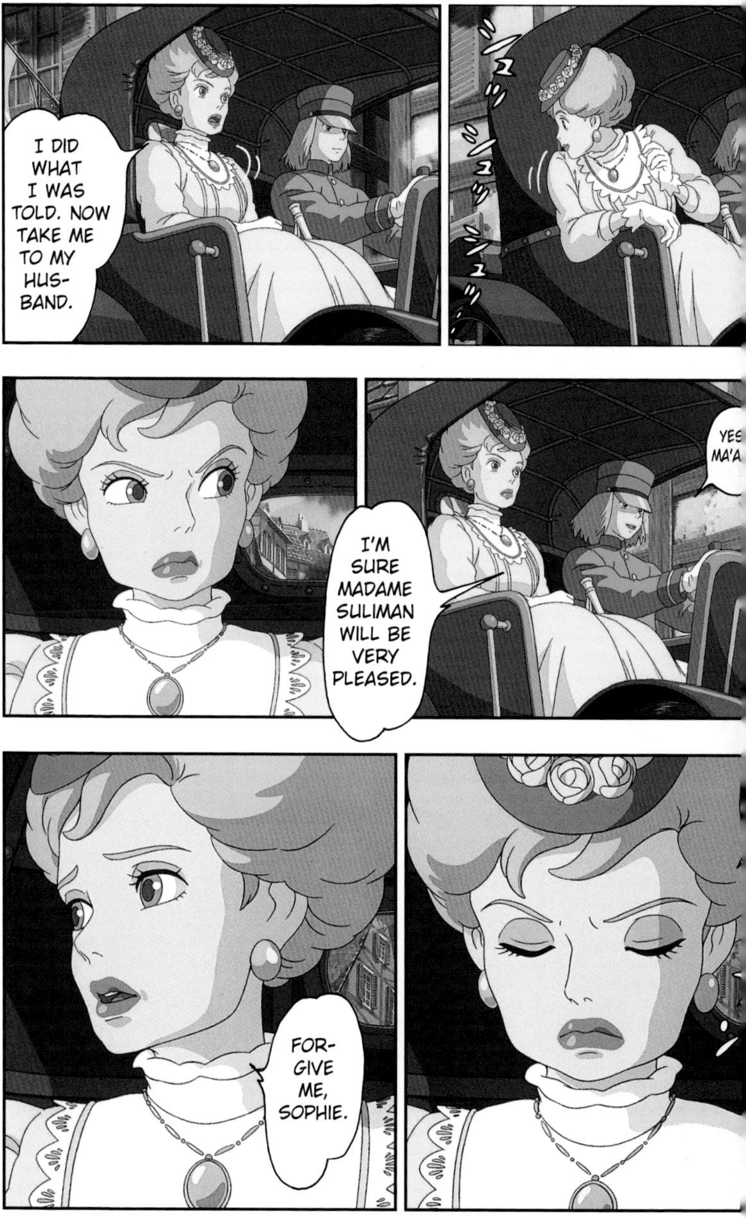

I DID WHAT I WAS TOLD. NOW TAKE ME TO MY HUS-BAND.
I'M SURE MADAME SULIMAN WILL BE VERY PLEASED.
YES MA'A
FOR-GIVE ME, SOPHIE.

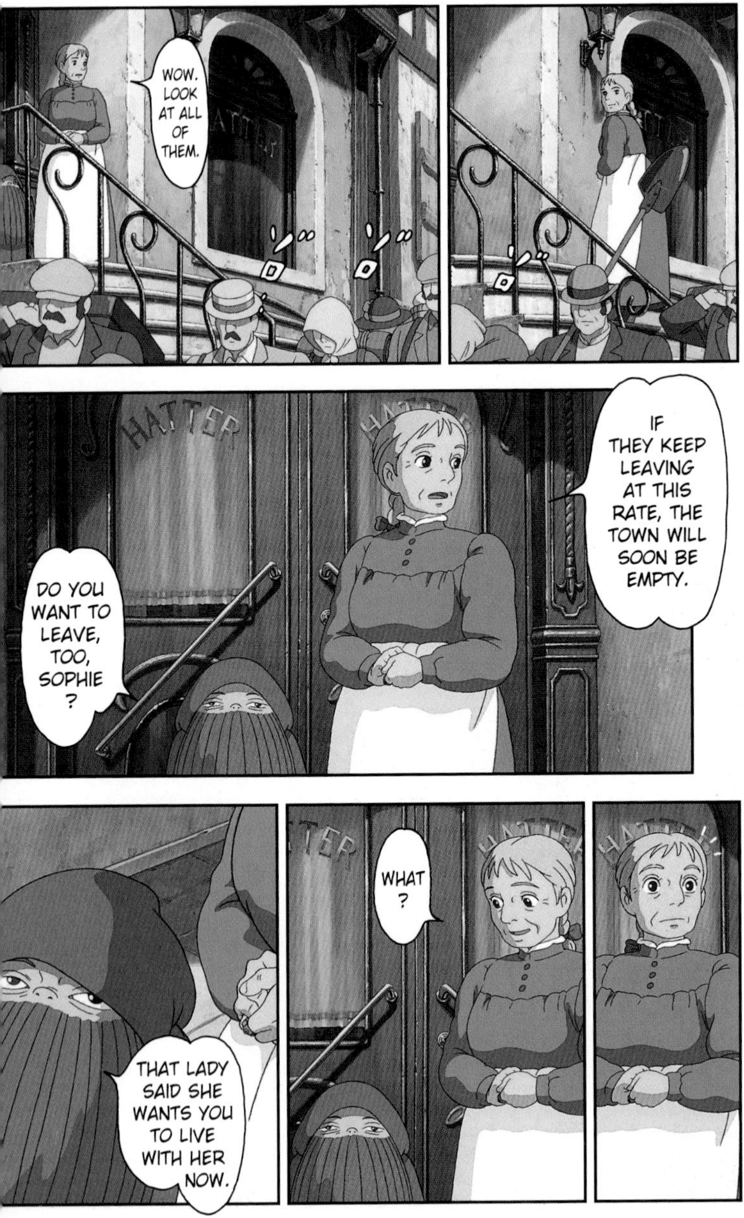
WOW. LOOK AT ALL OF THEM.
IF THEY KEEP LEAVING AT THIS RATE, THE TOWN WILL SOON BE EMPTY.
DO YOU WANT TO LEAVE, TOO, SOPHIE?
WHAT?
THAT LADY SAID SHE WANTS YOU TO LIVE WITH HER NOW.

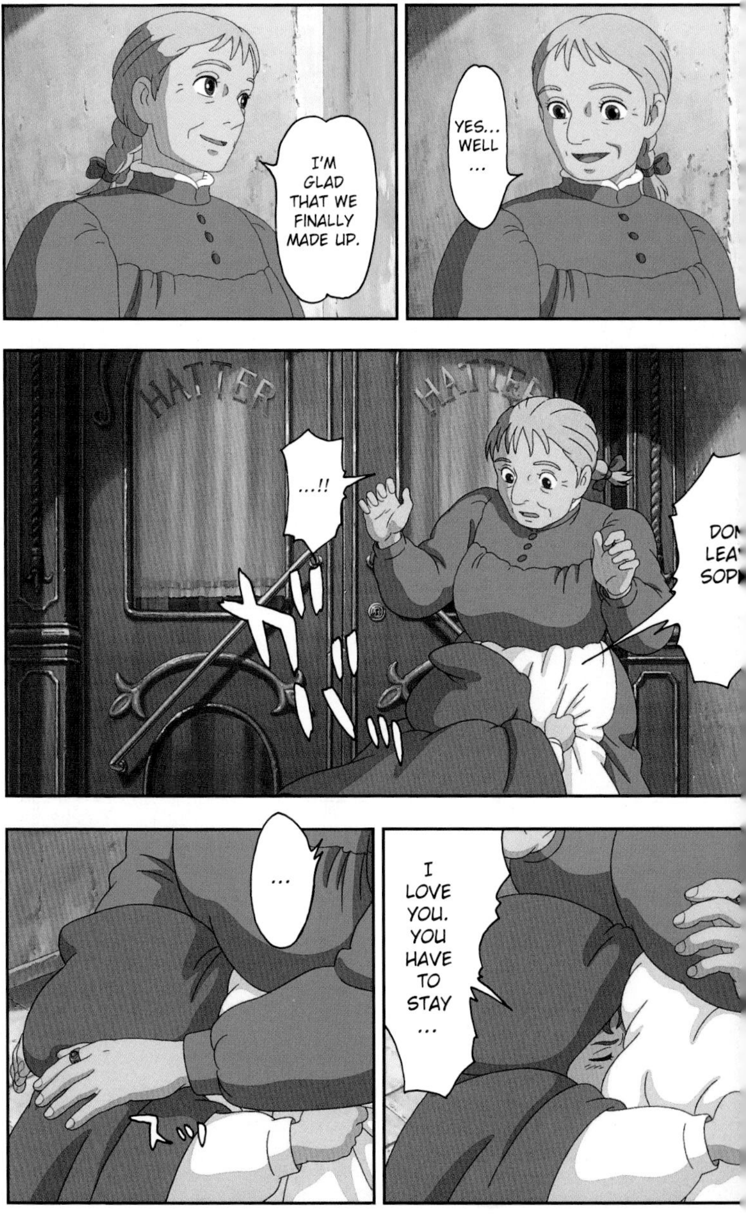
I'M GLAD THAT WE FINALLY MADE UP.
YES... WELL ...
...!!
DON
LEA
SOP
...
I LOVE YOU. YOU HAVE TO STAY ...

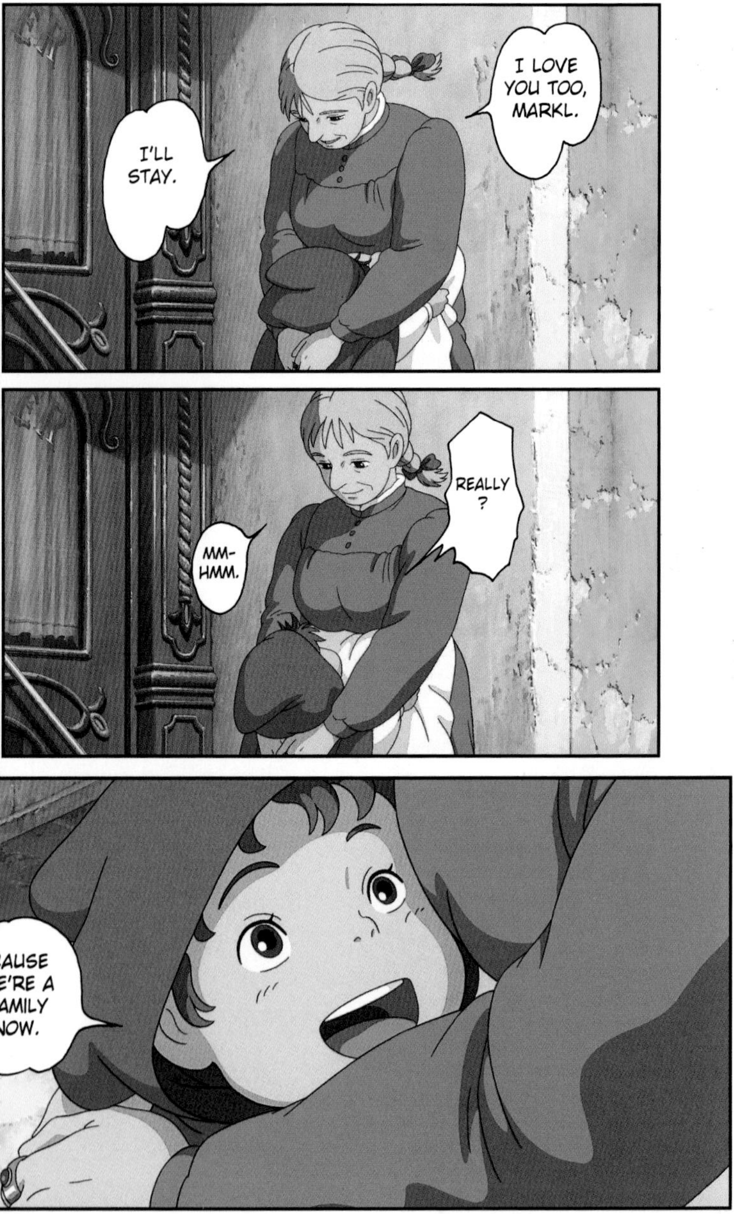
I LOVE YOU TOO, MARKL.
I'LL STAY.
REALLY?
MM-HMM.
CAUSE 'E'RE A AMILY NOW.

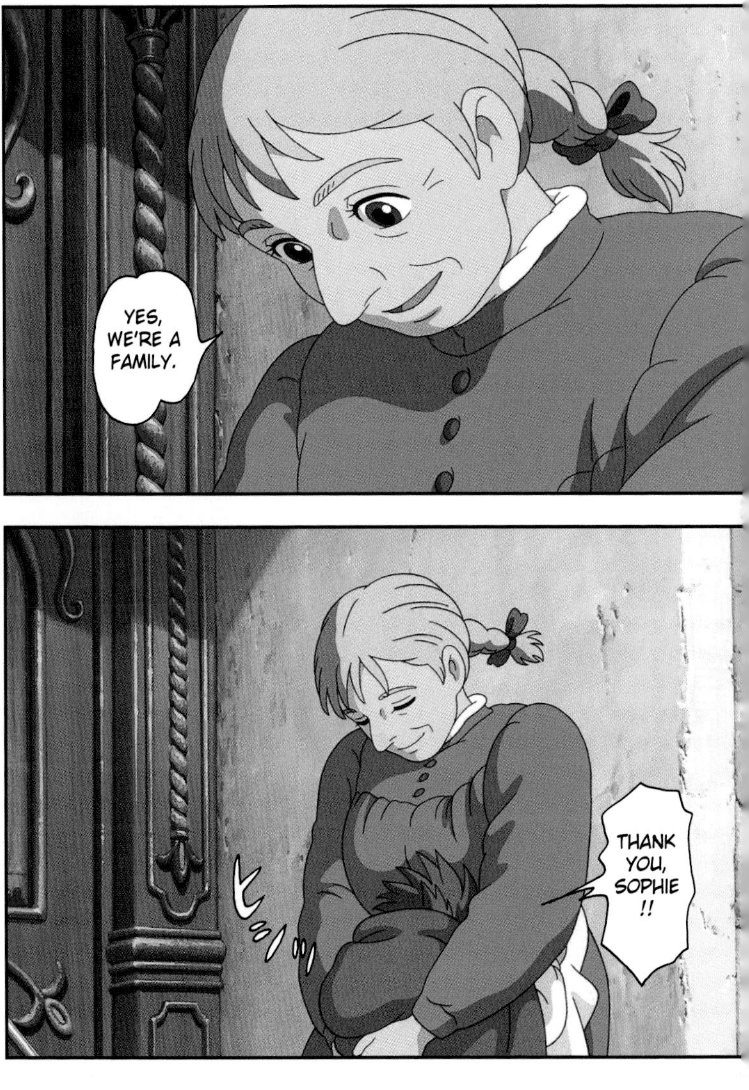
YES, WE'RE A FAMILY.
THANK YOU, SOPHIE !!

TO BE CONTINUED...

Guide to HOWL'S MOVING CASTLE Sound Effects!

your enjoyment of the distinctive Japanese visual style of HOWL'S MOVING CASTLE we've included a listing of and guide to the sound effects comic adaptation of the movie. In the comic, these sound effects are written in the Japanese phonetic characters called katakana.

d effects glossary for HOWL'S MOVING CASTLE, sound effects are listed by page and panel number, for example, 6.1 means page 6, panel 1 — if re than one sound effect in a panel, the sound effects are listed in order (so, 12.1.1 means page 12, panel 1, first sound effect). Remember that all e given in the original Japanese reading order: right-to-left.

age and panel numbers, you'll see the literally translated sound spelled out by the katakana, followed by how this sound effect might have been or what it stands for, in English — it is interesting to see the different ways Japanese people describe the sounds of things!

times see a long dash at the end of a sound effects listing. This is just a way of showing that the sound is the kind that lasts for a while; similarly, fade-out are indicated by three dots. When a sound effect goes through more than one panel, a hyphen and number indicate the panels affected.

'e ready to use the HOWL'S MOVING CASTLE Sound Effects Guide!

X: BASA BASA BASA... [fwip fwip fwip...]	19.6	FX: BASA BASA [fwip fwip]	5.5	FX: GU [tugg]		
X: GASHAAN [krrrrsh]	20.1	FX: BYUUUU [whooo]	6.1	FX: SHA SHA SHA SHA... [fwoosh fwoosh fwoosh fwoosh...]		
X: SU [fsh]	21.2-6	FX: GOOOOOH [rrrrrrr...]				
X: HYUUUU... [whoooo...]	21.7	FX: SHAA [zinng]	7.2	FX: SHIKU SHIKU SHIKU... [tup tup tup]		
	21.8-9	FX: PASSSHAAN [plisssh]	7.3	FX: SU [fsh]		
X: DOSA DOSA [whud whud]	22.1	FX: SHAAN [zinng]	7.4	FX: KATSU KATSU [tak tak]		
X: SHA SHA SHA SHA [whirr whirr whirr whirr]	22.2	FX: SHAAN [zinng]	7.5	FX: KATSU KATSU [tak tak]		
X: TATATA [tp tp tp tp]	22.3	FX: SHAAN [zinng]	9.2	FX: KATSU [tak]		
X: BA [fwoosh]	22.4	FX: SHAAN [zinng]	9.3	FX: KATSU [tak]		
X: DON [tump]	22.5	FX: SHAAN [zinng]				
	22.6	FX: PASSSHAAN [plisssh]	11.2	FX: KATSU KATSU [tak tak]		
X: SHA SHA SHA SHA SHA SHA... [whirr whirr whirr whirr whirr whirr...]	22.7.1	FX: SHAAN [zinng]	13.1	FX: HA HA HA HA HA... [ha ha ha ha ha...]		
	22.7.2	FX: SHAAN [zinng]				
X: SHA SHA SHA SHA [whirr whirr whirr whirr]	23.1	FX: SHAAN [zinng]	13.3	FX: SU [fsh]		
X: SHA SHA SHA... [whirr whirr whirr...]	23.2	FX: SHAAN [zinng]	13.5	FX: KATSU KATSU KATSU [tak tak tak]		
	23.3	FX: SHAAN [zinng]				
X: SHA SHA SHA [whirr whirr whirr]	24.5-6	FX: BARI BARI [rrip rrip]	15.2	FX: SA [fsh]		
X: SHA SHA SHA [whirr whirr whirr]	25.5	FX: GUWA [fwap]	16.1	FX: SU [fsh]		
X: HIN! [heen!]	25.6	FX: BA [fwoosh]	16.2	FX: TON! [tump!]		
			16.5	FX: GO [rrr]		
X: SHA SHA SHA... [whirr whirr whirr...]	26.3	FX: SU [fsh]	17.1-4	FX: GOOOH... [rrrrrr...]		
X: SHA SHA SHA SHA... [whirr whirr whirr whirr...]	27.1	FX: BA [thup]	18.1	FX: GOOOH [rrrrrr]		
	27.2	FX: SA [fwoosh]	18.2	FX: DOBAAH [fwissh]		
	27.3	FX: KA [zing]	18.3	FX: GOBO GOBO [glug glug]		
X: SHA SHA SHA... [whirr whirr whirr...]	27.4	FX: BYU [fwish]	18.4	FX: GOBO... [glug...]		
	27.5	FX: DOSU [thud]				
X: SHA SHA SHA SHA... [whirr whirr whirr whirr...]	28.1-3	FX: BASA BASA BASA BASA BASA [fwip fwip fwip fwip fwip]	19.3	FX: BUWA [fwoop]		
			19.3-5	FX: BYUUUU [whoooo]		

61.5 FX: POI [fwip]
61.6 FX: GYU... [tugg...]

62.1 FX: GASHA GASHA [klang klang]
62.2.1 FX: GUOOH [schnorr]
62.2.2 FX: OOH [rrrr]
62.3.1 FX: GUOOH [schnorr]
62.3.2 FX: OOH [rrrr]
62.5 FX: KACHA... [chak...]

63.1 FX: BETA BETA [plip plip]
63.2 FX: BETA... [plip...]
63.5 FX: BETA BETA [plip plip]

64.1 FX: BETA BETA [plip plip]
64.2 FX: BETA... [plip...]
64.3 FX: GISHI GISHI [kreek kreek]
64.4 FX: GISHI GISHI... [kreek kreek...]
64.6 FX: GABA [fsh]

65.1 FX: PATAN... [thump...]

66.4 FX: PARA [fwik]
66.5 FX: PAAA... [fwik fwik...]
66.8 FX: SA [fwip]

67.1 FX: SHU [fsh]

68.1 FX: KOTSU [tok]
68.2 FX: KOTSU KOTSU [tok tok]
68.5 FX: SU [fsh]
68.6 FX: KORI... [snik...]
68.7 FX: GI... [krik...]

69.3 FX: HYUOHH... [fweeeoooh...]

70.2 FX: SU [fsh]
70.3-4 FX: HYUOOOOH... [whoooooo...]

71.1 FX: KASA [fwik]
71.2-5 FX: OOOOOOOOOH... [wooooooom...]

72.1-3 FX: OOOH... [wooom...]
72.4 FX: OOH... [woom...]

73.3 FX: OOH... [wooom...]

75.1-2 FX: BUOOOH... [fwooooom...]
75.3-4 FX: ZUZAZAZA... [swish swish swish]

50.1 FX: DOGA [thunk]
50.2 FX: DA [tmp]
50.3 FX: DA DA DA... [tmp tmp tmp...]

51.1 FX: ZAAA... [fssssh...]

52.2-3 FX: SHA SHA SHA SHA SHA SHA... [whirr whirr whirr whirr whirr whirr...]
52.4 FX: SHA SHA SHA... [whirr whirr whirr...]

53.2.1 FX: MOZO... [fup...]
53.2.2 FX: HIN! [heen!]
53.5 FX: SHA SHA SHA... [whirr whirr whirr...]

54.1-3 FX: SHA SHA SHA SHA SHA SHA... [whirr whirr whirr whirr whirr whirr...]

55.1 FX: SHA SHA SHA... [whirr whirr whirr...]
55.2 FX: SHA SHA SHA... [whirr whirr whirr...]
55.3 FX: HIN! [heen!]
55.4.1 FX: PII [tweep]
55.4.2 FX: BUOHH [vrroom]

56.1 FX: SHA SHA SHA... [whirr whirr whirr...]
56.3 FX: SHA SHA SHA SHA [whirr whirr whirr whirr]

57.1 FX: SHA SHA SHA... [whirr whirr whirr...]
57.2 FX: SHA SHA... [whirr whirr...]
57.3 FX: KAPU [mwunch]

58.2 FX: DOKAAN [buwaam]
58.3 FX: DOKA [krrsh]
58.4 FX: DOSU [thud]

59.2 FX: DA [tmp]
59.3 FX: TA TA TA... [tp tp tp...]

60.4.1 FX: HIN!! [heen!!]
60.4.2 FX: GABA [fwoosh]
60.7 FX: GARA GARA [klak klak]

61.1 FX: GARA [klak]
61.2 FX: GARA GARA [klak klak]
61.3 FX: BA [fup]

38.3 FX: SU [fsh]
38.4 FX: GURA [fwoom]

39.1 FX: SHA SHA SHA... [whirr whirr whirr...]
39.2 FX: FUWA [fwoop]
39.3 FX: GURA [vwom]
39.4-5 FX: SHA SHA SHA SHA SH [whirr whirr whirr whi whirr...]

40.2 FX: KARA KARA KARA... [klak klak klak...]
40.3 FX: SHA SHA SHA [whirr v
40.4 FX: SHA SHA SHA [whirr v
40.5 FX: CHIIIN! [ding!] FX: SHA SHA [whirr whirr]

41.2 FX: SHA SHA SHA [whirr v

42.2 FX: SA [fsh]
42.4 FX: SUU [foosh]

43.2-3 FX: SHA SHA SHA SHA SH [whirr whirr whirr whirr whirr...]

44.3-4 FX: SHA SHA SHA SHA SH. [whirr whirr whirr whirr]
44.5-6 FX: SHA SHA SHA SHA... [whirr whirr whirr whirr]

45.2 FX: GUI [tugg]
45.3-5 FX: SHA SHA SHA SHA SH. [whirr whirr whirr whirr whirr]
45.5 FX: BASA [fwish]
45.6 FX: SHA SHA SHA... [whirr whirr whirr...]

46.1 FX: GUGU [tugg tugg]
46.2 FX: ZUBO [thup]

48.1 FX: KA [tak]
48.2 FX: ZA ZA ZA [tromp tromp
48.3 FX: DAN DAN DAN [tmp tmp
48.4 FX: GAN GAN GAN [thunk thunk thunk]

49.1 FX: DOKA DOKA [wak wak]
49.2 FX: BARIN! [krakk!]
49.3 FX: DA [tmp]
49.4 FX: DA DA [tmp tmp]

X: GARA GARA [klak klak]
X: GOTO GOTO [tunk tunk]
X: GOTON [thunk]
X: BUUN [fwoom]
X: PISHI [zipp]

X: GUGII [fwing]
X: GUNYU [fwoosh]
X: BAN [thud]
X: DON [thmp]
X: KOTON [tunk]
X: GYOOOOH... [fwoooom...]
X: BATAN [thud]

FX: DOHN [thuunk]
FX: TOTON [tutunk]
FX: TON [tmp]
FX: PASA [thup]
FX: GOOOH... [rrrrrr...]

FX: DON [tmp]
FX: BATA BATA [tump tump]

FX: TA TA... [tp tp...]

FX: POOOH... [prooot...]
FX: BA BA BA [shoop shoop shoop]
FX: GOTON GOTON GOTON
[klaketta klaketta klaketta]

FX: KACHA [chak]

FX: AHA HA HA... [ha ha ha ha...]

FX: TA TA TA... [tmp tmp tmp...]
FX: KACHIRI [chak]
FX: KURI [zwing]

FX: KACHA... [chak...]

FX: SA [fsh]
FX: SA [fsh]

FX: OOHN OOHN OOHN
[womm womm womm]

FX: OOHN OOHN OOHN
[womm womm womm]

FX: KI [hmm]

FX: OHN OHN [wom wom]

FX: OHN OHN [wom wom]

88.4.3 FX: KYAHAHAHAHAHA...
[ha ha ha ha ha ha...]
88.4.4 FX: PYON [bwing]

89.1 FX: ZA [fwik]
89.2 FX: ZA ZA [fwik fwik]
89.3 FX: HA HA HA... [ha ha ha...]

90.1 FX: PACHI PACHI [krakkl krakkl]
90.2 FX: MOGU MOGU [mnch mnch]
90.3 FX: PACHI PACHI [krakkl krakkl]

91.2 FX: MOGU MOGU [mnch mnch]
91.4 FX: BOWAAN [fwohm]
91.5 FX: GISHI GISHI [kreek kreek]
91.6 FX: GISHI GISHI [kreek kreek]
91.7 FX: GISHI GISHI... [kreek kreek...]

93.3 FX: HA HA HA... [ha ha ha...]
93.5 FX: KURU [fwip]

95.1 FX: KARA KARA... [klak klak...]
95.4.1 FX: BUOHH [vrroom]
95.4.2 FX: SHUU [fsssh]

96.1.1 FX: GASHA [klang]
96.1.2 FX: BUSHUU [fwoooosh]
96.2.1 FX: GASHA GASHA [klang klang]
96.2.2 FX: GOHE [burrp]
96.2.3 FX: GOKI [krrik]
96.3.1 FX: DOKO [twunk]
96.3.2 FX: KUUU [krrrr]
96.3.2 FX: GOHE [burrp]
96.4 FX: KATSU KATSU [tak tak]
96.5 FX: SU [fsh]

97.3 FX: KA KA [tak tak]
97.4 FX: GOTO [tunk]

98.4 FX: SU [fsh]
98.5-6 FX: OOOOOH... [wooom...]
98.6 FX: GUWAAA [arrrr]

99.2-3 FX: DORO DORO DORO...
[glug glug glug...]
99.3 FX: MISHI MISHI MISHI...
[krrnch krrnch krrnch...]
99.4.1 FX: MU MU MU MU MU
[hmm hmm hmm hmm hmm]
99.4.2 FX: MISHI MISHI MISHI...
[krrnch krrnch krrnch...]
99.4.3 FX: GO GO GO GO GO [rr rr rr rr rr rr]

76.1 FX: DOOH [fsssh]
76.2 FX: DOOOH... [fsssh...]
76.3-4 FX: DOOOOH... [fssssssh...]
76.5 FX: GABA [fwip]
76.5-6 FX: DOOOOH... [fsssssssh...]
76.7 FX: DOOH... [fsssh...]

77.1 FX: GUOOH... [schnorrr...]
77.3 FX: PACHI PACHI [krakkl krakkl]

79.3 FX: !
79.4 FX: BON! [bomp!]

80.5 FX: ZAA... ZAA...
[fssh... fssh...]

81.1 FX: PYON [bwing]
81.2 FX: TON [tmp]

82.1 FX: TA TA TA [tmp tmp tmp]
82.2 FX: TA [tmp]

83.1 FX: GUHEE [blaah]
83.2 FX: TA [tmp]
83.3 FX: GU [tugg]
83.4 FX: GUI [tugg]

84.1 FX: GU GU [tugg tugg]
84.2 FX: GU GU GU [tugg tugg tugg...]
84.3 FX: GU GU... [tugg tugg...]

85.2 FX: GONI!! [thunk!!]
85.3 FX: BI BI BI BI BI [krr krr krr krr krr]
85.4 FX: GA GA GA [tunk tunk tunk]
85.5 FX: BI BI BI... [krr krr krr...]
FX: DOGA [thunk]

86.1.1 FX: DOGAGAGA [kathunk thunk]
86.1.2 FX: BATA BATA BATA [tunk tunk tunk]
86.2 FX: BARA [fwom]
86.3 FX: GATA KATA KATA KATA
[tunk tunk tunk tunk]
FX: DOTEN [whump]

87.1 FX: TA TA TA [tmp tmp tmp]
86.2 FX: GAAAN [thonk]
86.3 FX: JAAA [fizzz]
86.4.1 FX: PUSUN [ploop]
86.4.2 FX: GOTO [thunk]

88.4.1 FX: PYON PYON [bwing bwing]
88.4.2 FX: AHAHAHAHAHA
[ha ha ha ha ha ha]

158.1 FX: SA [fsh]
158.2 FX: SUTATATATA… [tp tp tp tp tp…]
158.3 FX: PA [fip]
158.5 FX: SUTATATATA [tp tp tp tp…]
158.6.1 FX: DOSUN [fump]
158.6.2 FX: BIKU [urk]
158.7 FX: PYUU… [fip]

159.1 FX: SU [fsh]
159.2.1 FX: GOSO GOSO [shf shf]
159.2.2 FX: NYUWAA [gwoom]
159.3.1 FX: GASHI [fip]
159.3.2 FX: KYUU [skwinch]
159.4 FX: UNYU UNYU [gwoo gwoo]
159.6 FX: POI [fwip]

160.2-3 FX: PAKU… [mnch…]
160.4 FX: BOMU [bom]

161.1 FX: POI… [fip…]
161.2 FX: POI… [fip]
161.3 FX: GOSO GOSO [shf shf]

162.2 FX: SHU [poof]
162.3 FX: SHU SHU SHU… [poof poof poof…]

163.1 FX: SHU SHU SHU… [poof poof poof…]
163.5 FX: FUN [hmph]

164.1 FX: ZORO [tromp]
164.2 FX: ZORO ZORO… [tromp tromp …]

165.3 FX: GABA [fwoosh]
165.5 FX: SU [fsh]

167.2 FX: HISHI [tugg]

145.2 FX: UU UU [urr urr]
145.3.1 FX: UU UU [urr urr]
145.3.2 FX: KANKAAN KANKAAN [klaang klaang]
145.4 FX: KARAN KARAAN [klaang klaang]

146.4.1 FX: BUUUN [fwoooom]
146.4.2 FX: KANKAAN [klaang klaang]
146.4.3 FX: UU UU [urr urr]
146.5.1 FX: PICHA [plissh]
146.5.2 FX: KANKAAN [klaang klaang]

147.1 FX: PACHI PACHI PACHI [krakkl krakkl krakkl]

148.1 FX: GOOOHN [rrrrrrrr]
148.2.1 FX: ZUZUUN [buwaam]
148.2.2 FX: DON DON [boom boom]
148.3 FX: ZORO ZORO… [fwich fwich…]
148.4 FX: DOHN DOHN [bwoom bwoom]
148.5 FX: GOOOOH… [rrrrrrr…]

149.3-4 FX: ZAAAAAA… [fwooosh…]

150.1.1 FX: GOTO GOTO GOTO [tunk tunk tunk]
150.1.2 FX: GARA GARA GARA [klak klak klak]
150.3 FX: GACHA [chak]
150.4 FX: PATAN [thud]
150.5 FX: PUPPUU [beep beep]
150.6 FX: KI [kreech]
FX: GOTON [tunk]

151.1 FX: TATATA… [tmp tmp tmp…]

152.3 FX: BA [fwoosh]
152.5 FX: DO [tump]
152.6 FX: DOTA DOTA [tump tump]
FX: BATAN [thud]

154.3 FX: HISHI [tugg]

155.2 FX: GUUU… [zzzz…]
155.3 FX: GUUU… [zzzz…]

157.3 FX: GUUU… [zzzz…]
157.4.1 FX: BATA BATA BATA [tump tump tump]
157.4.2 FX: KATSU KATSU [tak tak]
157.4.3 FX: CHIRA [glance]
157.4.3 FX: BATAN [thud]

127.3 FX: OHN OHN OHN [wom w

128.1 FX: OHN OHN OHN [wom w

129.2 FX: SU… [fsh…]
129.3 FX: OHN OHN [wom wom]
129.4.1 FX: OHN [wom…]
129.4.2 FX: SAA [fssh]

130.2-5 FX: BYUUUU… [fwoooosh
130.6-10 FX: BYUUUU… [fwoooosh
130.11 FX: BACHI BACHI [krakkl k

131.1 FX: BUUN BUUN [vrom vro
131.4 FX: PITA… [stop]
131.5.1 FX: ZU ZU ZU… [rrr rrr rr.
131.5.2 FX: FUII FUII FUII [foom foo
131.7 FX: SU [fsh]

132.5 FX: WANA WANA [chirr ch

133.2 FX: FUII FUII FUII [foom foo
133.3 FX: PUI PUI PUI [ploop ploo

134.1 FX: BASA BASA [fwip fwi
134.2 FX: BUUUN [fwoom]
134.3 FX: BUUUUUN [fwoooom]
134.5 FX: SA [fsh]

135.1-2 FX: TA TA TA TA… [tmp tmp tmp tmp…]
135.3 FX: BA [fsh]
135.4 FX: BASA [fwip]
135.6-8 FX: BASA BASA BASA BAS [fwip fwip fwip fwip fw

136.2 FX: BUUUN [fwooom]
136.3 FX: BASA BASA [fwip fwip
136.4 FX: BUUUN [fwooom]

137.5 FX: PA [foop]

138.1-4 FX: AAAH [ahhhh]
138.7 FX: BA [fwoosh]
138.8 FX: BATAN [thud]

139.2 FX: KURIRIN [zwing]
139.3.1 FX: BA [fsh]
139.3.2 FX: GACHA [chak]

140.3 FX: KON KON [tok tok]

143.3 FX: FUU [hmm]

This book should be read in its original Japanese right-to-left format.
Please turn it around to begin!

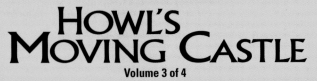

HOWL'S MOVING CASTLE

Volume 3 of 4

From the novel by Diana Wynne Jones
Screenplay written and directed by Hayao Miyazaki

ıedited English-Language Adaptation/Cindy Davis Hewitt & Donald H. Hewitt
Original Japanese Script Translation/Jim Hubbert
Film Comic Adaptation/Yuji Oniki
Lettering/John Clark
Design/Hidemi Sahara
Editor/Pancha Diaz

Managing Editor/Masumi Washington
Director of Production/Noboru Watanabe
Vice President of Publishing/Alvin Lu
Sr. Director of Acquisitions/Rika Inouye
VP of Sales & Marketing/Liza Coppola
Publisher/Hyoe Narita

Printed in Singapore.

Published by VIZ Media, LLC
P.O.Box 77010
San Francisco, CA 94107

First Printing, September 2005

VIZ media

RATED A FOR ALL AGES
PARENTAL ADVISORY
HOWL'S MOVING CASTLE
is suitable for all ages.

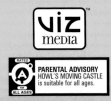